The Quest for Meaning VE DEC 2011

ENOY R

VE SEPT 18

TARIQ RAMADAN

The Quest for Meaning

Developing a Philosophy of Pluralism

ALLEN LANE
an imprint of
PENGUIN BOOKS

ALLEN LANE

Published by the Penguin Group
Penguin Books Ltd, 80 Strand, London WC2R ORL, England
Penguin Group (USA) Inc., 375 Hudson Street, New York, New York 10014, USA
Penguin Group (Canada), 90 Eglinton Avenue East, Suite 700, Toronto, Ontario,
Canada M4P 2Y3 (a division of Pearson Canada Inc.)
Penguin Ireland, 25 St Stephen's Green, Dublin 2, Ireland (a division of Penguin Books Ltd)
Penguin Group (Australia), 250 Camberwell Road, Camberwell, Victoria 3124, Australia
(a division of Pearson Australia Group Pty Ltd)
Penguin Books India Pvt Ltd, 11 Community Centre, Panchsheel Park,
New Delhi – 110 017, India
Penguin Group (NZ), 67 Apollo Drive, North Shore 0632, New Zealand
(a division of Pearson New Zealand Ltd)
Penguin Books (South Africa) (Pty) Ltd, 24 Sturdee Avenue, Rosebank 2196, South Africa

Penguin Books Ltd, Registered Offices: 80 Strand, London WC2R ORL, England

www.penguin.com

First published 2010
3

Copyright © Tariq Ramadan, 2010

The moral right of the author has been asserted

Set in 10.5/14 pt Sabon LT Std
Typeset by TexTech International
Printed in Great Britain by Clays Ltd, St Ives plc

ISBN: 978-1-846-14152-2

To the semi-colon;

Despite the diversity of languages, there is some form of punctuation that is universal and common to them all.

In a world of simplified communications and simplistic binary judgements, the semi-colon reconciles us with the plurality of propositions, and with the welcome nuances of the sentence and of complex realities.

To my former students, who will rediscover here the fragrances of a teaching of philosophy.

And who will not forget to 'say to those they love that they love them'.

Life is fragile.

Contents

Ocean and Windows

This book is a journey, and an initiation. It is actually about setting out and travelling the paths of the heart, the mind and the imaginary.

There has never been more talk of diversity and plurality than in this era of globalization and modernization, and yet, more so than ever before, we seem to be trapped into our identities and differences. The global world is a village; they say ... a village of villagers who know nothing of each other. In more senses than one: they do not know who they are, and they do not know who they are living with. This situation can only lead to half-hearted, fearful and dormant conflicts rather than a confident celebration of our riches: Edward Said suggested it would lead to 'the clash of ignorance'; I propose it will lead to a 'conflict of perceptions'. Perceptions are more telling than ignorance: perceptions can certainly result from ignorance, but they express a relationship with ourselves and others that has to do with more than knowledge. Perceptions have to do with feelings, emotions, convictions and psychology. We are lacking in confidence. Confidence in ourselves, confidence in others, confidence in God and/or man, and/or the future. We are lacking in confidence, no shadow of a doubt about that. Fear, doubt and distrust are imperceptibly colonizing our hearts and minds. And so the other becomes our negative mirror, and the other's difference allows us to define ourselves, to 'identify' ourselves and, basically, gives us some reassurance. The other becomes our 'diversion', in Blaise Pascal's sense of the term. The other distracts us from ourselves, our ignorance, our fears and our doubts, whilst the presence of the other justifies and explains our suspicions. We have projections, but at the same time we have to admit that we have no projects.

We therefore have to get back to some elementary truths. Simple, profound truths. We have to set out, ask the essential questions and look for a meaning. We have to travel towards ourselves and rediscover a taste for questions, constructive criticism and complexity. We begin by establishing a first thesis of truth that should naturally foster an attitude of intellectual modesty and humility: we all observe the world through our own windows. A window is a viewpoint over a horizon, a framework, a piece of glass that is always tinted to some extent, and it has its orientation and its limitations: all this, together, imparts its colour and qualities to the surrounding landscape. We have to begin, humbly, by admitting that we have nothing more than *points of view*, in the literal sense, and that they shape our ideas, our perceptions and our imagination. Coming to terms with the very essence of the relativity of our gaze does not imply that we have to doubt everything and can be sure of nothing. It might mean quite the opposite, and the outcome might be a non-arrogant confidence, and a healthy, energetic and creative curiosity about the infinite number of windows from which we all observe the same world. The plurality is such that we have doubts as to whether we are talking about the same world, the same questions and the same humanity. Within the 'global village', in the meantime, our increasingly pronounced individualism even leads us to doubt the fact that there are such things as fragments of philosophy behind the calculations of our respective drive for power and self-interest. And what can the ego make out of egoisms?

The point I am making is that we cannot go on standing at our windows. Off we go, we said, along the paths of the heart, the mind and the imaginary! The horizon ahead of us offers us a choice between two paths: we can go from window to window, from one philosophy to another and from one religion to another, and try to understand, one by one, traditions and schools, their teachings and their principles. As we go from one to another, from ourselves to others, we will find many similarities, many things in common and many shared values. Or we can take the other path, which leads us into the very heart of the landscape and then invites us to turn our gaze on the windows around us. Once we take that path, it is no longer a question of considering the multiplicity of the observers but of plunging into the object we are all observing, and then apprehending the diversity of our points of view and the essence of their similarity. Once we have accepted the existence of our window, we therefore have to travel, set ourselves free, plunge into the ocean, set sail, go on, stop, founder, resist, set off again, set sail once more, and remember that the ocean exists only because of the presence of the many shores that make it one ocean, and that their presence is also our only hope of survival. And vice versa.

We have chosen the second path, and we wish to accompany our reader to the heart of what we are observing, so as to apprehend with confidence and humility the myriad observers. This is what I call a philosophy of pluralism, which states that, by immersion in the object per se, we will be able to meet human beings, or subjects, with their traditions, their religions, their philosophies, their aesthetics and/or their psychologies. Each chapter will therefore deal with one theme, with one element in the landscape of philosophy: the quest for meaning, the universal, freedom, fraternity, education, memory, forgiveness, love, and so on, and we will try, as we stand in the centre, to address and understand the diversity and creativity that well up from the windows. The notions of equality, freedom, humanity, emotion and memories belong, for instance, to all traditions and all philosophies, but their absolute truth is in no one's possession. And, as we shall demonstrate, the universal can only be a universal that is shared.

In the course of this initiation, which works backwards from existential questions and shared philosophical notions to the pluralism of answers and points of view, the reader will begin to see the contours of a philosophy of pluralism. By recognizing the existence of one's window, and then taking the risk of moving away from it and becoming decentred, one will, thanks to the essence of debates about one notion, gain access to the shared fate and hopes of subjects, men and women from all walks of life, throughout the whole of history. Like any initiate, the reader will sometimes wonder: 'Where am I being taken?' There is no one answer, and no final answer. We are heading for that realm of consciousness and mind where all wisdoms remind us that it is its shores that make the ocean one, and that it is the plurality of human journeys that shapes the common humanity of men.

Ella Maillard (1903–1997), who was one of the twentieth century's greatest travel writers, once said: 'The hardest part is getting to the station.' And the first steps are indeed the hardest: leaving behind your family and friends, your habits, your comfort, your certainties, and setting off for new horizons. It takes an effort, will power . . . the appeal of travelling and discovering distant shores is incompatible with laziness, self-importance and arrogance. It takes self-awareness, determination, humility, modesty, curiosity and a certain taste for risk to venture into strange worlds, new references and new vocabularies. It means accepting insecurity and appreciating empathy.

I have tried to introduce these complex notions in the simplest and most approachable way so as to ensure that the reader does not get out of her or his depth. No philosophical or religious knowledge is required before setting off. And besides, the reader will quickly understand that this initiation takes place in stages and that every reader will get something out of it and will discover the luggage and supplies he or she set out with. I have tried not to make complexity needlessly complex, or to confuse simplicity with the absence of profundity. The poverty of the landscape mirrors that of our gaze, murmured the German poet Rainer Maria Rilke, and the same is true of its wealth. A man who is lost is vulnerable, and rarely complacent. It is therefore a good thing if the reader sometimes gets lost, finds his way again, thinks he has understood and then finally understands that he does not understand, or does not understand enough. This is a good school of wisdom. On its benches, we learn to reserve and to suspend our judgement. These chapters open a thousand windows but they do not offer absolute truths or definite answers; they offer perspectives that remind us that, ultimately, human beings are all alike in their joys, their sufferings and their loves. And in their quest for truth and peace.

The goal of the journey is the journey itself . . . poetically put, it is a journey that takes us far away, and back to ourselves. In order to find there our being, a liberated ego, God, reason, the heart, or the void. But always, always tenderness and love. And hope too: the last of evils according to the myth of Pandora, and the first act of faith in God or man. By setting out from these shared ideals, values and principles, the traveller who goes in search of initiation sets foot on the shores of a rich diversity and of pluralism, begins to find a path and sees doors and windows opening. He lives the paradox of travelling to the periphery of traditions and of settling into the essence of their teachings. And then he can murmur, confidently and with an open mind: my philosophy is travel, and pluralism is my destination. Humility is my table, respect is my garment, empathy is my food and curiosity is my drink. As for love, it has a thousand names and is by my side at every window.

I

The Quest for Meaning

In the beginning, there is childhood. Life has already begun, and childhood is its most immediate, most material, liveliest and most exuberant expression. It is sometimes said that this is its most beautiful expression. Babies and children express life with a sort of crystalline purity. 'Life is there, simple and serene,' says the poet Paul Verlaine in his *Sagesse*. Childhood is innocence. That might be a universal truth, if we did not recall the words of St Augustine in the *Confessions* when he observes that even a baby at the breast feels jealousy and already bears the stigmata of sin that runs through the human condition from the very beginning.[1] The innocence of being and of origins is therefore neither a fact nor a universal postulate. Childhood may even be, as in the Hindu or Buddhist tradition, the new beginning of 'something' or of a life that came before it. If that is the case, origins, purity and innocence are so many illusions that are fostered by our shortsightedness and/or ignorance.

So, it is very complicated from the very beginning. Where do we begin? And how can we speak of 'apparent' origins, or of childhood as it is lived, and not as we observe it, from our viewpoint, with our reason, our judgements, our philosophies or our religions? If childhood is neither primal, pure nor even innocent . . . then is there such a thing as a truth that can express it or a quality that can describe it? That is a difficult question, and yet the extraordinary thing that attracts and fascinates us to the point of moving us to tears is palpable as we sit at the bedside of a child and of life: childhood is life, but it asks no questions

---

1. Augustine, *Confessions*, trans. R. S. Pine-Coffin, Harmondsworth: Penguin, 1961, 1: vii.

about life. The 'being of being' immediately clings . . . to life. It asks no questions and is not mediated by either consciousness or the intellect.

Childhood is carefree in the literal sense: a child lives but has no worries about life. That does not mean that a child feels no pain, is never hurt and never suffers. It does not mean that a child experiences only pure joy and happiness. No. Children do experience pleasure and pain, laughter and tears, fullness and lack, but they do so unquestioningly. Childhood does not need answers or philosophies. It falls short of that, or perhaps it is beyond that. The painter Pablo Picasso used to say how difficult it was to 'become young again' because he was so eager to rediscover a carefree creativeness – and finally outgrow his precocious mastery of forms and colours. Friedrich Nietzsche, the philosopher who was so in love with art, had already described childhood as the final stage in three basic transformations: his prophet Zarathustra proclaimed that human beings had to become rebellious lions and no longer submissive camels if they wished to accede at last to the free and carefree liberty of a child.[2] Nietzsche did believe in innocence, but what looked like the final completion of the philosophical quest was a combination of lack of concern and freedom: the freedom of the carefree, of those who are not worried about life, the freedom of the child. He thought that we have to get beyond useless questions about meaning if we are to experience the fullness of being in its immediacy. The philosopher's only hope of success was to transform himself into a child-artist. He was not hoping for an answer to questions about life but trying to get beyond them, and that is a much more profound experience. Nietzsche's insight was profound, and so true: in philosophy, the ideal of childhood is the end of philosophy.

QUESTIONS, A QUESTION

Escaping consciousness is, however, difficult. And perhaps we can never really do so. The intellect gradually awakens as it discovers the realities of life and asks the first questions: why, or why not, are there

2. Friedrich Nietzsche, *Thus Spoke Zarathustra*, trans. R. J. Hollingdale, Harmondsworth: Penguin, 1969, pp. 54–6.

things to eat? Why, or why not, are there toys, a swimming pool and rain, presence or absence? The first 'whys' are about immediate causalities that are obvious at an immediate level – at the heart of the life that is given us – and not about life itself. Time passes, and the questions become deeper and more focused as our consciousness has to deal with the real: our carefree existence, and part of childhood vanishes as we begin to ask the basic existential question: why life? Why me, here and there?

We reach the age of reason as we take the path that leads to maturity. We have to become adults whether we like it or not. This journey – these stages, the immediacy of the carefree existence that ceases as we approach the mediation of conscience is the most intimate and the most universal experience of all. It is a universal intimacy, or the universal nature of human intimacy. Ancestral traditions punctuated this journey with rites and/or initiations, rites of passage, symbolic ordeals and new responsibilities. They helped being, consciousness and the intellect to enter the world of meaning. Religions and prophecies, like traditions, spiritualities and philosophies, find their *raison d'être* at the very threshold of this question of meaning: they are so many of the answers that are given to human consciousness – either in advance (by a family or community) or in the course of the personal quest – when consciousness accedes the existential preoccupation (life's worries about life) and asks the question 'Why?'

The essence and the prospect remain the same, from the tribal religions of Asia to the Aztecs and the Mayas, from the religions of the Andes to the traditions of Africa: understanding, doing and giving meaning. Egyptian, Greek and Roman polytheisms, like Hinduism and Buddhism, and even the Jewish, Christian and Muslim monotheisms, offer frameworks and systems that allow us to answer the basic existential question, and then all the other related questions: what is the meaning of death, suffering, love, morality, and so on? Philosophers and philosophies try to reconstruct what religions have already grappled with by asking the initial question, by using their autonomous reason and exploring truths that have, to some extent, been established or verified (postulates). They try to arrive at a meaning by asking questions and in the process elaborate systems that strive for consistency and for answers. Socrates has often – and quite wrongly, as it happens – been described as the first systematic philosopher, but he is the first and emblematic representative of the philosophical project and the philosophical experience. The Socratic dialectic is a pedagogy based upon a series of leading questions. The thousands of questions he asks are designed to elicit from his interlocutor truths he did not know were in his possession. And those truths allow the interlocutor to apprehend, with the intellectual gentleness that is implicit in logical reasoning, the question of questions: the question of meaning, and the question of truth.

The geneticist Albert Jacquard observed, with a certain humour, that human beings are born too early, and quite incomplete. It is impossible for a baby to survive without help. Left to its own devices, it is physically doomed to die. It is therefore naturally in a state of need. The physical need to be cared for, fed and protected until it reaches physiological maturity is most obvious and most pressing at the very moment when it is most carefree. Total physical dependency in order to stay alive is associated with an absolute freedom and lightness: our being is part of life. And then time passes and perspectives are inverted: as we become physically independent, we gradually begin to ask existential questions, and those questions are so many needs. At the very moment when the body realizes its potential and becomes autonomous, the mind becomes aware of its questions, limitations, needs because its dependency mirrors its incompleteness, doubts and truths. We spend our time coming to terms with our physical, emotional and intellectual dependency. We move perpetually from one state to the other: man is a being who is 'in need'. That is why our relationship with peace – inner or collective – is always a question of autonomy and power. That is as true of individuals and couples as it is of social relations. 'Why?' expresses the quest for meaning, and an awareness of our needs, limitations and powers.

TIME

All religions, all spiritualities and all philosophies take a natural interest in the question of time. It is perhaps the experience of passing time that gives consciousness access to life's first questions about life. Life is there, time passes, and life passes away. The question of time shapes an awareness of death. The awareness of death is reflected in and reflects the essence of existence, its origins and future, and the meaning of destiny and hope. The three basic philosophical questions formulated by the German philosopher Immanuel Kant clearly relate the awareness of time to the existential quest: *What can I know? What should I do? What may I hope for?*[3] This very last question encompasses the others and has to do with time. Our origins, our being in time, our hopes for the future and our death inscribe the human consciousness in time, and the nature of the answers to these questions will necessarily determine its relationship with space, with Nature and with human beings, in both their similarities and their differences. There is no spirituality, tradition or religion – or at least none that is systematic – that does not provide answers to these questions. The metaphysical philosophers never imagined that they could be avoided, while more recent philosophies (such as phenomenological and analytic philosophies) which posit these existential questions are, by their very nature, problematical and debatable.

Without getting lost in these complex debates, which are sometimes quite pointlessly technical and nebulous, we do have to dwell on the question of origins. It is, in both religious and philosophical terms, essential and concrete. 'Source' points us toward the 'meaning'. If we know where we come from, we know our way. The human consciousness has a very special relationship with the question of origins, of beginnings, or the beginning: that is the secret or truth we have to succeed in apprehending in spiritual and intellectual terms. Basically, Kant's three questions could be summed up in one other question whose essence holds the key to all the others: where do I come from? It synthesizes all the others: is there a Creator, Spirit, Being, Substance or Cause? Is meaning determined from the origin? Are we products of a will, an accident or chance? These questions are the very substance of the search for meaning. Time asks questions, and consciousness tries to answer them, or fails to answer them. The meaning that is produced by the question of passing time and approaching death naturally transforms our relationship with space, Nature and the

3. Immanuel Kant, *Critique of Pure Reason*, A805.

elements. If life does have a meaning and if the source does show a way, then the elements are transformed into signs . . . and they reveal that meaning because they are individual and singular.

The origin is always the axis and/or refuge of those who believe in meaning. If life is an accident, a chance event – or a mistake – then origins express nothing more than its brute, unfathomable reality: it is an event of which nothing can be said and from which nothing can be learned. The origin of meaning always seems more ideal or more alive than the meanings we encounter on our path. That is the source of the nostalgia for origins that runs through all traditions and all religions; at the origin, meaning seems to appear pure and complete in all its fullness and then, as time passes, it becomes corrupt, perverted and self-destructive and self-contradictory or even becomes lost. We advance towards the horizon so as to return to our origin. Hindu, Buddhist, Jewish, Christian and Muslim mysticisms all give out the same message: we have to go forth in order to come back, plunge into time in order to be born anew, and roam the world in order to get back to ourselves at last. This universal experience is summed up as simply and as profoundly as it could be by Paolo Coelho's novel *The Alchemist*: leave Andalusia to look for a treasure that is hidden in Egypt and discover, once in Egypt, that you have to go back to Andalusia. Andalusia is not, however, self-sufficient, and requires the mediation of Egypt. The source is not sufficient unto itself; the Andalusia from which we come is not the same as the Andalusia to which we return. In the order of spirituality, the Andalusia we come from needs the path that leads to it and thus reveals its meaning and essence. It exists thanks to the discernment of the consciousness that gives and restores its meaning.

When we are haunted by questions and driven by the quest for answers and meanings standing between the origin and the destination, we are in a better position to understand spiritual, religious or philosophical representations of circular or linear time. Is man advancing freely towards an indeterminate future? Or is he tirelessly retracing his steps? Given that birth and death are celebrated in an eternal renewal, isn't an individual life just one more illusion. Shouldn't our consciousness of the singularity of the self and of the path begin by grasping the truth of repetition, of the return of the same and of the eternity of renewal? These questions too have never stopped being repeated in all ancestral, spiritual, religious or philosophical traditions. They all speak of and express the quest, the initiation and the way: the Lesser or Great Vehicle (*Hînayâna, mahâyâna*), the Kabbalah, mysticism and Sufism are methodical and systematized expressions of that same truth. For some of them, however, cosmic time is cyclical, and we must both apprehend it and escape from it in its essence, as in the determinations of the Hindu and Buddhist *samsâra*. For others, it is linear time that makes sense because it speaks of origins and determines destinations: gods, God, a judgement. For still others, linear time is in fact a disguised form of a cyclical time, or perhaps it is the other way round and perhaps cyclical time evolves in linear fashion: 'we never bathe twice in the same river', remarked Heraclitus. Everything is repeated, but never in the same way. This is another way of speaking of the experience of the quest: we must walk down roads and through towns as we seek, and that is a temporal experience. A being will live what others have already experienced, the days will repeat themselves, experiences will be similar, as will the questions, the doubts and the suffering . . . we will even return to our place of origin, to ourselves, but nothing – the self, the questions, the experiences or the quest – will ever be the same. The quest for meaning, which is always begun again by every human intellect, is to human consciousness what a fingerprint is to the body: shared by all, and unique to every individual. A universal singularity.

BACK TO THE SELF

As we have said, the quest for meaning is a journey through time and across the world, but it always ends by bringing us back to ourselves. All paths lead us back to ourselves. In his *Muqaddimah*, which is aptly subtitled *An Introduction to History*, the mystic and philosopher Ibn Kaldun (1322–1406), who was the first sociologist, concludes from his study of history and the macrocosm that the evolution and demise of civilizations are cyclical. The past is the future, and the future is the road to a new past. The microcosm of consciousness reveals the same truths. Human beings, be they believers or atheists, idealists or rationalists, philosophers or scientists, are on what Ibn Qayyim called 'the seekers' way' (*Madarrij Saalikeen* ('Stations of the Seekers')), and it leads us back to ourselves. In the face of self-awareness, in the face of death or love, in the face of loneliness or suffering, in the face of doubt or absences . . . on the road, and in the heart of life, we must return to ourselves one day.

Who am I? asks the human being, the believer, the atheist, the philosopher or the poet. All religions and all philosophies convey the same truth: wherever you are, whatever your origins, your colour or your social status, your very humanity means that you must become introspective – for a moment or for life. 'Know thyself,' the Delphic oracle told the philosopher, and, from the Epicureans to the monotheistic religions, we find the same basic concern for the self, for the ego. It causes us pleasure and pain, and the first apprehensions of consciousness reveal that it is always in a state of tension. Knowledge of God lies 'between man and his heart', says the Quran ('The Spoils, VIII 24), and it also locates the quest for the One and His peace (*islâm, salâm*) in immersion in the heart's tensions. All the paths of life lead to the heart. They teach us to understand ourselves, our being, qualities and weaknesses in the light of our own aspiration, of others and of the world. In his quest for the truth, the philosopher Descartes asked himself what he could be certain of, in the same way that the Brahmans before him sought to identify the prisons of the inner self. Every human being must one day take stock of what she/he is, of her/his being, beliefs, certainties and contradictions, and of both her/his freedoms and prisons. We can decide to choose a philosophy of introspection, a faith, morality or religion, the practice of initiation or self-denial, but we must choose: and one day, for all that, life will force us to question our choice. As we have said, existence cannot escape consciousness.

We then have to make allowance for acquired characteristics. What we get from our parents and what shapes us: the strange way in which we resemble them physically, our body-language, the emotions we feel and express, and even some aspects of our intellectual dispositions. Our past, which is always so present, our experiences, our questions, our encounters and our wounds make us what we are, determine us and decide part of our identity. Our contradictory aspirations, our doubts, our dark side, often perturb and disturb us: Who are we? Who decides who we are? Do we have the ability to change, to transform ourselves? 'We cannot remake ourselves,' says the adage that places limitations on our freedom. Getting back to ourselves and to the heart of our consciousness means entering the natural world of tension, of contradictory 'postulations', of the battlefield described by the novelist-psychologist Dostoyevsky. It means knowing where we come from and asking the simple question of what we want, what we can do and what we can make of ourselves. It means accepting that something about us is indeterminate and, like Rimbaud, stating that 'I is an other', taking stock of our qualities, of what we are lacking and of what we need, and of setting off. We have no choice: we have already set sail on our existential journey. We already have our convictions, and the die has already been cast. We have to give things a meaning, even if we postulate that they have none. In the light of that meaning (or non-meaning), we must try to know ourselves better (or to know nothing of ourselves), take decisions (or take no decisions) and make choices (or decide not to choose). A human being is a being 'in need' and who must make choices: when it comes to making existential choices, deciding not to choose is still a choice. The return to the self is the first and the final stage of all human experience: the reflections of the 'I', of the ego, of consciousness and the unconscious, of the emotions and the mind mirror the adult's questions about freedom, meaning and truth.

IN SEARCH OF PEACE

Our conscious adult state is naturally a state of tension. Our doubts, our aspiration towards the ideal and (perhaps) immateriality, the calls of our instincts and their potential for what can be a bestial violence, our dreams, our imaginary, our fantasies and even our conscious or unconscious traumas all indicate that our origins are fraught with problems. We are looking for peace: for answers to our questions, for a few certainties beyond our doubts and for solutions to our tensions. The quest for meaning is indeed a quest for peace.

The oldest Asian and African tribal religions project on to the world and the elements meanings and signs that tame the world, make it less hostile and allow communications that soften the relationship between human being and Nature. Both spiritualities and religions teach the way and the means to be at peace with oneself, with God, with others and also with the environment and/or Creation. Theoretical and metaphysical theory seeks to explain and, therefore, to answer and appease analytical reason. Dante's *Divine Comedy*, which is midway between philosophy, religion and art, is in that sense an imaginary description of a beyond that answers the painful and serious questions of an awakened consciousness which inevitably experiences angst. The existentialists openly describe the same experience: the Christian Kierkegaard could not help but acknowledge the fatal disease and the heartbreaking inner conflict that lies at the very heart of faith in the experience of Abraham, torn between his love for God and his love for his son. The atheist Sartre also held that anxiety was central to human experience: we have to recognize it, accept it and transcend it. What are we to make of our doubts, contradictions, fears and anxieties, with or without God? How can we contemplate death calmly, live and then pass away in peace? What is the ultimate meaning of the last question asked by the biblical Jesus – 'My God, why hast thou forsaken me?' – of Socrates' request to be allowed to settle his debts before he passed on, or of Kant's 'It is good' as he closed his eyes for ever?

Throughout the ages, we find the same questions, the same thirst and the same hope that we will find a spring that can at last quench it. This is how we manage our tensions and this is how we achieve fullness. And that is, as it happens, the true meaning of *jihad* in the Islamic tradition: managing our natural, individual and/or collective contradictions, and seeking peace. The very word for faith – *imân* – expresses not the idea of 'faith', but a state of security, well-being and peace (*al-amân*). This answer echoes the personal and universal experience of every consciousness, whatever choices it makes. Modern psychology, in all its forms, and psychoanalysis, with all its schools, serve the same function: observing, seeking, finding the key, an event, or a rift that explains and allows us to transcend distress, imbalance or neurosis. Making peace, feeling well. The promise of *nirvana*, complete faith, communion, unconditional love . . . a return, yet again, to the fullness of childhood: an instant of life that takes away the cares of life. A consciousness that is as assured and as free as the child's carefree existence. Do we return to the self in order to transcend the ego, or are we trying to draw closer to the One and lucidly face up to the loneliness of our consciousness and our indeterminate destiny? The answer is never, ever, strictly rational: as we travel the road that leads to the origin, follow the meanders of cyclical and/or linear time, and come back to the self, we discover both a horizon of tensions and a hope for harmony and peace; the road we travel, therefore, always involves emotions, affection and well-being. Spiritualities, religions and philosophies, whatever they may be, cannot escape either the questions of reason or those of the heart. Those questions exist, and they owe as much to consciousness as they do to love.

2

Of the Universal

There is a lot of talk these days about which values and principles are universal and which are not. It is as though, in these times of general relativity, we needed to recall that there is some form of absolute, or some point of reference, that can transcend our many different points of view or, more indirectly, our loss of points of reference. In an age of postmodernity, deconstruction and postmodernism (of a conceptual inflation that causes our old relations with truth to implode), and in which so many concepts speak of the end of orders and logical systems, of narrations and coherent narratives, and, finally, of ideologies of political totality and human finalities, we suddenly begin to describe the status of certain values and principles as 'universal'. If we look at things from afar, or even a little more closely, it seems that the feeling of loss of meaning and all points of reference internally is overcompensated for externally (i.e., vis-à-vis other civilizations), by a strong, determined will to speak out, express or even possess the universal. Perhaps the claim that we, as opposed to the Other, are in possession of universals restores to us what the postmodernist experience has taken away from us. There is a certain intellectual, and even psychological, logic to these communicating vases: this has to do with doubts. And it always has to do with power.

But what do we mean by 'universal'? Given that, as we have seen, we are all – each and every one of us – searching for meaning, truth and peace ... then where will we place that which is universal in human experience? In the nature of the questions we all ask, or in the possible similarities between our different answers? Or in both? Where does he or she who sees, defines and speaks of universals speak from? These are not new questions, and they were formulated increasingly naturally (and recurrently) in Western philosophy with the emergence of the autonomous rationalism of Descartes and especially Spinoza. An answer had to be found to what is, after all, a basic question: do we discover universals 'top down' by identifying a Being, Essence or Idea that is the cause of everything, or thanks to a 'bottom-up' process which allows human reason to identify common features that we all share, despite the diversity of human beings and elements? Hegel used the term 'concrete universal' to describe the idea of a Type or ideal Being (or a transcendental Given) that is the cause of beings and things as opposed to the 'abstract universals' we construct thanks to the use of a reason that identifies the generic characteristics of beings and things. This is also the meaning of Schopenhauer's distinction between Ideas and Concepts: the very essence of the universal means that it has different origins and a different nature. Even at the very heart of Western philosophy, or in the dialogue between civilizations and religions, we cannot get away from these questions about the origin and nature of the universal. The simplicity of this exposition might give the impression that Socrates, who postulated the existence of Ideas, opted for 'top down' or a concrete universal, whilst the Kant who described the categories and qualities of pure Reason opted for an abstract universal constructed by rational deduction. But if we look more closely, we find that things are much more complex than that: Socrates deduced his a prioris from what he thought were inductions, just as Kant clearly had an a priori idea of what he thought he had discovered thanks to the rigour of his deductions. All this is highly complex and paradoxical. There is, nonetheless, a simple truth, and we must have the wisdom to accept it: the way in which we say we accede to the universal says a lot about our preconceptions (or even our state of mind) when we begin to think. We should remember that.

All (non-theistic) spiritual or religious traditions have some notion of the universal. The concept of a universal refers, in one way or another, to a Being, Idea or Way (a concrete universal) that speaks, a priori, of the essence of human experience. No matter whether we believe that Nature is inhabited by a soul or souls, that we must free ourselves from the ego and the prison of the eternal rebirth through an initiation or self-transcendence, or that we must recognize the One

13

and practise a rite ... each and every one of us implicitly assumes that truths and ritual and ethical exigencies must, respectively, be regarded as universally true. Truth (insofar as it is a value) and meaning (for itself) are, quite logically, regarded as the truth and meaning of everything. The assumption that there is such a thing as an a priori universal does not, however, necessarily imply that, for spiritualities and religions, there is no legitimacy in constructing the universal on a rational basis, or that the two paths can never converge. As we shall see, the two approaches are not mutually exclusive, but that depends, once again, on the mental attitude of the thinker or seeker in question. This is not simply a matter of determining how *we* believe we can discover the universal, but of being able to listen to (though one might not always understand) the other's apprehension of the universal. It is a matter of listening to what she/he says about it, of understanding where she/he is speaking from, and of learning to apprehend different forms of the universal: the transcendental universal, the immanent universal, the inner universal, the universal of the heart, the universal of reason ... and even the nihilist universal of nothingness and non-meaning. The question of the universal is therefore primarily a question of ways, paths and states of minds.

PATHS

If we follow a path of initiation and fulfilment, or we believe in God the Creator, then that path or God is an expression of the universal that grants human beings truths, values, ethics and rules for behaviour. Idealist or rationalist philosophies use the human faculties, sense-data, intuition and sometimes even the image-stock common to archetypes, symbols and signs to elaborate constructs whose universality is, to a greater or lesser extent, either abstract or concrete. As we have seen, these are not the only ways of elaborating the universal. We can do so also by relying upon human faculties, and spiritualities and religions insist on doing this because their goal is to reveal the correspondence between the macrocosm of the universe and the microcosm of our innermost being. The universal of meanings, of consciousness, of the heart and the ego, for example, is present in mysticisms and rituals

14

that relate to our relationship with knowledge, the gnosis, truth and liberation. We can thus understand that the universal, which reveals the transcendent cause of All, also reveals common qualities and values that are immanent in everything, or identifies the similar essence of the human faculties of all human beings, and that, as we were saying, the universality of what we have in common, and which is expressed in the name of a faith or postulate, actually expresses the undisputed truth of the plurality, of the multiplicity and diversity of the ways that lead to it and its representation. There can be no universal without diversity: the quest for the ultimate commonality would be pointless if we did not recognize the initial differences that explain just why we have to go in search of the universal. We often tend to forget that when we set out on our quest because we are already convinced of the certainties or doubts we have come to accept.

Ancient traditions and contemporary spiritualities, like religions, have a similar relationship with the real on to which they project meanings, directions, destinations or teachings. The Spirit or universal spirits and the paths to liberation or God give birth to truths that are meant to be shared by all and to be true for all men. They are universal in a primary sense. The essence of each of these traditions or religions is that they call upon our consciousness to find a way, to make choices and to act accordingly. The universal that calls upon us to choose a path should, for example, never, by definition, deny either the reality of the essential necessity – which is quasi-ontological – of other paths. I must experience other truths if my responsibility for having chosen my truth in all conscience is to be meaningful. Without the truth – or errors – of others, my truth is no longer my choice or my responsibility. If it were forced upon me in its uniqueness, it would lose its meaning, and there would be no justification for its existence. That is the profound intuition we find in the teachings of Hinduism and Buddhism, but it is also central to the most profound messages of the monotheisms. The mystical and Sufi traditions constantly remind us that there are many ways, just as there are many paths up the mountainsides that their initiates scale to reach the same summit, ideal or truth. That there are many ways does not detract from the nature of the essential truth, just as the fact that there are different paths up the mountain does not mean that the peak is not transcendent – quite the contrary. The absolute is not relative to the paths that lead to it. Not everything is relative.

When we set out to look for the universal or affirm its existence, it is, then, important to remember that we are on a quest, progressing along a path, and to recall that our hearts and our reasons aspire to something. We have to remember that we are on the side of a mountain and remain aware that the absolute of the peak is a goal, an ideal and a hope. That should be our original state of mind, no matter whether we are believers or unbelievers, rationalist, idealist, materialist or mystical philosophers. And even if we prefer the symbol of the desert of immanence to that of the mountain of elevation and transcendence, the perspective does not change: the infinity of the desert also reveals the many paths along which we can go in search of ourselves or lose ourselves. The desert appears to have no summit and no centre, but it too can unveil the essence of its absolute thanks to its infinity, which stretches as far as the eye can see. A hint of the universal is present everywhere, which means that we must not be too self-confident and must be suspicious of our tendency to think that our road – or lack of one – is the only road there is. That is why we must rise in spiritual and intellectual terms to a third level of doubt when we are talking about the universal: what does my summit or my desert, my truth or my Way, say about the truth of others? What does my path say about paths, and what does my singular universal say about diversity? What, for instance, does this Quranic assertion-revelation say to the Muslim consciousness and to believers in general: 'Had God so willed, He would have made you a single community' (The Table Spread V 48). This implicit recognition of diversity seems to echo the essence of the ancient teachings of Hinduism, Buddhism and Confucianism. Knowing that we are on a quest, recognizing the existence of many different ways, and doubting the essence of our way, as opposed to that of others: these are the three basic elements of humility. If we discover them on our path, they will transform and reshape our being; if they are lacking at both the beginning of the journey and its destination, it is because they have deserted a reason and a heart that are imprisoned in arrogance and blindness.

NEEDS AND POWERS

Human beings always have contradictory aspirations: their will to assert their singularity is expressed with as much force as they need to discover both common truths and an absolute that transcends diversity and differences. Whilst the heart seems to desire a love that is like no other, reason wants to discover the essence that is common to all loves. The singular is universal and the universal is common, but the contradictions and paradoxes are no more than apparent. The universal is a need as much as a necessity: modern philosophies may well deconstruct systems and orders, and conceptualize a postmodernity in which points of view and truths are at once multiple and relative, but the individual and collective consciousness always come back to the need for meaning, certainty and a community of heart and/or of mind, perhaps of fate (such as a civilization, a nation, a culture or even an identity). The Spirits reveal 'the universal language of Nature', we are told by an African tradition that echoes the spirituality of the Sioux Indians as they strive to listen to the language of the earth to which all humans belong. According to the wisdom of the Sioux, the 'White Man' is afflicted by an optical illusion that makes him think that the earth belongs to him. The need for a commonality that reveals a truth (or an essence, or immutable elements that signify and structure) is a constant from Socrates to Kant, from Hinduism to Islam, from the bridge-building Nietzsche to the post-structuralists of deconstruction. The concrete universal is the axis of the origin, in the same way that the abstract universal sets up milestones along the road. The need for a universal is another name for the need for truth, defined here not as a value, but as a confident and definitive knowledge. That is, as it happens, why the human intellect tirelessly tries to formulate universal values that make it possible to explain reality in a priori terms or in terms of a rational construct. The advocates of both universals use weighty arguments to defend their respective theses: if there is a God, He is in a better position than any individual man to speak the universal truth about man; if, on the other hand, man is left to his own devices, then he must rely upon reason, which is a faculty common to all human beings, if he hopes to deduce universal truths that apply to all human beings. For such very different minds as Saint Augustine and Luther it was a matter of faith that the former thesis was self-evident, whilst the philosophers of the Enlightenment were convinced that only the intellect could enlighten us with common truths. Midway between these two positions, both the twelfth-century Muslim scholar Abû Hâmid al-Ghazâli (in his search for *Deliverance from Error*) and Thomas Aquinas (in his Averroist rereading of Aristotle) tried to reconcile these two aspects of the universal: that of the transcendent Being and that of immanent reason, the two orders of the concrete and the abstract universal.

Which leaves the question of power. When he discusses the 'origin of inequality among men', and therefore of power relations, Jean-Jacques Rousseau imagines the event that marked the historical birth of property: 'The first man who, having enclosed a piece of ground, bethought himself of saying "This is mine", and found people simple enough to believe him, was the real founder of civil society.' He then adds: 'From how many crimes, wars and murders, from how many horrors and misfortunes might not anyone have saved mankind, by pulling up the stakes, or filling up the ditch, and crying to his fellows: "Beware of listening to this impostor; you are undone if you once forget that the fruits of the earth belong to us all, and the earth itself to nobody."'[1] We find in Rousseau the ideal of sharing that we find in both African and Sioux spiritualities and in the critiques of private property that later finds expression in the thought of Marx, Engels, utopian and scientific socialism. What he is describing here, namely the seizure of power through its illegitimate appropriation, is to common property what the claim to have a monopoly on the universal is to values. In his *Pilote de guerre* (1942), the French writer and aviator Saint-Exupéry states with unexpected optimism that 'the cult of the Universal exalts and binds together particular riches'. Now it is possible that this celebration of the universal results in an unfortunate confusion between the cult of the Universal and the cult of the self. Some have no qualms about arrogating to themselves the ground of universal values and stating, forcefully and arrogantly, 'this is mine . . .

1. Jean-Jacques Rousseau, *The Social Construct and Discourses*, trans. G. D. H. Cole, London: Everyman, 1973 (revised edn), p. 84.

nly centre of what is seen and what there is to see.
s territory and its property, and the universal is its
lone is true, its reasons alone are rational, and only its
fied.

ic mind displays, moreover, one further characteristic.
istake to think that it accepts the existence of only one
the dogmatic mind is a binary mind. Whilst it states
is the only truth, that its Way is exclusive and that its
he only universal, that is because it stipulates – at the
that anything that does not partake of that truth, that
at universal is, at best, absolutely 'other' and, at worst,
staken. This simplistic state of mind can sometimes be
ly sophisticated; it is, to say the least, disturbing to observe,
t of postmodernity and globalization, the rise of mass
s that are, in varying degrees, intellectualized or emotive,
dogmatic and binary minds that are increasingly incapable
ng the complex multiplicity of points of view, paths and
is as though mass communications, with their colossal
heir capacity to bring psychological pressures to bear and
ntrolled complexity of their power to influence us, had shaped
dinary human being, in both the East and the West, the North
South. This increasingly universal human being is, like his
in danger of becoming simplified: we are seeing the global
f a binary mind that is increasingly devoid of complex ideas
ances, easily convinced of the truths it is told again and again,
zed by perceptions and impressions that are as intellectually
as the way it judges others is cut and dried and final.

THE UNIVERSAL SHARED

re are other dangers. The minds that do accept the existence
many categories and of many paths are primarily interested in
mparisons, and sometimes competition, and often conduct the
bate about the universal in terms of power relations. What matters
them is comparing values and principles and establishing a hier-
rchy of 'better' and 'best'. We often find that the advocates of these

and my people's'. The quest for the universal is sometimes – and all
too often – transformed from being a need to being a close and exclusive property, into an instrument of power and domination that has
provoked wars and deaths, crusades, offensive and expansionist
jihâds, forced conversions, civilizing missions, colonizations and so
many other 'misfortunes' and 'horrors'. Someone should indeed have
pointed out that that which is universal (and which, by definition,
cannot be appropriated) is summed up by the simple formula 'the
fruits belong to all' and 'the earth to nobody' . . . and those values are
everyone's property and everyone's exclusive right.

THE DOGMATIC MIND

There are various ways of appropriating the universal, claiming to
have a monopoly on it and then establishing a hierarchy of values,
civilizations and cultures. This sometimes involves forcing it on others
without further ado . . . 'for their own good', of course. In the realm
of the universal, the most natural, if not the least dangerous, attitude
consists in reducing the range of possibilities to one's own point of
view: my truth is everyone's Truth, and the truth for everyone, and the
values that derive from it are, a fortiori, universal. In that case, order
is imposed from on high and man adopts, for himself and with
confidence, the viewpoint of God or the absolute. All religions or
spiritualities run the risk of being distorted in this way: because we
look down the mountain from the summit, we deny the very existence
of the many slopes that constitute its very essence and give it its human
perspective. If we attempt to use the common faculty of reason to
elaborate a universal, the phenomenon is markedly different, but
the outcome is the same. As we make our way to the common good
of men, we accept, by definition, the existence of a multiplicity of
viewpoints, the need for postulates, doubts and even the paradoxical
contradictions of analytical reason, irrespective of whether or not we
believe in the existence of a truth or meaning. We can establish the
principles of immutability and change in the same way as Socrates
or Aristotle, or establish a framework of reference and hierarchies
of truth as we go in search of the first Reality, like al-Kindî (801–873)

and then Ibn Sîna (Avicenna: 980–1037). We can, like Descartes, determine a strictly rational method and maxims, or begin by observing the truths empiricists like Berkeley and Hume derive from what they call sense-data. We can in fact start out from a thousand philosophical postulates and theses, and construct so many truth-systems that their very number signals their relativity. When we are climbing a mountain, we accept that only one side of it can be observed. There is still a danger that we will think that, whilst we accept that the mountain has many slopes, only one path actually leads to the summit . . . the path we are taking. Even though we accept, in theory, that there are many hypotheses and many truths, there is a danger that, in practice, we will assume that our certainties and truths are exclusive. Or that we will pass a final judgement on those who seem to have taken a different path: they are 'alienated', to use Feuerbach's categories, or what Sartre describes as minds that have been colonized by 'bad faith', or even as 'cowards' or 'bastards'. Given that we alone can reach the summit, even though we are armed with the faculty of a reason that is shared by all, it therefore seems almost logical to think that the values that *we* discover or elaborate are naturally those of *everyone*. The terms of the equation are perfectly clear: the universal of reason quite naturally has to be accepted by all rational beings. If that is not immediately obvious, the passage of time will make it so. That is the meaning of Auguste Comte's theory of the three stages (theology, metaphysics and positivism). According to Comte, there is ultimately only one path, and not several, and some civilizations are simply ahead of others. For Comte, positivism is the ultimate realization of philosophy. Fukuyama translates this idea into political terms when he announces the 'end of history' and claims that the West is showing the way. This is not, then, a matter of diversity, but of temporality and historicity. It is quite simple: some are seen to have gone further down the road of human progress's linear evolution and will reach the universal before others. We cannot criticize those who support this approach for appropriating anything, for having established illegitimate property rights or for claiming to have a monopoly on the universal: like Rousseau, they accept that the fruits belong to all, and the earth and the summit to no one . . . the only problem being that only their path leads to the earth, the fruits and

the summit. And tha[...] of view.

It has often been sa[...] tions are the most likel[...] the universal and to as[...] quite true: if we believe[...] truth and fulfilment, ther[...] place of the God in whom[...] Truth we support; the histo[...] proof of that. And yet we ha[...] ent stance. There are religious[...] aware of the danger of beco[...] they have always striven to en[...] listening to others, who have fir[...] respected the multiplicity of relig[...] opposite extreme, we have seen ra[...] ist thinkers claiming to be open-m[...] the view that the very idea of their[...] status and their values a natural su[...] emerged from the French Revolutio[...] Because they confuse self-doubt with[...] some rationalists and sceptics succum[...] exclusivism, not in terms of the univers[...] one path that leads to it. That is the para[...] there is only one way to have an open m[...]

The common feature of the various atti[...] monopolization of the path to the univer[...] object of the quest than with the dispositio[...] on it. Points of view are determined by stat[...] tudes have succumbed to the dogmatic temp[...] intellect. In that sense, the dogmatic mind is n[...] or a believer's mind, and it is quite capable of in[...] intellects. The characteristic feature of the dog[...] dency to see things from one exclusive angle, and[...] absolutes: the dogmatic mind thinks that it is Go[...] ment from on high and in the name of eternity, jus[...] is the absolute viewpoint (Bergson sees this as a[...]

comparison–confrontation-based approaches have one thing in common: they often compare their values and their ideals with the practices and behaviours of others, and the latter are inevitably far less ideal. *Our* values of justice, freedom, equality and dignity are much more beautiful than *their* practices, contradictions or decadence. This intellectual character trait is universal. When we compare *our* theoretical ideals with *their* weaknesses and *their* inconsistencies, we become involved in a theologico-philosophical competition, and we have already won it: the intention behind the comparison is malicious and its terms are biased. The illusion of recognition is probably more dangerous than the absence of recognition.

We therefore have to get back to some simple or primal truths. Without any illusions, without any naivety and without any arrogance. As we have already said, the universal amongst human beings means, by its very nature, that we have to conceive and accept diversity, multiplicity, difference and singularities. Let me be more specific. Some have, as we have seen, defined universal values in terms of what they are in themselves, in terms of their revealed origins, or as being born of the innermost being that exists behind the illusory envelope of the ego. Spiritualities and monotheisms, for instance, associate the universal and the truth with an *a priori* and/or the transcendent. Others take the view that the universal is by definition that which is common to all Men, and that it must be discovered and formulated thanks to the mediation of reason, which is common to all Men. The *Universal Declaration of Human Rights*, for instance, is a product of a common Human reason, and it produces values that are shared by and universal to all Men. Others, finally, take the view that the two paths can converge and together determine what we all have in common. We can refute these points of view, dogmas and postulates by asserting that a belief in God is necessarily exclusive and expansionist, that reason is never cleansed of historical and/or cultural influences, or even that it is impossible to reconcile these two realms. Yes, we can do that ... but the essential point is still to reconcile ourselves with elementary logic.

No matter whether it comes from God, lies hidden beneath the veils of initiation, or is the work of reason; no matter whether it is the light that shines from heaven, from the peak of a many-sided

THE QUEST FOR MEANING

mountain, or from a desert where we go in search of ourselves or lose ourselves; no matter where the universal is, as we were saying, the product of these sources or the expression of these symbolic images, all the evidence and all our experiences reveal that there can be no universals unless they are *shared*. Acknowledging the existence of the universal does not preclude the possibility that it might be appropriated, monopolized or transformed into an instrument of power or even oppression. We have already stated that. Asserting and recognizing the existence of a *shared universal* implies, in contrast, a twofold recognition of both the common (the universal) and diversity (the shared). We must therefore regard the universal as a common space where several roads, several paths, several religions meet, and where reason, the heart and the senses meet. Appropriating the centre by denying the legitimacy of other points of view is out of the question. The important thing is to remember that we are always on the road from the periphery, where everything is by definition multiple, and where my truth needs the truth of others in order to protect my humanity from my angelic and/or bestial temptations. Blaise Pascal was quite right: 'Man is neither angel nor beast, and it is unfortunately the case that anyone trying to act the angel acts the beast.'[2] Others protect my humanity; their truth sustains my truth, and their difference enhances my singularity. Whatever our destination may be, our common humanity inevitably means that our paths will cross.

We must be, or become, curious. The idea of sharing obviously implies that of meeting, but also that of equality. Whilst believing with our hearts and minds in the greatness of our truth, we must recognize with our reason and in our hearts the legitimacy and contribution of the truths and values of others. Besides, the only values that are universally true are those that are shared in the centre, on the peak and in the common space to which the different paths lead. The point is not to *integrate* systems, values and cultures with other systems, values and customs, but to determine – in human terms – spaces of intersection where we can meet on equal terms. The intersection of what we have in common, rather than the integration of differences.

2. Blaise Pascal, *Pensées*, trans. A. J. Krailsheimer, Harmondsworth: Penguin, 1996, 678.

That changes everything: we all have to learn to bring about a real Copernican revolution within ourselves. We must learn, as we start out on the periphery, to develop a healthy curiosity about diversity and multiplicity, and freely commit ourselves to the quest for the centre. That takes humility, coherence, the ability to listen, respect and love. We must love human beings, with their qualities, their beauties and their difference, but also with their weaknesses, their doubts and their fears. This means acknowledging that they, like us, are capable of the best and the worst. They are so beautiful and so ugly, so worthy and so unworthy. Whilst we must never accept the unacceptable, we must nonetheless patiently arm ourselves with a lucid and curious love that has no illusions and that is full of hope. Our love must be resolutely universal, and eager to share.

3

Faith and Reason

What can I know? And what is the basis for what I know, what I think I know, or what I hope to know and understand? One major question about the essence and meaning of human knowledge stands out from the myriad questions that arise as we pursue our quest for meaning. Consciousness queries the nature of the known even as it apprehends the horizons of the unknown: death and what comes after death reveal, by a process of induction, our inability to understand its meaning and many 'whys', and our very limited understanding of so many 'hows'. The ocean of what is unfathomable is disturbing; the mystical crisis of the rationalist, mathematical and scientific mind of Blaise Pascal comes at the precise point where the philosophic-religious quest for meaning encounters the doubts of a reason that has realized that both infinities (the infinitely great and the infinitely small) are beyond its descriptive powers. 'The eternal silence of these infinite spaces fills me with dread.'[1] Here, 'silence' is another name for my lack of knowledge, and the 'infinite spaces' reveal the extent of my ignorance. It is truly dreadful.

Are there any self-evident truths that we can rely upon? Even before we raise the question of what we can know, it is probably helpful to determine which faculties allow us access to knowledge. The simple question of means (faculties), their existence and their capacities has, from the very beginning, been the source of disagreements, disputes and tensions within and between spiritual traditions, religions and schools of philosophy. My consciousness becomes conscious of the real, observes that my senses hear, feel, touch and so on, and that they

1. Pascal, *Pensées*, 201.

26

are the first 'means of knowledge', or at least its first mediators. The empiricists regarded them as the essential source of all rational and complex knowledge: they thought that my mind cannot understand the principle of causality if my eye has not observed it. The second source of knowledge is, therefore, obviously my reason, which observes, makes connections and tries to understand the world: it seems to make some progress where the 'hows' are concerned, but breaks down when it comes to the 'whys' of the world and of life. Another, inner faculty reveals that: the heart that feels and experiences (in a different way from the senses) and that apprehends and understands (in a different way from the mind). The faculty of reason very quickly reveals, in the most intimate proximity, its limitations: it is quite unable to understand the realm of the heart, its knowledge, its truths and even its loves, and is quite bewildered by it. The senses, reason and the heart: are we destined to have three types of knowledge produced by three distinct faculties? Are they complementary or contradictory? Is it possible to overcome the inevitable tensions that exist between them, and to reconcile them? That is the question raised by the typology of the three brothers Karamazov in Dostoyevsky's novel. They represent Pascal's three realms, and there is both a tension and love between them. The similarities and differences between them lie at the heart of the human tragedy and human hope. Dimitri and the exuberance of the senses, Ivan and the critical tensions of reason and Alyosha and the transparency of the heart shed a moral light on the order of our faculties and knowledge. This brings us to the heart of the real debate. It is indeed a debate about knowledge and understanding, but it is primarily a matter of deciding what is good for us, for our society and for humanity. Knowledge and ethics converge, as do science and philosophy, science and religion, and philosophy and religion. Is this a question of reason, or a question of faith? Who can tell us how, and who can tell us why?

Reason, of course, relies upon the senses and observation, and then establishes relations of similarity, genre and causality. It determines categories, works deductively and inductively and tries to understand 'how' the elements are set in place, and 'how' Nature and its realm are determined. It accepts the existence of relative truths and hypotheses, which it will (or will not) verify, and is aware of its own limitations when it comes to mathematical conventions, which are (like *langue*'s signs, according to Saussure) sometimes completely arbitrary. The important thing is to observe the real, to describe it, understand it and, in the long term, master it. That is the object of science. No matter whether it is bound up with a spiritual tradition or with God, faith is concerned with a different realm: what matters is not observing 'how', but answering the question 'why'. In that sense, faith is more concerned with the legitimacy of postulates, conventions and hypotheses than with the theoretical or technical explanations that derive from them. When described rationally (and therefore observed from outside), faith could be defined as a choice, a stance, that is based on postulates that reason cannot verify and on finalities of existence that it cannot grasp. Seen from the outside, faith would thus appear to be a more or less free choice of primary truths and ultimate ends. In his lectures on religious beliefs, Wittgenstein quite rightly demonstrates the non-pertinence of such 'external' descriptions: languages and meaning are only accessible from within, and a rationalist description of faith has already ceased to be faith.

In the Tao, for example, faith or belief, which comes from within, is concerned with the order of the world because it is a way of establishing a correspondence between being and the cosmos. There is no question of answering the 'why' (which both precedes and follows the 'how'). Taoism projects the meaning of that essential harmony on to the totality of knowledge: the 'why' in effect explains the 'how'. Such an approach combines philosophy, science and poetry. This is also Siddhârta's basic teaching: introspection, liberation from within and the escape from the ego prevent all forms of knowledge from being transformed into instruments of domination. There is no question of knowing in order to dominate. The point is that faith and our hearts allow us to understand the profound meaning of the Whole, to espouse its essence and to transcend individuation. This faith is a mystery, and this is what all the monotheisms express, from within and each in its own way. Grace, a call or a conversion: the heart seems to change its disposition, to be illuminated by a light that makes the world look different. The world makes sense. Seen from within, faith is therefore neither a postulate, a principle nor an end, but a light that is not the light of reason. A light of meaning. Faith is an inspiration, an impetus, a belief without reason (and/or with every reason in the world) that projects meaning everywhere and sacredness at all times: no faith, no sacred. Faith, like love (or precisely because it is love), is also belief: to love is to believe, without any shadow of a doubt. Faith takes many forms: some are associated with the immediacy of love, others with a disciplined self-liberation that gradually reveals the harmony of the whole, and still others with the essence of the purification of faith itself. In the course of his studies and peregrinations, Mircea Eliade concluded when he looked into the production of the sacred that it was 'an element in the structure of consciousness'.[2] There is therefore no avoiding the question of the relationship between reason and faith, as it concerns both our relationship with truth and the management of human affairs. At the point where metaphysics and the sciences meet, religion asks questions of practical and theoretical philosophy, and has questions asked of it.

DOGMAS AND POSTULATES

No human being can live without faith, belief or reason. Unless we are mad or completely inebriated, we all always believe in something, and we are all always trying to understand and master the principle of causality. That is a minimum. The countless actions of our day-to-day lives are permeated with both faith and reason, even if we are not always aware of that. We therefore have to stand back and look for a moment at the question of knowledge and truth. What do faith and reason teach us when we try to go beyond sense-perception or the realm of instinct? In the oldest spiritual and religious traditions, reason is integrated into a system which, as it projects meaning on to human experience, tries to exert a twofold influence: it explains the 'why' of things before it observes their 'how' (and to that extent, objective observations may be distorted), but it also attempts to determine first principles and truths that are legitimated by the system and not by analytic rationality.

2. See Mircea Eliade, *The Sacred and the Profane: The Nature of Religion*, trans. W. R. Task, New York: Harcourt Brace.

In the beginning, there are always truths that cannot be proven or verified: in the realm of faith, which, according to Christian ecumenicism, can be experienced as a 'setting off' on a journey, reason is invited to recognize its own limitations, and to include in its elaborations feelings, intuitions, spiritual discernment and, more generally, mystery, dogma or destiny. We are, to a greater or lesser extent, free to use our reason, but everything it tells us about the how of things must be integrated into what faith and belief reveal as to their why. Believing in a spiritual Way or having faith in God or a system of a priori values inevitably gives rise to a particular relationship with rationality, understanding and knowledge: our understanding of the world fuses with, and is illuminated by, the values we adopt: the science of facts is concerned with the science of ends, and knowledge aspires to serve the cause of hope. This may of course pose a threat to the autonomy of reason or the objectivity of reason. As we shall see, that has sometimes been the case in history, but the threat has not always materialized. And besides, it is possible that, as in our contemporary period, it is the absolute autonomy of the sciences that obliges us to reconsider the marriage between analytic reason and applied ethics.

Analytic reason does not recognize any dogma, or any of the a priori givens of a belief or faith in a Way, a God or a Revelation. In the absence of faith, reason does not have to come to terms with intuitions, mysteries, dogmas, hopes of revealed Texts. It observes that which exists and tries to establish its own truths for itself. Descartes' hyperbolic doubt is an attempt to construct a body of knowledge and truth on the basis of rationally established certainties. That is why he asserts that 'clear and distinct ideas' are true, and establishes the substance of the cogito in stages: the 'I think therefore I am' of the *Discourse on the Method*, and then the 'I am, I exist', which is necessarily true, of the *Meditations on First Philosophy*. Kant, Nietzsche and then the phenomenologist Husserl, among others, make a critique of both the first principle and the method itself, and see in the cogito a debatable initial postulate, whereas Descartes saw it as establishing a primary truth. Rationalism had, from its very beginnings, already established the potential limitations of the faculty of reason. Could reason claim to establish an absolute order of knowledge? Few philosophers or scientists had actually argued in categorical terms that it could, and, increasingly many of them insisted that reason must at least be autonomous within the field of scientific knowledge. They therefore defended their freedom to criticize the certainties and dogmas established by spiritualities and religions when they had some direct or indirect effects of scientific analyses. Even when it is based upon hypotheses, reason has the right to ask questions of systems, religions, sacred Texts, mysteries and all dogmas. Whilst there is a danger that faith will bind reason to an order that is imposed by a system of thought or a religion, it is clear that, *a contario*, a free reason that has been liberated from questions about the 'whys' and ends must be able to extend its powers of observation and its scientific and technical mastery to the whole of the real and to all human beings, without any limits and without any ethics. The contemporary period teaches us not only that the danger is real, but that the excesses are always apparent. 'Knowledge without conscience is but the ruin of the soul,' remarks Rabelais in Chapter VIII of *Pantagruel*,[3] as though to warn us against such divorces and potential acts of negligence.

We can see that the dualistic thought developed by the Greek philosophers has sometimes clarified the nature of these different realms, but that it has also caused the very rifts it wanted to prevent. For Socrates, Plato and Aristotle, the order of knowledge necessarily found its coherence in the realm of action. Philosophers, like practising believers, must know in order to be able to act and must act in the light of their knowledge. Such was the meaning of Greek wisdom. The paradox was, however, that it was indeed a dualist thought: the two realms of knowledge were linked together by the reason of the philosopher, and only his dialectical intellect could establish correspondences between the two. We are a long way from the spiritual traditions of Taoism, Hinduism and Buddhism. According to their inner logic, the microcosm reflects the macrocosm, and they have never given rise to an intellectual dualism. The important thing is not to consider the tension between body and soul, but to find within ourselves the correspondence between them and the Whole of the universe. Greek rationalism, on which Western philosophy is still so reliant, believes in

3. François Rabelais, *The Histories of Gargantua and Pantagruel*, trans. J. M. Cohen, Harmondsworth: Penguin, 1955, p. 196.

individuation and a multiplicity of dualist relations (the world of ideas and the world of the senses, body and soul, mind and instinct, wisdom and passion, and so on), whereas the ancient spiritualities hold that freedom consists in escaping from the individuated ego and in seeing ourselves as part of the interdependence of intimate and multidimensional relationships that have to be harmonized (but never only in intellectual terms). The monotheistic religions have not been subjected to the same Greek influence. It is probably Christianity that has borrowed most from Hellenistic logic (in the very exposition of its theology and humanism), whereas Judaism and Islam do not necessarily accept its basic dualism. Christianity itself, with its central assertion of 'the faith is love', has succeeded in distancing itself from its own dualist theology: its paradoxical rationality about the being of God and the mystery of the Trinity is shot through with outbursts of the love of God, in God and through Jesus that enfolds spiritual experience within an aspiration similar to that of the ancient spiritualities. We find in the French philosopher Henri Bergson (1859–1941) the same desire to escape dualism, to be free of the contradictions of the intellect and language (which spatialize movement, and codify and relativize what they claim to be transcending) by relying on the faculty of intuition, which penetrates its object from within. We can understand that this concerns not only the object of knowledge and the sum of knowledge that I can acquire but also the faculties and their hierarchy: what do my senses, my mind and my heart transmit to me even before I concern myself with the order and meaning of the world? The basic difference between faith, belief and reason is what these modes of knowledge have to say, individually or collectively, about the subject, before they turn to the question of the object.

As we can see, both the faith that enlightens and the reason that criticizes make demands and express hopes, but there is also a danger that dogma will become suffocating and that technical reason will come to be dominant. Basically, once the relationship between faith and reason is seen as a dualism (a clash between the two, the integration of one into the other, or the reconciliation of the heart and reason), it is only natural that we should observe tensions, struggles and a balance of power. Once again, it is a question of power.

AUTHORITY

The story of Galileo says it all. The Church, with its interpretation of the Bible, its beliefs and its dogmas, dictated its truths: the geocentric thesis was not open to debate, the earth was at the centre, and everything revolved around it. Galileo's research and descriptions of what he had observed, with reference to the Copernican theory, established that the earth, like the other planets in the system, revolved around the sun and was not the centre of the universe. His discoveries were challenged, rejected and condemned; he was judged and finally had to recant in 1633. The truths of religion contradicted the truths of science, and faith contradicted reason: power was at the time in the hands of the Church, and the claims of reason and science had to bow before its authority. This opposition and condemnation are part of one of the West's most important historical experiences. It was a sort of trauma that had a lasting influence on debates about human beings, knowledge, autonomy, freedom, power and, obviously, social and political organization. Whilst other civilizations, from India to China, and other spiritualities and religions, from Hinduism to Buddhism and from Judaism to Islam, have never experienced such a traumatic conflict-tension (or at least not in the same terms or in the same traumatic form), it is quite impossible to understand the West and Christianity (the influence of the West's Christian roots) without understanding the terms of the equation of Galileo's trial.

The Roman Catholic Church dictated a truth that was refuted by objective and scientific observation of the world. So who was to have the last word? For centuries, the clerical institution had held the power of both political and scientific authority: it dictated the order of truth. Thanks to the rediscovery of Greek rationalism, the Renaissance, humanism and the birth of the scientific mind, the basis of clerical authority was being slowly undermined: the West was witnessing the emancipation and autonomization of reason, and therefore the birth of the new epistemological authority of the sciences. The fear that faith would lose its meaning and pre-eminence lasted for centuries, and affected even those who seemed best placed to challenge rationalism. More than one hundred years later, Pascal warned, with

Descartes in mind: 'Write against those who probe science too deeply.'[4]
He warned against the reason and sciences that imperilled religious
authority by challenging the truths of faith and institutional authority.
Galileo had lost, and won.

As we have said, other spiritualities, religions or civilizations did not
experience this crisis or this epic confrontation. There are several reasons for this: the very nature of the spiritual and religious teachings,
the absence of a dominant hierarchical authority and the nature of the
bodies of knowledge that had been acquired or promoted the civilizational zones in question. Sometimes, several different factors came
into play at the same time, but the fact remains that the Western, and
Catholic, experience, of a conflict between faith (belief) and reason,
between spiritual givens and scientific facts is much more the exception
than the rule in the history of civilizations and of man. And yet these
questions are still of interest and are central to all of us, everywhere.
Are there two orders of truth? And if so, how are we to distinguish
between the truths of faith and those of reason, and how are we to
circumscribe the authority of religion and that of science? Does
metaphysics have anything to teach us about physics? Do we have to
distinguish between, and contrast and/or reconcile, faith and reason?
The texts of spiritual traditions from the Bhagavad-Gita to the
Upanishads do, as we have said, concern themselves with the science
of meaning and with self-liberation in the light of the Vedas and hymns
that reveal an absolute understanding of origins. Throughout all the
developments that led up to Hinduism, and even more so Buddhism,
we find a constant *de facto* principle: spiritual teachings concern
themselves with the scientific and objective observation of facts and
elements to only a very marginal extent. Implicitly, and in the end quite
explicitly, there are two different orders of knowledge. Meaning,
essence, enlightenment and freedom come within the remit of spiritual
teachings, whereas scientific observation reveals the order and the
'how' of things and describes itself as a means and never as an end.
By acknowledging their essential difference, those traditions assert
their imperative complementarity. Much later, we find that this is
still the case for the Jewish theologian, philosopher and physician

4. Pascal, *Pensées*, 553.

Maïmonides (1135–1204), who established distinctions and promoted correspondences between the realms of physics and medicine, and between those of theology and metaphysics. His *Guide for the Perplexed* is an attempt to make the science of faith and of (religious) law as rigorous as the science of physics. And conversely, he attempts to work backwards 'scientifically' from the rationality that is projected on to the world, to the necessary proof of the existence of the Creator of order and causalities. Faith and reason are clearly distinct faculties, as are religion and philosophy on the one hand and science on the other, but convergences are possible and, ultimately, necessary: we must never forget meaning when we observe the facts scientifically, and we must use the facts to ask rational questions about the meaning of faith. We find in Maïmonides the questions that run through the work of al-Ghazâlî (1058–1111), who had such an influence on him: the distinction between the two realms is a fact. Faith (which means trust and conviction) and reason (which means observation and analysis) should therefore not be contrasted when it comes to authoritative knowledge, but should complement one another as terms of reference for action. This is the primary focus of al-Ghazâlî's aptly named *The Balance of Action* (*Mizân al-'Amal*). Even before philosophical questions are asked about the nature of the relationship between faith and reason, we find in the Islamic legal tradition a methodological difference between the spheres of creed (*'aqida*) and ritual practices (*'ibadât*) on the one hand, and social affairs (*mu 'âmalât*) on the other. A distinction is made, within the very reading of Revelation, between what is revealed, which is clear and immutable, and injunctions of general orientation, which must be interpreted and contextualized in rational terms. From Abû Hanîfa (699–675) to Ja'far as-Sâdiq (702–765) and Ibn Hanbal (780–855), from the Sunnis to the Shias, and right down to contemporary scholars, there are indeed two realms within the practice of law. The realm of faith cannot do without the critical exercise of reason if it is to remain true to its own teaching: the union of the two is imperative, and harmony between the two is essential.

We find precisely the same problematic at the heart of the question of political authority. The separation of Church and State is a political expression of the resolution – by divorce – of the philosophic-religious crisis that Galileo experienced at the scientific level. A distinction is made between practices and powers in both spheres (the scientific and the political). Whilst the Church and faith determine and recognize authority from the top (God, Revelation, the clergy), it is imperative to recognize another authority that emerges from below, from the scientific observation and analysis of the real, from critical debate and from the plural negotiations required by science, philosophy and politics. The principle of distinction is fundamental, and the separation is both multidimensional and global. When asked about the separation of Church and State and the distinction between religion and politics, some Muslim scholars and intellectuals reply that, as in Judaism, there is no Church in Islam, and that it is therefore impossible to separate the State from an entity that does not exist. They miss – or avoid – the point. The important point is whether or not there is a distinction between the realm of faith and that of rationality, between dogma and science, between the revealed truth and the rational truth that is negotiated. Islam, like the spiritualities that came before it, like Hinduism and Buddhism and, in even more explicit terms, Judaism, establishes (through the work of its scholars and classical philosophers) an implicit distinction between these realms and an explicit categorization of the methodologies that establish the distinction between spheres and authorities. And besides, both the oldest spiritual and religious traditions and the most modern philosophies and ideologies have always tried to avoid two extreme solutions: confusing the realm of faith (and sometimes that of philosophy and belief) with that of scientific reasons to such an extent as to stifle and muzzle reason in the name of a meaning or system that is determined a priori; and divorcing the two realms to such an extent that the autonomy of analytic and technical reason, and its scientific and/or political logic, had nothing to say about questions about meaning, ethics and ends. We have encountered the quest for meaning, and then the quest for the universal. We now encounter the quest for harmony.

REASONS AND ENDS

The oldest African and Asian traditions taught the art of living in phase and harmony with the souls of the elements and with Nature. The Vedas and then the teachings of Hinduism and Buddhism all emphasized that there are correspondences between the macrocosm and the self-transcendence that could be achieved by becoming as one with the soul of the cosmos. The projection of the Greek Logos, which reflects the rationality that strives to apprehend it, is clearly a quest for harmony. The meaning of the Law, exile and the principles of faith that lie at the heart of Jewish orthopraxis call upon believers to remain true to their 'chosen' status in the light of the One, just as the teachings of the Christian faith and salvation through Jesus bring the gospel of the possibility of redemption through grace and love, which are faith and fusion. The Muslim tradition of proximity, memory and trust, with the heart and understanding of 'those who are endowed with insight', appeals for the same quest for harmony between the senses, the intellect and the heart. The involvement of Muslim scholars in the experimental sciences thanks to the rise of medicine, physics, chemistry and even astronomy from the Middle Ages onwards was a response to this fundamental intuition: the how of the world reveals or confirms to us all or part of its why: 'Only those among his servants who have knowledge are truly conscious of God' (Quran 35: 28). The link could not but be established.

Some philosophers have attempted to establish links between the realm of belief and that of reason by other means, or by grounding the rationale for belief or faith in rationality. Socrates tried to prove that the soul is immortal, and thinkers like al-Kindi (801–873), al-Farabî (c.872–950) and Ibn Rushd (Averroës: 1126–1198), who were all influenced by Greek thought, also tried to use logic to prove the necessity of the divine and/or Revelation. The proof of God's existence advanced by Descartes reveals the same desire: establishing faith on a rational basis and establishing links is a way of establishing the truth and achieving harmony. When he refutes Descartes' ontological proof of the existence of God, Kant reformulates for both himself and posterity the terms of the debate. As he moves from a description of pure reason to that of the judgements of practical reason, he has to abandon knowledge and replace it with belief. The science of the heart is not the science of reason, and we have to decide how to reconcile the two.

Spiritualities, religions and many contemporary philosophers (atheists, agnostics and believers) agree that we need to think about the ends of human action. Religion should therefore not meddle with scientific hypotheses, methods, theories or knowledge: the big bang or the theory of evolution (which, according to some contemporary biologists, must not be reduced to Darwinian interpretations) cannot be refuted by means of the 'proofs' of the creationism that is promoted by the most literal readings of the religious texts. That is simply not tenable. It would, however, be madness to give complete autonomy to an analytic and technical reason that sees no need to ask questions about the ends of human knowledge and actions. As many philosophers and humanists down to Descartes, Kant, Heidegger, Sartre and Camus have all said, faith must recognize the autonomy of reason and its ability to produce a rational, secular ethics. By the same criterion, reason must accept that it is legitimate for the heart, consciousness and faith to believe in an order and ends that exist prior to its observations, discoveries and hypotheses. Once the distinction between the realms of faith and reason, and religion and science, has been accepted, it is therefore futile to debate, and still less to dispute, the hierarchy of first truths (dogmas and postulates) or the nature of the authority granted to their methods and/or references (rational logic or Revelation). The religious or spiritual mind cannot recognize the primacy of the principle of reason that is invoked by the atheist, just as the atheist cannot accept the existence of the realm of faith, spirituality or the heart that is invoked by the Brahman, the believer or the initiate. Whilst it is impossible to agree about origins, sources, hierarchies and methods, it is possible to agree about necessary finalities. That faith or spirituality refers to an a priori ethics (which governs human rationality and acts) whilst an autonomous analytic reason produces an a posteriori rational ethics is not in itself a problem: it should allow us to reconcile the two perspectives and to participate in the production of the *shared universal* discussed in the last chapter. Faith should not meddle with scientific postulates, hypotheses and conclusions, just as reason must not discredit the essence and substance of faith in the name of a supposedly superior positivism. It is vital to preserve the human choice – and right – to believe, just as we must guarantee the human right to debate, question and describe the world as it is. Harmony must therefore emerge a posteriori: we have to think together (on the basis of our multiple references) about both the ends of how we act upon the world and the values and principles that constitute the applied ethics we have to elaborate in a pluralistic, collective way. The world now obliges us to think about ends. Michel Serres demonstrates in his *Contrat naturel* that the state of the planet means that we have to reconsider the nature of the autonomy of science. If we do not include the third party – Nature – in our human, social, political and economic contracts, we will destroy ourselves. We have no choice. We are back to the basic intuition of the earliest spiritualities: harmony between the self and the self, and between the self and the world, is the ultimate goal, and the senses, the heart and reason must play their respective parts in the general symphony. Pointless disputes about sources and origins make us lose sight of the need to reconcile ethics and ends. Reason must remain free and critical, but it also has a duty to question its own power and its potential self-importance. Science needs ethics in the same way that reason needs the heart. An atheist is, it is said, a believer who does not realize that he believes, for it is true that no one has ever been completely devoid of faith or of some belief. Knowing ourselves means having the humility to measure the substance of what we know and the tenor of what we believe . . . without ever allowing our beliefs to stifle our ability to remain curious, to ask probing questions and to never tire of criticism . . . and without ever allowing our analytic reason to trap us into the arrogance of those who despise, in themselves or others, the grammar of signs, the prayers of love and the knowledge of the heart.

4

Tolerance and Respect

Observing the horizon of one's life, infinities and finalities; seeking meaning, harmony and peace; the need is personal, but the quest is universal. We set out on our journey with our consciousness, our convictions, our questions, our loves and our hopes. Along the way, there will be joys, happiness, tears, pain and many doubts about the meaning of life, signs, absences and death. When we begin to look around us, to observe individuals and societies, and to study philosophies and religions, we realize that our loneliness is shared. Our solitude is plural, and our singularity is the similarity between us. And yet, from the earliest times down to our own day, there have always been many ways and an infinite number of paths through our cities, streets and neighbourhoods: the distinguishing feature of this one humanity is its diversity and differences. Ultimately, we have no choice.

And yet, is this intellectual disposition all it takes to make us accept the real and its diversity? Is observing and knowing that our quests and hopes are the same all it takes for us to come to terms with our differences, actually recognize our similarities and manage our differences in a positive way? Sitting at a desk, at a café, over a meal, in our classrooms, our lounges, our living rooms, our lecture halls or conference centres . . . all that is possible has been said over and over again with all the conviction and wisdom of our intellects and our humanities. In theory, or when our day-to-day life or wealth exposes us to the other's difference to only a very marginal extent, the magnanimity of human beings is certainly welcome, but it tells us nothing about life and does nothing to resolve the difficulties of diversity. When our ways of life trap us into a closed world of friends who look or believe like us, elaborating great and beautiful philosophies of tolerance and pluralism is a highly virtual petition of generosity, an extremely subtle way of avoiding the need to be open-minded. Those are but good intentions that amount to making a show of being anti-racist in intellectual terms, even though we come across no – or almost no – Blacks, Arabs or Asians (or Whites, or others, if you are Black, Arab or Asian) in our day-to-day lives. Being opposed to anti-Semitism or Islamophobia whilst living, deliberately or otherwise, at a respectable distance from Jews and Muslims is certainly an honourable intellectual stance, but basically it tells us nothing about the real personal attitudes of the human being who theorizes in that way. Ghettoes have their own characteristics and consequences: be they physical, social, intellectual or mental, those who live in them always nurture projections of themselves or the world around them that are more imaginary than true. In the ghettoes of the intellect and idealistic theories, there are a lot of intolerant and racist people who do not realize that they are. There are quite a few indeed.

Observing the horizon and apprehending, consciously and intellectually, the necessary diversity of human beings, and of ways and paths, is merely the beginning of the challenge. It is not enough; it never is. Facing up to and handling diversity requires us to abandon our high-minded theoretical and idealistic notions and to plunge into real life; it requires us to free ourselves from the ghetto of our noble, secure mind in order to enter the world of raw, tenacious and sometimes mad and dangerous emotions. It requires us to move from the controlled order of the mind to the chaotic tensions and disorders of the heart and entrails – of 'the guts', to use an ordinary but a far more expressive phrase. Living with and meeting the other, with his differences in terms of skin-colour, dress, beliefs, customs, habits, psychology and intellectual logic, refers us back to ourselves, to our inner horizons and to our subjectivity. Our minds do not control everything: our certainties and habits may be merely unsettled, but our emotions too react and express themselves. Away from our lounges and lecture halls, they can easily take possession of us. The other, all 'the others' and all their visible and/or supposed differences, reveal both the light and the dark dimensions of our humanity. When 'the others' seem to be confident and serene when we ourselves are unsure of our truths; when their visibility disturbs our living space and their presence upsets our habits; when they seem to steal the few jobs available; when their prosperity reminds us of our difficulties or even poverty ... then they stir up within us emotions that are to human beings what the survival instinct is to animals. The reaction is almost uncontrollable: all our fine words become meaningless, and we are back to our raw humanity. We have to come to terms with emotions, dispositions of the heart and our 'gut' reactions that colonize our minds with fear, suspicion, rejection and prejudices. Purely intellectual racism is a minority, and often marginal, phenomenon. The rejection – conscious or otherwise – of the other always feeds on a mixture of doubts, fear, insecurity and habits that have been upset, combined with real or fantasized rivalry for wealth, numbers or strength: the day-to-day problems of immigration, unemployment, poverty, of the feeling of being dispossessed, invaded and so on. We are indeed at the heart of humanity and of life: we may well despise and denounce the dogmatists and the racists in our cosy spaces, but it is most unfair not to take full account of the often highly instinctive fears and doubts which, in concrete situations, produce the worst rejections of the other. This is not a matter of justifying or minimizing racism, intolerance and xenophobia, but rather a matter of understanding where they come from, how they develop and how, finally, they can be fuelled and instrumentalized. The strength of the populist discourses that reject the other lies precisely in their ability to arouse and touch upon raw emotions, fears and 'the guts', and to provide them with simplistic reasons and explanations. Idealistic theoretical discourses must reconcile themselves to life and must not scorn the realist dimensions of the human in any sense.

THE OTHER WITHIN ME

And so, we are invited to go back to the inner self. The presence of the other speaks to me. It speaks to my intellect, to my heart and to my emotions: I therefore have to take the time to listen to how I listen to *them*. This journey to within the self and to the encounter with the other is the basic lesson of all spiritualities and religions. It is a way of directing the attention of human beings to their conduct and behaviour, and of making them examine causes of their actions, controlled or otherwise. The teachings of Hinduism place great emphasis on the inner dispositions which make 'good life' a balanced life. We must comprehend both the moral prescriptions that apply to all of use and those that are more specific to the stages and states of moral evolution (*varnasharanadharma*), and then identify their inner causes, which are also both collective (*dharma*) and quite individual (*karma*). Whilst everyone, Hindu or non-Hindu, shares with others an essential Self (*atman*) that exists beyond their imprisoned ego, every *karma* gives birth to a unique, individual psychological and moral disposition (*swabhava*) that the individual consciousness must apprehend and understand if it is to reform and improve itself. It is that quest, that reform and that inner liberation that will make it possible, after the necessary work on oneself to transcend the ego, to go towards the other. We must master ourselves and transcend the blind dispositions of the ego before we can grasp the principle of universal causality: the difference between roads, paths, minds and colours can then be understood from within through the disposition of the heart and the mind as they master the illusions and potential blindness of the emotions.

The parable of the blind men and the elephant, which we also find in the Buddhist tradition, reveals this same truth: when he touches some part of the elephant, each blind man believes he can describe the whole animal and is in possession of the whole truth. A superficial interpretation might lead us to believe that the important thing about this parable has to do with the fact that it teaches us that no one is in possession of the whole truth and that the ways are many. In fact, it also teaches us something else: men are blind, or have been blinded, and the problem of their relationship with truth and diversity has to do with their inner blindness. Only through fundamental introspection can they hope to reach the essential truth about the elephant and about points of view. What matters is not what the other is, or what the other tells me, but what, in me, prevents me from seeing, hearing, understanding and recognizing the other for what he is. What the other reveals about my problems, my deafness and my blindness, is what matters. The encounter with the other, and recognition of the other, are not the outcome of an intellectual approach, but of an initiation into the inner self, of introspection or a journey into the self

43

that should allow me to reconcile and harmonize the dimensions of my being: my consciousness and my heart, my mind and my emotions. More importantly, my rejection of the other reveals the blindness that is within me: on the periphery of the 'ego', the other is an accidental threat; at the heart of the quest, the other is a positive necessity.

This was the intuition of Socrates and his teachings about temperance. Whilst philosophy can lead us to the truth, it is also an exercise in mastering the self and its passions, a quest for the inner peace that alone can, in the long term, bring social and political peace. Indeed, according to Socrates, it is the philosophers who should be in charge of the affairs of the *polis*: by the time they have reached the age of fifty, their quest is well under way, and their initiation into the secrets of the soul and the dangers of innermost passions enables them to enter public life in all serenity. It is in *The Republic* that Plato develops part of his reflections on the inner self, and it is no coincidence that we find Aristotle's introduction to purification and catharsis not only in *The Poetics* but also in his account of *The Politics*. Art, and public performances of music and plays are collective instruments or social mirrors that refer us back to ourselves, our introspection and to the moral imperatives to transcend blind passions, and unhealthy fears and emotions. Aristotle's catharsis is an anti-populism: it teaches us and calls upon us to cultivate attitudes that are quite the opposite to those induced the populist discourses that are now undermining us. The former refer us to ourselves – profoundly and demandingly – so that we can acquire the wisdom we need to open up to the other in wisdom; the latter give us a superficial and frightening image of others in order to turn us in on ourselves in a closed and selfish way.

The same teaching is present in the three monotheistic religions. The presence of God, the Creator of all things and all men, is an appeal to the individual consciousness: all moral teachings are in fact meaningful only because they demand that we work upon ourselves, upon our behaviour, our feelings, our emotions and our fears. From Hinduism to the monotheisms and through Socrates, Plato and Aristotle, the common message is that we are all, naturally and potentially, inclined to reject the other, and to be intolerant and racist. Left to our own devices and our raw emotions, we can be deaf, blind, dogmatic, closed and xenophobic: we are not born open-minded, respectful and pluralist. We become so through personal effort, education, self-mastery and knowledge. As we have said, faith means confidence, a state of peace and balance and being at ease with ourselves. The quest for that inner peace is regarded as one of the preconditions for a serene relationship with the other and with differences. The universal message we find in the maxim 'Love thy neighbour as thyself' is an ideal that reveals three dimensions: first, it is indeed a question of love, or a disposition of the heart; second, love for the other means paying special attention to a love for oneself ('as thyself') which must be experienced, and deepened, as an invitation to look outwards, and not as a prison; and lastly, loving ourselves and finding inner peace is an implicit precondition for loving and welcoming others into the peace of our hearts. This is a love story. It is also a story about consciousness and demands: it is about knowing ourselves, recognizing our darkest natural temptations and going in search of our hearts' noblest aspirations. The price for a serene, respectful encounter with the other is the engagement in an encounter with oneself. When the Quran demonstrates that God wills a universal plurality ('We have made you into nations and tribes') it recalls the meaning of excellence in mastering and managing it: 'the noblest among you is the most deeply conscious of God [the most pious]' (49:13). This is the universal message of all philosophies, spiritual traditions and religions. They call upon us to examine our conscience, to work upon ourselves, and never to forget the need for trust and love, in oneself, of oneself, and in others.

TOLERANCE

And yet, is this enough? Have not religious institutions and spiritual authorities, in the course of history, advocated a message in direct contradiction with the above? In the name of the Truth they possessed, women, children and men have been persecuted, tortured and killed: no tradition can boast that it has never experienced excess on the part of its established authorities or on the part of some of its faithful followers. Beside the necessary mastery of emotions in one-self, what is also required is a solid rational framework for managing diversity. This is all the more important when power relations are established and institutionalized. When, in 1689, John Locke wrote his *Letter Concerning Toleration*, it took the form of advice and recommendations to a Church that possessed an almost exclusive political and religious authority. He argued against Hobbes (who, in *Leviathan*, took the view that civil peace was possible only when there was only one religion in society) and defended the idea of the need to accept religious plurality (he made an exception of atheism, which he regarded as both unacceptable and dangerous). He was trying to make a distinction between the authority of the State and that of the Church: the temporal power of the State established laws and managed the social contract and civil peace between citizens who had to be free to choose their religion and dogmas. Locke was addressing both powers and developing an argument based on the need to separate them: the State must manage the diversity of its citizens by protecting their freedom (both individual and civil), whilst the Church must 'tolerate' other religions within civil society and recognize their individual freedoms. Toleration is, therefore, seen here as a way of distinguishing between and limiting powers that sometimes merged and became exclusive and potentially prone to excess.

One hundred years later, Voltaire was inspired by the same concerns: written after the death of Calas and in order to denounce a miscarriage of justice, the *Treatise on Tolerance* also calls upon us to resist abuses of power and appeals to the conscience of men. It calls upon the State, the Church and God to ensure that all agencies of power promote the acceptance of differences and tolerance as a humanitarian principle. Its reflections and arguments are based upon the contention that man and human relations must be conceptualized and defended on the basis of a demanding rationality. It is once more a question of resisting abuses of power and of sending the authorities a strong and well-argued message based upon the power of reason and common sense, one that urges them to reject intolerance and the wars, deaths and injustices it brings in its wake. An autonomous and critical reason rebels against absolute authority, imposed dogmas, blind certainties and human pretensions to the absolute. It reminds human beings who are quite capable of seeing themselves as gods – or of acting in the name of God – that they are mere human beings, and that the claim to be in possession of the only truth leads to horrors and unacceptable miscarriages of justice that contradict the messages of goodness that they claim to be defending. Like Locke, Voltaire (and all the philosophers of the Enlightenment) lay siege to the citadel of a politico-religious authority that has to choose tolerance at the very point where it takes decisions and resolves how to act. Power must learn to tolerate – in the primary, rational, social, religious and political sense of the word – the existence of others, to 'suffer their presence' in the literal sense and to come to terms with plurality.

What was once an act of resistance in the face of powers (which can also be represented by the majority, the elite, the rich, and so on), and a brave, determined call inviting them to be tolerant, changes its meaning and import when we are dealing with equal relationships between free human beings, relations between the citizens of civil society, or even relations between different cultures and civilizations. Calling upon powers to be tolerant once meant asking them to moderate their strength and to limit their ability to do harm: this actually implied an acceptance of a power relationship, of a potential relationship of authority, such as the relationship that might exist between the State and individuals, the police and citizens, or between colonizers and the colonized. Deviations, infractions and a few differences could be 'tolerated' . . . they were 'suffered or endured'. But when it is no longer a question of resisting and limiting power, the positive dimension of tolerance is inverted: it becomes a disinterested generosity on the part of those who dominate and hold political, religious and/or symbolic authority, the authority of the majority or of wealth. Tolerance is intellectual charity on the part of the powerful. Locke, Voltaire and all the philosophers of the Enlightenment laid the first landmarks of resistance and called upon Church and State to be tolerant. They used their critical reason to undermine certainties and challenged dogmatic justifications for the dogmatic and autocratic management of difference. The critical, rational and reasonable appeal for tolerance from resistance thinkers, victims and the dominated is understandable, but it cannot be anything more than a stage in a process, and we must get beyond it. When standing on equal footing, one does not expect to be merely tolerated or grudgingly accepted: that others endure and 'suffer' one's presence is inadequate for oneself and detrimental to them.

RESPECT

When it comes to relations between free and equal human beings, autonomous and independent nations, or civilizations, religions and cultures, appeals for the tolerance of others are.no longer relevant. When we are on equal terms, it is no longer a matter of *conceding* tolerance, but of rising above that and educating ourselves to respect others. This requires a very different intellectual and emotional attitude. It begins with the recognition that the presence of the other within my own conception of the world is both a fact and a necessity. As we have seen, the oldest African and Asian traditions, like Hinduism, Buddhism and then the monotheisms, recognize, explicitly or implicitly, the necessary presence of other Ways, either because they stipulate that several paths can lead to the truth, or because that presence influences and shapes the way I conceive my own relationship with my truth. Pluralism is a precondition for humility and a defence against potential excesses. Islam confirms their transversal teaching by synthesizing the two dimensions. The verse 'Had God so willed, He would have made you a single community' (5: 48) expresses the essence and finality of this diversity in no uncertain terms. This message is echoed elsewhere in the Quran: 'Had not God checked some groups of people [nations, societies, religions] by means of others . . . the earth would have been corrupted' (2: 251) and 'monasteries would have been pulled down as well as synagogues, churches and mosques' (22: 40). Diversity, balance of powers, certainly implies the possibility of conflicts and disturbances, but the survival of men depends upon it, and it teaches us both a sense of proportion and humility. When it looks out on to the world and at societies as they are, consciousness looks inwards and has to reckon with its own tendency to take the view that 'my truth' is the only truth: we never stop being drawn to the sirens of the dogmatic spirit and its haughty smugness, which insists that our relationship with the other is only meaningful if we try to convince the other that we alone are in possession of the truth. Dialogue then consists in talking, and never in listening: the other is the privileged field for my proselytism. My truth has become a blind and blinding passion: it imprisons me when it should set me free; an alienation.

An act of reason is therefore necessary, first of all, to teach us to become reasonable. Recognizing the diversity of paths and the equality of all human beings are the two preconditions for the respect that allows us to get beyond the power relationship characteristic of relations of tolerance. In addition to that factual and objective recognition, we also need an intellectual disposition: if I can *tolerate* and 'suffer' the presence of someone I do not know, I cannot come to respect others without making any attempt to know them. Respect, therefore, implies an active and proactive attitude towards others, rather than a passive attitude: we have to be curious about the other's presence and being, and try to know the other once we have learned to recognize him. Recognition, active curiosity and knowledge introduce our intellects and hearts to the world of the complexity of others. We begin to gain access to their principles, hopes, tensions and contradictions, as well as the diversity of currents that run through their universe of reference. Tolerance can reduce the other to a mere presence; respect opens up to us the complexity of his being. At the same time, it teaches us to recognize that the other is as complex as we are: he is our equal, our mirror, our question. The other exists within me, and I exist within the other.

Reason thus brings us back to the path of the heart, to the path we were talking about at the beginning of this chapter. Philosophies, spiritualities, religions and currents within psychology have never been so unanimous as on the role the self-to-self relationship plays in the relationship between self and others. Nature and humanity, with their uniqueness and their colours, refer us back to our innermost being: with or without a microcosm, with or without God and with or without the unconscious, we must seek harmony and peace with ourselves, and accede to the other, within us . . . and discover ourselves in the other. Reason, which allows our consciousness to move from mere recognition to an understanding of, and respect for, the other, gradually opens up the way of the heart which, because it understands, appreciates and, because it appreciates, learns to love. The path is difficult, and the educational process is long: an encounter with the other, a return to the self, self-transcendence, initiation. The path of tolerance ends as the mind becomes more resolute; the way of respect is the key to a heart that is open. The reason that has become reasonable must learn to understand the essence and reasons of affection and love.

And yet nothing can ever be taken for granted: rejection, intolerance, xenophobia, individual and institutional racism, missionary proselytism, the temptation to colonize, truths that are not open to debate and collective, strong, even hysterical and deaf passions will always pose a threat to men, rich and poor, and to societies, industrialized or not. Human beings will never be totally safe from this dark side of their humanity. The spiritualities, philosophies and religions that have been present throughout history are there to remind us of these fragilities, these vulnerabilities and these dangers: they are so many reminders on the way, and their own excesses must also be there to remind us. We have to watch the world, and watch ourselves, with the humility of those who know, in the very depths of their being, that learning to become human is a process that never ends. Learn to listen, and to listen to ourselves, every day, always. And always recall one truth: nothing can ever really be taken for granted . . . neither respect, nor love.

5

Freedom

On his desert island in the Indian Ocean, Hayy Ibn Yaqzân ('Alive, Son of the Awake') discovers life, Nature and the elements, and learns to understand both his destiny and the universe. Brought up by a gazelle, he establishes the stages of knowledge by himself, and sets out, armed only with his reason. Inspired by the work of Ibn Sîna (Avicenna), Ibn Tufayl's twelfth-century *Hayy ibn Yaqzân* is probably one of the first philosophical novels. It deals with access to knowledge and the truth, but also with experience, determinism and human freedom. It was translated into Latin (*Philosophus autodidactus*) as early as the seventeenth century and then into English (*The Improvement of Human Reason*). The substance of its argument is immediately clear: who are we when we are alone? What can we know? What is the nature of our relationship with others? To what extent are we free? The novel also asks many other questions. Despite the lacunae of the European memory, the influence of Ibn Tufayl's work persists in many books produced all over the world, and especially in the West. Defoe with his Robinson Crusoe, shipwrecked on a desert island, al-Ghazâlî and Descartes, with their approach to doubt, Locke and Hume with their empiricist theory, and even Marx, Engels and historical materialism all return, directly or indirectly, to the themes of this seminal novel. It is indeed about knowledge and understanding, but it also tries to determine what I can do, what I want . . . and what I am in what I want.

In the heart of Nature, alone and living amongst animals and their instincts, a human being seeks to understand the real powers of his mind and the essence of his freedom (the feeling, or even the illusion, of freedom). The natural laws he discovers, and then the rules he establishes, refer him back to the conditions of his own existence: he is trapped in a body and ruled by needs and by instincts, and they decide for him, within him and before him. It is, paradoxically, external laws that make him aware of both his freedom and its limitations. My nature decides for me, but it is when I am confronted with the external law that I become aware of what I can decide and of what the law reveals about what I can and/or want to undertake. Much later, Rousseau and Kant will assert that there is no such thing as freedom without the establishment of the law ... and the imaginary experience of Hayy ibn Yaqzân or Robinson tends to demonstrate that the law (of instinct, of Nature, or even of the social order) comes first, and that it is the law that allows us to determine whether or not there is such a thing as freedom. In other words, and in both cases, human freedom exists only in relation to that which limits and/or permits it: it is and exists only if it can be measured. The natural law and the natural order, like instinct, give birth to the substance of freedom in the same way that the need for a law expresses the aspiration towards order and freedom. The novelist Michel Tournier intuitively grasps this seeming paradox in an original way in his *Friday and Robinson: Life on Speranza Island*: alone and free, Robinson suddenly feels that he is imprisoned in the order of Nature and the great cosmos, and it is his decision to establish laws for himself and his servant Friday (social laws) that gives him access to the meaning of his freedom. Any reflection on freedom thus raises difficult, complex, paradoxical and contradictory questions: every consciousness knows that it is to some extent determined by its body, its instincts, its parents, its past and even its feeling ... and yet every mind is inspired and driven by a freedom that has the ability to understand the world thanks to the strength of reason, and to repaint it thanks to the power of the imagination. We cannot decide everything, but we know that we can decide so many things ...

POWER AND WILL

We must set off down the winding path that leads to freedom. It begins on the periphery of social experience and insensibly takes us inwards, to the inner self. The French novelist Honoré de Balzac developed a highly original theory of description. It consisted in hovering around his characters, describing their town, their neighbourhood and then their homes, their bedrooms and finally focusing in on their clothes, their physical appearance, their hands, their eyes and the most minute details of their faces. This 'circular description' owes nothing to chance and is based upon an underlying philosophy: no matter whether we choose them or not, external details (our town, the way we arrange our bedrooms, the expression of our hands ...) say something about us, about our inner being and psychology, and they inevitably shape us. They are part of the individual's being and personality. A reflection upon freedom reveals something similar: it is by beginning with the periphery, with what determines us from outside, that we can best understand – and understand most deeply – the meaning of and preconditions for our inner freedom, in ourselves and for ourselves. Freedom, with its multiple dimensions and paradoxes, invites us to study it in circular fashion and then to close in on it so that we can make a better analysis of its conditions and potential manifestations ... and, above all, to learn to distinguish between realities and illusions.

In Balzac's philosophical and fantastic novel *The Wild Ass's Skin*, the young Raphaël has a disturbing and revealing experience. Born into a ruined family that is crushed by the authority of a despotic father, he studies hard in the hope of winning his social freedom. Ambitious and eager to climb the ladder of success, he meets the wealthy Feodora – the 'golden fairy' (*fée dorée*) – who very quickly takes over his whole being. She represents both the upward mobility that determines him from on high and the love that now chains him down. It is a Faustian pact, and possession is never far away. Lost and destroyed, he is thinking of suicide when he meets an old antiques dealer who gives him a talisman and reveals the secret of life to him. The talisman – the skin of a wild ass – will allow him to gratify his every desire, but it will shrink in size whenever he expresses his desires. The power of his apparent freedom chains him and will lead him inexorably to death. The old antiques dealer whispers to him that the secret of freedom and happiness lies in self-control and in a marriage between knowledge, will and power. We must choose, even and especially when we have to face up to what appears to be forced upon us: the objective conditions of life, our aspirations and even the impulses of our hearts. Raphaël's fate raises the first major question about freedom: even before I know what I want, I must ask myself – from where I stand objectively – what I can do. Two hundred years later and on a very different continent, the same question runs through the family saga of the Buendias in Gabriel García Márquez's novel *One Hundred Years of Solitude*. Six generations of lives, cyclical repetitions and the inevitable return of the same – which is always different. Living in solitude like Raphaël, Aureliano finally understands that the prophecy on Melquiades' parchments has come true with him. He could only do what had to be.

The myth of the 'noble savage', like the stories of Hayy and Robinson, was meant to represent man outside all social determinations and to raise the first question: what could the individual do in such circumstances? There were already many determinations: the needs of the body, the instincts and desires, not to mention the limitations of the intellect and the understanding. Whilst Rousseau held that human beings were not necessarily destined to become social animals, the intuition of most philosophers and novelists was different: the only justification for the solitary experience of Hayy or Robinson was that it allowed an extrapolated study of what made them beings who were naturally and eminently social. The imaginary projections of an individual who is left in solitude with nature reveal the sum total of the conditions that are required to make him human. Over and beyond his ability to construct the edifice of truth on a rational basis, it is indeed a question of determining the a prioris of his humanity by establishing the sum of his needs and his abilities. As the antiques dealer suggests to Raphaël, we can certainly resolve to master our will by preserving a minimal degree of will power (and thus finding peace); but if it is a matter of being inspired by a will that has no power, then we must learn to live in perpetual, and almost inhuman, suffering. That is what Buddhist teachings tell us when they codify the stages of our possible release from the cycles of suffering. And besides, we always want more than we can have. The important thing is therefore to determine the conditions of our power in order to then ask questions about the source and essence of our will.

SOCIETY

Having raised these initial philosophical questions (about being), we come to the second circle on the paradoxical road that leads to freedom. What can thinking about freedom and society mean, if society does not guarantee me the preconditions for my humanity? At the halfway point between a sociological approach and a philosophical study, we must begin by formulating these simple but essential truths: there can be no freedom and no power unless the human need for basic necessities has been satisfied. Like the projections inspired by Montaigne's myth of the 'noble savage', the stories of Hayy and Robinson Crusoe abound in implicit a prioris about the status of man. In his state of nature, man eats, drinks and satisfies his elementary needs, and that allows him to move to the higher stage of asking philosophical questions. By satisfying his physical needs, the environment frees the individual from the first objective causalities that inevitably determine human behaviour. Now what seems to be taken for granted in the state of nature (and it is clearly absent from the reflections of too many philosophers) has never been a day-to-day, objective reality for millions of people throughout history and all over the contemporary world. Poverty, want and injustice in societies sometimes force human beings to regress to a status that is even lower than that of the noble 'savage'.

Before looking into our freedom to act and think, we should therefore look at the world and respond to the priorities of our times. At the human and physiological level, the first freedom is the freedom we acquire once we have satisfied our elementary natural needs: being able to eat and drink, having the wherewithal to protect ourselves against the threats posed by the environment, and sexual fulfilment are *sine qua non* preconditions for access to even the idea of freedom. Depriving human beings of their elementary rights and powers actually means leaving them to the mercies of the things that will determine them, take over their entire being and imprison them before they have even achieved human status: they are individuals without any real freedom, and the 'freedoms' their thoughts and imaginations may enjoy make no difference. A human society that does not provide its members with that minimum deprives them of their rights, their dignity and their humanity. Billions of individuals are now in that position. As we start off down our circular path in search of 'freedom', it is here that we encounter the first stumbling block, the first real, palpable and crude obstacle that stands in our way: to speak of freedom in the midst of poverty is like philosophizing about humanity in the midst of the inhuman. And here, the social sciences call philosophy to order, and that is how we should read and understand the philosophic-political, economic and sociological reflections that punctuated the nineteenth century in the West: frenzied industrialization, growing poverty, a deepening gulf between classes, and a feeling that systems of production and society in general were being dehumanized. The utopian socialism of Fourier, Owen and Proudhon, the scientific socialism of Marx and Engels and even the thought of the anarchist Bakunin were primarily responses to these brute and brutal social and economic realities. The preamble to the Universal Declaration of Human Rights alludes to these realities because they influence all our attempts to promote rights, freedoms and peace.

When human reason has at last been freed from the constraints of instincts, bodily needs and its own survival, it discovers the world, discovers itself and seeks to understand. The natural aspiration, desire and need to learn and understand are some of the most immediate attributes of the human consciousness. Interacting with the environment and other humans, discussing and pondering the self and others, and mastering the elementary principles of natural causality are the first spheres of the education that, once the need for prime necessities has been met, develop and complete man's humanity. Whilst the first precondition for freedom has to do with guaranteeing men the right to satisfy their vital needs, the second is education, which determines the very essence of that freedom at the intellectual and psychological level. Education means giving individuals the tools they need if their minds, being and individuality are to be autonomous; this is not simply a matter of acknowledging the power of their will, but of becoming its agent. Education is what allows human beings to become the true 'subject' of freedom. It is a necessity, and it is a right. Extending and going beyond his reflections on the state of nature, Rousseau is inspired, in the idealist project of *Emile, or, On Education*, by this basic intuition: education is the essence of social man's humanity and a precondition for his autonomy and freedom among his fellow men.

We then have to introduce the notion of inalienable rights. As we have said, a society that denies the elementary needs of human beings and that does not guarantee them a minimal education dehumanizes them. And if, incidentally, it does not allow them to make use of their freedom of conscience, thought, expression and action, it imprisons them. Common laws and an acceptance – willing or not – of the constraints that are needed if we are to live in a society nevertheless presuppose the establishment of principles that ensure that no individual – man or woman – can be deprived of his or her status as a rational and autonomous subject. At this point, and as we noted at the beginning of this chapter, laws allow us, conversely, to determine the extent of the freedoms that are granted to the individual and the community. Individual and civil freedoms are so many rights that human communities must defend: by allowing individuals to fulfil all the potential of their being, they grant them powers relating to their humanity and their status as subjects, or as human beings who know that they exist, that they are free and that they are not alone. That is the meaning of Rousseau's formula: 'One person's freedom ends where another's begins.' Its spirit is already present in the oldest philosophies of law, from the *Twelve Tables* of Roman law (inspired by Greek practice), which recognize the rights of plebs, to medieval Jewish juridical traditions (and especially Maïmonides) and medieval Islamic traditions (which made a distinction between the rights of God and the rights of men towards each other as early as the eighth century). Despite their differences of opinion about God, reason and faith, Thomas Aquinas and the medieval philosopher Duns Scotus extend and elaborate this line of thinking in the Christian world, with particular reference to the rationality and meaning of the contractual relationship.

Even before we turn to philosophies of being, freedom and responsibility, the equation is very clear: any society that does not guarantee the conditions for the survival and life of all, education for all and the rule of law to defend individual freedoms (in the handling of interpersonal relationships) is a society that fails to respect basic human rights. It deprives its members of their potential and their powers, and, at best, encourages their illusions as to the immensity of the power offered by the virtuality of their will, their dreams and their imagination.

FREEDOM AND RESPONSIBILITY

We have now reached the third circle: that of the individual and his intellect when he no longer asks questions about the meaning of his power in an absolute sense, as Raphaël and Aureliano did, but about the nature of his responsibilities in his day-to-day life. These debates and disputes are long-standing and profoundly universal: all spiritual traditions, schools of philosophy and religions have been confronted with the complex and paradoxical relationship between freedom and determinism. Do we experience an illusion of freedom at the heart of the unavoidable reality of overall determinism? Or is it the opposite of that, and are we basically free, even though we appear to be the prisoners of our destiny? Every consciousness is, at one moment or another, preoccupied with this question. Every consciousness asks questions about the choices it has made, its relationship with its past and present and, of course, about the nature of its responsibilities at the existential and social level. Who decides? Do I choose for myself? Am I really free to decide? Having gone beyond the questions of survival we discussed earlier, the human intellect now has to address questions of a different order, and they are difficult, complex and disturbing. Some learn to live with them by simply concluding that they appear to be free, and therefore feel free, whilst others suffer as they struggle with their doubts, with painful events and with the feeling that they are so trapped and confined as to question the very idea of freedom.

One recalls the young Rimbaud trying to understand the curse that has been laid upon him in *A Season in Hell*. In his quest for freedom, peace and silence, he goes back to his origins, to his *Bad Blood*, and concludes: 'I belong to a race that has been inferior throughout all eternity.' That is why he rejects the order 'of jobs' and of God. He is not responsible for his destiny, and nor, at bottom, did he decide to be a poet: haunted by his past, he is haunted by that other 'I' that makes him watch the 'development of [his] thought' as a bystander. He has decided nothing: neither the intensity of his curse, nor the essence of his election. He endures, suffers, rebels and finally loses heart. So much so that he wishes to remain silent for ever. 'I am the one who suffers and who rebelled,' he writes, as though to signal the meaning of the chains that bind him. More serene and older, the German poet Rainer Maria Rilke reveals the same feeling and the same demands to the young poet who wrote to him: writing is not a free act. It must be prompted and driven by a higher necessity that one does not choose. Diderot's character *Jacques the Fatalist* reached the same conclusion about the illusion of freedom: 'Everything is written up there.' He wanted to be serene, fatalistic and rational: why suffer and cry over what one cannot decide? 'It is written', '*Maktûb*', to use the well-known Arabic expression . . . there is no reason to suffer or to feel pity. All the philosophers of the Enlightenment, from Germany to England and France, tried to solve this existential equation. The German philosopher Leibniz tried to reconcile an overall determinism (as to the principle of causality) with the human ability to act within it. Voltaire caricatured his thought in *Candide*, but Leibniz was, basically, making an objective statement and raising the central question asked by all spiritualities, philosophies and religions: the determination of things and events is beyond question just as my freedom to act is beyond question. How can we reconcile these objective givens? Where does fate end, and where does my free will begin? What am I responsible for?

There can be no human responsibility without freedom. He who has no choice cannot be judged in any way or sense. That is the question that colonized so many minds in the three monotheistic religions: if God knows everything and His knowledge encompasses the past, the present and the future, then He knows what will come to pass, and knows my choices and my destiny. How can we reconcile that proposition with my freedom and, a fortiori, my moral responsibility towards men and in the face of God's judgement? The mainstream Jewish tradition distances itself from the concept of original sin, and clearly opts for the principle of free will: man is free and responsible for the choices he makes. Jewish orthodoxy and the more mystical currents agree on one basic idea that echoes the theses of Hinduism and Buddhism. We also find it in the Christian and Muslim traditions. We will come back to this, but for the moment let us recall the sharp debates about the question of grace and free will that run through the whole of Christianity, both Catholic and Protestant. In the sixteenth century, the Jesuit Luis Molina attempted to reconcile the thesis of predestination, which was defended by Saint Augustine (who had argued against the monk Pelagius and his defence of freedom), and the idea of effective free will, and brought the wrath of the Dominican order down upon himself. He also rejected the theses of Luther and Calvin, who invoked the authority of the same Augustine in order to assert that predestination was the essence of the experience of faith. The Jansenists, who were so central to the Catholic Reform movement, tried to reappropriate Augustine's heritage and developed a theory of grace that radically contradicted theories of free will: only God's 'efficacious grace' could allow human beings to come to terms with their status and a state that was tainted by original sin. We are a long way from the conclusions of the Council of Trent (1547), the positions adopted by the Jesuits and, as it happens, the theology of Thomas Aquinas, all of whom attempted to reconcile human freedom with the power of God. These theologians postulated that, through his will power and reason, man, unlike animals and objects, had the ability to act freely. According to Aquinas, that was in fact a precondition for religion itself. Were it not, he argued in his *Summa Theologica*, 'advice, exhortations, precepts, prohibitions, rewards and punishments would be in vain'. We find the same debates, probably influenced by the encounter with Christianity, in the Islamic tradition. Belief in fate (*an-qadr*) is one of the pillars of faith, but schools of thought differed over the nature and limits of the freedom bestowed upon man. The Ash'arites, who defend the idea of predestination, are contradicted by the rationalist Mu'tazlites, who defend the free-will thesis. Two schools emerged from these debates, *al-qadariyya*, which defends the latter thesis, and *al-jabariyya*, which asserts that the very essence of God, who knows and understands everything about men and the future, means that men are completely predestined. Both Sunni and Shiite jurists have attempted to reconcile the two theses. In the fourteenth century, Ibn Taymiyya made a distinction between two realms: God knows all things and everything and established the order and laws of nature, but He granted man the freedom to make moral choices, to act and therefore to influence his destiny. What God knows, man does not know, and he must therefore not seek to go beyond the limits of his knowledge. He must come to terms with that and act as best he can as a being who is free and responsible in the light of God's prescriptions. As we can see, the theses of Thomas Aquinas and of the Jesuit order are close to that position.

The fourth circle is that of the heart and of the paradoxical union of necessity and freedom. As we have said, man is responsible to God and his own conscience only when his freedom is guaranteed. This means resolving potential contradictions and, above all, resisting the temptation to succumb to certain illusions. Every human being knows that he or she has the rational ability to act freely, but it is difficult to deny the constraints of the body and, for believers, the logical implications of the presence and will of God. The paradox is profound. From that point of view, it has to be noted that the Hindu and Buddhist traditions, certain religious schools and some mystical and philosophical currents are in agreement here, and assert that true freedom does not correspond to such a superficial intellectual impression, and that it is a spiritual freedom that is to be found in the depths of being. We therefore have to undergo an inner conversion, enter into ourselves and free ourselves from the illusion that we are free even though we are imprisoned by causalities, the ego and our desires and drives. Just as social and collective laws refer us back to the substance of individual freedom, here it is immersion in being – in the self – that, over and beyond general determinism and the contingencies of its manifestations, allow us to penetrate the essence of the law that governs all things, of the Logos and/or that which animates it (in the sense of giving it a soul). This initiation into the fullness of being by transcending the self, the ego and the prison of desires is a liberation and gives us a subjective access to the freedom that exists at the heart of the Whole or in the proximity of God. It is a demanding freedom, from self to self, beyond oneself: an extinction of the ego to experience unfettered plenitude. Trapped by the intellect and by words, Hamlet concluded that death was the only escape, the only true extinction of the self and suffering; the above-mentioned traditions say the opposite by calling upon us to accede to the true Life that lies beyond the paradox of the disappearance of the ego. We have to enter into ourselves so profoundly that, as the Jewish tradition has it, the will of God (or of the cosmic order) becomes our own will, and that the two merge, fuse and become one. Christianity speaks of the same fusion through the love of God, and Islamic traditions evoke this proximity in love that reaches its paroxysm when the ear, the eye, the hand and the foot hear, see, hold and walk in and by the light of His presence. The French philosopher Bergson outlined an intellectual mysticism that bore similarities to this experience: in his view, intuition allows us access to the essence of time, to a time that is neither intellectualized nor spatialized, and to the movement that is the essence of beings and of life. This is the tabernacle of freedom. Like the artist, the philosopher knows, feels and penetrates, and can therefore go beyond his individuation and partake in the soul of the Whole. Although they follow different paths and hope for different ends, spiritualities, religions and mysticisms reveal here the meaning of the same experience: we gain access to inner freedom, to the freedom of being not by letting ourselves go (or doing what we apparently want to do), but after a demanding work of introspection and self-mastery. And in our introspection we go on asking questions about the source of our wanting, the finalities of power and the essence of freedom.

SAYING 'I' AND ART

The path that leads us to the fifth circle allows us to get beyond the remaining tensions, to celebrate the communion of mastery and freedom. First, we have to free ourselves from paradoxes, and even contradictions, by freeing ourselves from what determines us physically so as to attain the essence of what frees us spiritually. Each stage in this quest for the self requires mastery, discipline, choices and ethics. Each of these stages reproduces the same questions with more and more intensity: Why am I what I am? Why do I think what I think? True freedom can only be a liberation: freedom is an ideal in a process, an ever-renewed experience, it is never achieved. It is interesting to note the similarity between this mystical observation and Freud's theory of psychic determinism: we are bound, consciously and/or unconsciously, and we always have to go back to the source, to our blocks and repressions, if we are to overcome the tensions of the neuroses that inhabit us. We can never escape them, and we must never be deceived by even the most beautiful manifestations of sublimation (usually through art): sublimation is not freedom, but merely a way of expressing and managing our imprisonment and/or traumas.

Many philosophical theories share this sense of impotence, or this necessary awareness of the determination in the natural order, in societies and in the individual. Spinoza's determinism or Marx's historical materialism do not entail fatalism or an inevitable passivity; on the contrary, they essentially point to the nature and limits – and therefore the actual powers – of human action. It is not a matter of measuring power by the standards of the will, but of inverting the terms of the question: what can I want? The answer given by the existentialist Sartre is radical in two senses. Because 'existence precedes essence', I am condemned to be free and must assume the totality of both my will and my power. I am therefore fundamentally free, and absolutely responsible: attenuating circumstances exist only for minds in bad faith that try to hide behind 'circumstances' . . . or faith. In the name of that freedom, it is also natural and logical for the intellect to produce an ethics that is rational, autonomous, secular, individual and demanding, because it must never neglect the human community in which and for which it finds expression. We are a long way – a very long way – from the paths of mysticism, faith and the extinction of the ego; here, the subject knows that he is alone, says 'I' and assumes his freedom as an individual. As the Lithuanian-born French philosopher Sartre puts it, freedom is 'the ability to do what no one else can do in my place'. And yet, as we go down the road to freedom, we find the same hopes, the same demands, the same need for ethics, or even laws, to regulate and give substance to freedom itself. Freedom demands awareness, rigour and, paradoxically, discipline on the part of the subject, the ego/self, the believer and the philosopher as well as the mystic. No matter whether we are alone or part of a community, we enter the virtuous circle of the experience of freedom and liberation, and we never emerge from it to the extent that we are human. For whilst freedom is a precondition for responsibility, one of the dimensions of responsibility is that we are completely responsible for the use we make of our freedom. Whilst the law can regulate, it cannot codify everything: in human relationships, friendship, love or a mere encounter, two free beings must recognize their mutual sensibilities and aspirations. The law sometimes allows us to say things that humanity, or common decency, invites us not to express. The quest for a reasonable freedom consists as much in demanding legitimate powers as in learning to master them.

We are at last coming to the end, or perhaps it is the origin. Art is the privileged school for this encounter between mastery, freedom and liberation. A pianist or violinist who plays Mozart, Schubert or Beethoven spends years trying to master a difficult technique. The rules are constrictive. He or she must begin again and again to practise, to internalize a technique ... concentrate, master the emotions, the body, the fingers. The technique is gradually acquired. The rules are assimilated, and they give the man or woman who has mastered them an unexpected freedom. His or her hands fly and infinite realms of possibility, expression and improvisation open because the laws, rules and techniques of the genre have been so completely mastered that they appear to be natural, simple and easy. Mozart or Beethoven suddenly seem to be, to be there and to create being. In art, a technique that has been mastered is a liberation. When Baudelaire speaks of the 'evocative magic' of modern art, he expresses the same idea (and introduces the possibility of transgression): a complete mastery of the piano, the paintbrush or language grants access to a freedom that is made possible through the exercise of constraint itself. After having *studied* painstakingly, the musician, painter or poet suddenly *plays*, and his expressive and evocative powers appear to be both limitless and almost magical. The mastery of a technique and its external rules allow us to concentrate on the inner universe, with its emotional density and shades of intensity: we can set feelings, or words, or colours to music ... and even, through an alchemy of poetic correspondence, colour the sound of words, or put words to colour tones: The variations of this theme are endless. This expressive capacity is indeed freedom and a liberation: everything becomes possible. Religious and mystical experience has a lot in common with this kind of artistic asceticism: study, self-control, mastery of the ritual, the rules behind apparent forms is the path that leads us inside the self in order to encounter and transcend the self, and to experience the spiritual liberation of being. Just as there can be no free artistic improvisation without a mastery of technique, there can be no liberating spiritual experience without study, or without a codified and integrated ritual. This is, however, not without its dangers, as we must never lose sight of our goals: an artist who concentrates solely on technique destroys art, and the believer or mystic who becomes obsessed with ritual destroys both meaning and spirituality. Basically, the same is true of our public life and interpersonal relationships: the law and the rules certainly help to protect our respective freedoms, but too many laws eventually stifle and confine us. That is the price we pay for our freedom: we must experience paradoxes, reconcile opposites, establish balances and harmonies and never lose sight of either apparent illusions or profound ends.

6

Fraternity and Equality

Equality between human beings is an ideal. Religions, philosophies and political ideologies have made the equality of them the essence of their teachings, principles or systems. Individuals must be treated with dignity and fairness. And yet a journey through societies and nations is all it takes to convince us that we still have a very long way to go: political philosophies have been elaborated, Declarations and Charters have been drawn up, ratified and signed, and laws have been passed, but the reality of inequality and discrimination imposes itself on us. Universally. Whilst equality is a de facto legal principle, we cannot avoid the conclusion that the law is not enough to establish it. Before we talk about laws and rules, we have to discuss and evaluate the very idea of humanity, and of its unity and diversity. And besides, there can be no law without ethics . . . without a certain idea of man, of the good, and of social and political ideals, and there can therefore be no question of legal equality amongst men without a moral philosophy that establishes the nature of human relations. What is needed is not the elaboration of an ethical principle that would be added a posteriori to the order that establishes equality among men, but rather the determination of a founding principle, a priori, without which this order has no substance or reality. We must evaluate laws in terms of their philosophy and – always – their relationship with power.

Ancient philosophies or religions often established the basic principle that human beings had a common origin and were therefore equal. And yet the fact remains that the way they were interpreted often condoned inequalities and relations of intellectual, religious and/or political domination: between Greeks (and then Romans) and 'Barbarians', between those who were 'elected' and those who were 'reprobates', and between the 'civilized' and the colonized, some-times in the name of the philosophy of the Enlightenment. That the common Adamic origin may or may not be an act of faith, that the evolution of species is an established fact, or that science tells us that the concept of 'race' is a purely intellectual construct that has been scientifically and objectively refuted does not alter anything: philosophies, discourses and the way we view others and ourselves – explicitly or implicitly – condone inequality and the discrimination that comes in its wake. Even if laws do try to correct and regulate discrimination, their ability to establish a new balance is partial and imperfect. Once again, we must pursue the ethical question to its logical conclusion, set aside philosophical postulates, religious dogmas and scientific facts, and ask individuals and societies about what they think of man and human fraternity.

One thinks of Mahatma Gandhi's struggle at the heart of Hindu-ism and the caste system. No matter whether they are *pariahs*, the 'children of God' (*harijan*), as Gandhi affectionately called them, or the 'oppressed' (*dalit*), as some, like the lawyer and politician B. R. Ambedkar, described them, the 'untouchables' were marginalized and excluded from the four castes recognized by classical Hindu philoso-phy. According to that philosophy, the order of the cosmos is perfect and the universal law (*dharma*) establishes castes and categories. Castes are the perfect human representation of those categories and orders. They respect and mirror the *dharma*, which must be respected, perpetuated and promoted if we wish to act in harmony with the order of the macrocosm. Priests, teachers, intellectuals (*Brahmans*), warriors, kings and princes (*ksatriyas*), and artisans and merchants (*vaisya*) are the elect and can attain knowledge, whilst servants (*sûdras*) – who are themselves divided into a multitude of categories – obey the higher castes by pursuing activities that have less spiritual and social value. The *pariahs* represent yet another caste that exists outside the caste system at the very bottom of the cosmic hierarchy, and lives in a state of impurity, indignity and poverty. This is, then, an order or harmony that requires a hierarchy of superiors and inferiors, and its set of social relations – spaces, occupations, marriages, friend-ships, and so on – is so codified as to reflect that reality. Gandhi fought to give the untouchable or *harijan* access to education, to get them out of poverty and to ensure that they had fairer treatment. He waged a ceaseless struggle against the injustices and scorn those who were excluded from the system had to face. In January 1934, he interpreted the Bihar earthquake as a warning and a punishment for the higher castes, their arrogance and their 'sins' against the poor and the *pariahs*. When he died in January 1948, the caste system had been abolished for a year (with India's accession to independence), thanks to the Constitution drafted under the authority of Ambedkar, who was appointed by Nehru. He was a very early critic of Gandhi's 'over-condescending' attitude, wanted the untouchables to be called the 'oppressed' (*dalit*) and advocated the principle of 'affirmative action' or positive discrimination in favour of the marginalized castes. Reality, however, was not so fine. The law had no power to change mentalities. The system lived on in the silence of everyday life, far away from visible breaches of the law. Gandhi knew that and stressed (over fifty years ago now) that there was a need to work on the under-lying idea of man that was being taught in schools and elsewhere, on the moral meaning and even the conception of fraternity that lies at the heart of philosophies and religions. Unless that was done and unless people were re-educated, the law would be nothing more than a pretext or a dangerous instrument in the hands of those who held power (and/or the power of the word) and who defended their priv-ileges through laws that seemed in essence to be egalitarian but that were not egalitarian in practice. That issue was central to the debate between Ambedkar, who was himself a son of the untouchable caste, and who was demanding equality, resistance, justice, the right to interpret the law and access to confident and militant speech, and Gandhi, who advocated the love of the excluded and reform from within through active commitment of the elite and the wealthy.

A religious man as well as an activist, Gandhi described himself as 'Hindu, Christian, Muslim, Buddhist and Jewish' and challenged all those religions by looking at their day-to-day social practices. He warned: 'Once we lose our moral certainties, we cease to be religious.' Practices and philosophies must, in other words, be consistent and must be considered together. The same questions run through our modern societies, both North and South, with the same intensity as in Gandhi's day, even though the castes, classes and categories of our societies – be they 'developed' or 'developing' – seem to be less visible than they were in India in the first half of the twentieth century. The dialectical relationship is still the same, and the questions appear to be unchanged: the concrete inequalities of everyday life urge us to be critical of our basic philosophies and of our conception of human fraternity, just as they must challenge the consistency of systems that claim to be egalitarian. There can be no law without ethics, and there can be no ethics without the law: we find the same equation in all religions and, with or without God, in all spiritualities and humanist and/or political philosophies.

AFFILIATIONS

It is important to ask our religions, philosophies, cultures and societies what meaning they give to our loyalties. The fraternity that appeals to the heart and the equality that is based upon the law therefore demand an imperative critical involvement of the mind. We have to evaluate our postulates and beliefs, our idea of truth and men, and even, to be more specific, our personal philosophies, our nations and our societies. This conscious and critical attitude is a *sine qua non* condition if we are not to become trapped in our existing loyalties. When that happens, we deny, or greatly relativize, our primary membership of humanity. Any moral teaching, on the part of any religion, spirituality or philosophy, that might lead us to ignore the common humanity of all men, to deny the dignity of some men, or to establish distinctions and an ontological hierarchy between beings must, as we said, be critically evaluated because it can have serious and dangerous implications.

Many factors explain why such teachings have emerged. Sometimes, the problem lies in the very fundamentals of a tradition, as is the case with the theory of castes: Gandhi's criticisms, which we were discussing earlier, pertain essentially to the fact that he cannot imagine any teaching that establishes definitive hierarchies between human beings and justifies de facto discriminations. He queries the specific teachings of classical or orthodox Hinduism in the name of a higher conception of man. In most cases, however, it is dogmatic or reductive interpretations of the founding texts that lead to exclusivist, closed or inquisitorial approaches. The closed minds of certain scholars, specific cultural features or even historical circumstances – being in a position of power or, at the opposite extreme, experiencing oppression or rejection – may bring about interpretations or theories that reduce 'belonging' to meaning membership of one to a single religious community, or to the supposed supremacy of one ideology or to blind nationalism. The very idea of our common humanity is then called into question or even denied. We have to think critically and we always have to begin anew, because no religion, spirituality or human or political philosophy is immune to closed interpretations, to abuses of power or to the instrumentalization of the feeling of being a victim (or, for that matter, to biased projections from outside). Scholars, the-ologians, philosophers and intellectuals must constantly strive to recapture the essence of the human and humanist teachings that lie at the heart of every religion, philosophy or tradition. That is what the Rabbis and Jewish thinkers did when they tried to explain the pro-found meaning of the concept of a 'chosen people'. It means, in their view, that the Jewish people have been 'chosen' in a spiritual sense, and that they therefore have a great moral responsibility to transmit moral values to humanity. Being chosen is therefore not the arbitrary and exclusive privilege of the few, but a requirement of exemplarity and service for humankind at large. We find the same approach in the Christian tradition and the analyses of theologians who suggest a broader and more open reading of the idea of election and redemp-tion (which are possible only through the mediation of Jesus, or even the Church, according to the famous 'No salvation outside the Church'). Muslim scholars have done similar exegetical work on the formula 'you are the best community established among men' (Quran 3: 110). They explain that the precondition for this election is the promotion of the good, being a model and bearing witness, and dem-onstrating ethical consistency towards all men. Such interpretations attempt to get back to basic teachings and the rationality that lies beyond the temptations of dogmatism and exclusivism. This is a requirement of faith, the heart and the mind. In the name of our pri-mary membership of humanity, we must never deny the common and equal dignity of all human beings.

We cannot, however, leave things at that. Everyone is called upon to make a personal effort to move out of the reassuring world of their own community (be it religious, spiritual, philosophical, social or political), with its certainties, rules and shared intellectual and/or emotional values, and to encounter the common humanity of others in the very heart of its difference. Our religious and philosophical traditions may well, in theory, call upon us to recognize the principle of the common humanity of all men, but that in itself is not enough to allow us to experience it in our daily lives and still less to experience human fraternity. Doing so is indeed difficult, demanding and sometimes disturbing, and it requires both an intellectual disposition and strength of purpose. It is a question of developing, at the human level, what contemporary psychologists call empathy, and empathy is primarily an intellectual attitude. It all begins with an examination of the way we look at things: we have to stand back and look at ourselves and others in an intellectual sense in order to try to understand the other as he is, his way of thinking, his emotional and affective reactions from where he stands, without prejudging anything. This defines empathy more broadly than contemporary psychological theories; it is not a matter of understanding what the other 'feels' through a purely intellectual and 'cognitive' empathy (which is quite understandable in the context of psychology's functions) but of recognizing in the other an alter ego and a mirror, and of acquiring the ability to understand where he is thinking from, how he constructs his universe of reference, his coherence and even his loves and hopes. Trying to put ourselves in the other's place presupposes that we have already recognized that the other has a place. That is no small matter and, basically, it is the beginning of the process of recognition, and of a possible fraternity. It is interesting to note – and this is no coincidence – that humanist psychologists such as Abraham Maslow and Carl Rogers begin by categorizing our common needs (from hunger to the need for self-respect and self-actualization), and then determine the stages of our recognition of the other: recognition in the mirror of our respective humanities, verbalization – for ourselves and for the other – of what the other is saying, and finally what Rogers calls 'warmth', or giving a positive regard for the other (as he is). Whilst this exercise is codified and imposes some basic rules on the psychologists, within the limits of their function (especially as far as judgement or affective involvement are concerned), the same does not apply to human beings in their day-to-day lives. Human beings naturally belong to specific universes of references (to a spirituality, a religion, a philosophy, a nation, a party or whatever it may be), and it is the demanding exercise of empathy with the humanity of the other's being, beyond singular affiliations, that prevents them from being trapped in their certainties and judgements.

We could not be further removed from the individualism and/or complacency that results from laziness or ignorance: we are asking the self to make an effort to reach beyond itself, to meet the other and to become decentred in a final attempt to arrive at an intimate understanding of the other that is at once intellectual and respectful. Learning to observe, to listen (in the primary sense of listening actively) and to project ourselves (to the extent that it is possible to do so) into the being of the other, in order to try to understand, feel and experience. The method of the practising psychologist ends where the human commitment of the free individual begins. It begins with empathy, but does not preclude sympathy or even affection and then, at a deeper level, fraternity. Without claiming to understand everything, and without denying that questions and critical judgements may sometimes arise, the individual establishes communications with the other by listening, by learning the necessary humility of one who has left behind his ego, respecting his attempts to learn and above all by trusting in the one who welcomes and is welcomed. This is a fraternity of being, a fraternity of fate. We find one of the dimensions of empathy, of self-transcendence, through human fraternity in the basic teachings of spiritualities and religions. In *Mahâna* (Great Vehicle) Buddhism, the aspiration to achieve Enlightenment (*bodhicitta*) and release from suffering involves the practice of the four sublime states: benevolence (*maitri*), compassion (*karuna*), sympathy (*mudita*) and equanimity (*upeksa*). As suffering is our common lot at the heart of these cycles, compassion does not refer here to a relationship of power or condescension (towards a dependent potential victim in a state of want), but rather to a sense of sharing, of a shared destiny and of a common aspiration to be released, in love and through detachment, from the chains of the eternal return: indeed compassion begins with oneself. We can recognize here the essence of empathy and see that the principles of contemporary transpersonal and humanist psychology are already implicit in a spirituality grounded in the universal experience of suffering and the need for liberation through Enlightenment. What matters in the end lies in the will to reach out of oneself and recognize the other's humanity and common aspirations (before his distinctive choices). This human relationship and this moral disposition towards the other are the path that leads to fraternity. We find the same belief in the monotheisms. As David Sears and Rabbi Jonathan Sacks remind us, the Jewish tradition and the Midrash convey the same idea: this is the meaning of the messianic project, spiritual election and the notion of service. The Christian notion of love (and not compassion, which clearly relates to the order of charity) is the best expression of this experience of human empathy. In the same way, the Quranic verse commands and recommends us to open up to others in their similarity and differences: 'God does not forbid you, with regard to those who do not fight you for your faith nor drive you out of your homes, from dealing with affection and justice with them: for God loves those who are just' (60:8). We must first establish a relationship of love and affection (*al-birr*) that permits – as though it were an implicit precondition – a truly and profoundly equitable relationship. More specifically, we must ensure that the 'equity' that associates the trusting and reasonable disposition of the heart goes hand in hand with a fair and equitable application of the law.

LAW AND POWER

What the individual must acquire at the personal level – a sense of our shared dignity and human fraternity – communities and societies must organize through laws and regulations. Every individual must be treated equally before the law, without any discrimination as to sex, colour, religion, social status or anything else. This is as much a universal principle as an ideal: as we have said, certain philosophies and/ or certain interpretations of spiritual or religious traditions sometimes make distinctions (either internally or with respect to those who follow a different tradition) between the status of individuals, thus legitimizing de facto discrimination. In contemporary democracies, the application of equality of rights is still quite imperfect and sometimes borders on being purely theoretical where the poor, marginalized populations or populations that are perceived as foreign are concerned. This ideal in fact means that we must always adopt a critical approach to the way societies apply the law. The law is not an abstraction that applies to individuals who are socially 'free' and politically 'neutral': socio-economic relations, relations of power and domination, and control of the symbolic apparatus and the media are so many givens that influence the equal application of the law.

If we look beyond the complexity of all these analyses and positions, we find two basic theses that contradict one another. Some take the view that, whilst social equality implies that all individuals are equal in the eyes of the law, that must not prevent them from fully developing their potential and abilities. Equality cannot be enforced through the denial of individual specificities. On the other hand, there are those who, like Marxists, prioritize the community and argue, in the name of the equality of all, that individual aspirations must be subject to controls, or at least that the needs of society must take priority. Even though the ideological basis for the latter thesis appears to have lost its attraction in the course of recent history (due mainly to the general erosion of communist systems, of course), the issue remains the same: how can we both defend equal rights and recognize individual specificities and potentialities without perpetuating, whether we mean to or not, the natural or structural inequalities we claim we are trying to overcome? Nietzsche saw the defence of equality as a sort of egalitarianism of mediocrity produced by jealous weaklings who were primarily interested in seizing power. Without going to such extremes, Karl Popper, who saw Plato, Aristotle and Marx as the precursors of totalitarian thought, advocated an 'open' society or democracy in which indeterminacy is the rule and in which the individuals must have the power to make the best of their freedom and its potential.

Rejecting the ideal and deliberately 'anti-historicist' image outlined by Popper, Michel Foucault not only reintroduces history into the argument, but identifies the relations of power that orient, disorient and undermine relations of authority by projecting social mechanisms through time and distributing them across different spheres of authority. When it comes to the relationship between institutions and individuals,

74

relations are always subject to a seizure of power and, Foucault argues, the emergence of a real 'biopower': politics takes charge of the entire existence of individuals, from their leisure activities to their emotional lives and even their economic productivity. What is more, he argues, we are no longer dealing with common *laws* that are socially neutral, but with the establishment of *norms* whose tenor is subject to the discursive power ('micro-power') that gives them their authority. Even if laws were egalitarian, those who control discourse and have the power to give existence and meaning to norms are the real masters of the egalitarian system. According to Foucault, the historical process and the complex order of the social system determine competences and powers that should leave us with no illusions as to the real nature of social equality. By developing his theories of 'capital' and 'fields', Pierre Bourdieu demonstrates that powers are exercised in parallel and interact, and that there can never be a 'pure' relationship between the individual and the community and/or institutions. Not to mention the fact that their 'habitus', or that 'structured structure predisposed to become a structuring structure', naturally determines the potential of human subjects both in history and at the heart of society. What we thought was a law that regulated interpersonal relations and gave us access to equality is, in other words, actually a potential product and instrument of powers that are exercised through the interplay between the political, economic, religious and social 'fields', and the 'capital' that is invested in them. A most complex reality. Relations of domination are inevitably established, and they establish, legitimate and reproduce social hierarchies that are experienced as a 'symbolic violence' that is all the more effective in that its victims are sometimes unaware of its existence. A complex reality indeed.

The law supposedly regulates powers, but there is already an actual power in the very fact of drafting, mastering and applying laws. Given the density of history, the organization of the legal and social system and the reality of both structural and symbolic powers, we can understand that the legal response cannot be the only response when it comes to managing the equality of citizens. The reality of the inequality that lies at the heart of our democratic (and supposedly egalitarian) laws would appear to begin at school, and the intuitions of Foucault and Bourdieu have been confirmed by many studies.

Despite all the egalitarian laws that apply to schools, schools reproduce inequalities rather than doing away with them. Jeannie Oakes's study of American schools,[1] like the research of so many educationalists in Europe, reaches the same conclusions about both modern and traditional societies: educational systems reproduce and legitimate class and race inequalities. The discourses that celebrate freedom and equality of opportunity sometimes tend to mask the symbolic violence of the relations of domination that operate with the actual legal realm. We must therefore go still further. As we have seen, a law without a priori moral sense and that does not relate to fraternity is empty, whereas a law that is unaware of the power relations that are established a posteriori can become inoperative or even dangerous because of the illusions it fosters. Without an awareness and a continuous and systematic critique of the power relations that exist within society, be they symbolic (language, communications, the media, etc.), structural (schools, occupations, social spaces, etc.) or cultural (codes, clothes, religions, etc.), the principle of equality cannot be a reality. The law is a means and never an end, and equality is a very demanding ideal.

CONFIDENCE AND FEAR

As we can see, the conditions for equality are at once legal, philosophical (and/or religious) and psychological. Whilst the legal framework and the legal regulation of interpersonal relations are unavoidable imperatives, we also require preconditions relating to both individuals and the social environment. Recognition of the dignity and place of the other, and of human fraternity, implicitly supposes that this is already achieved for oneself . . . which is far from being the case. A system that is egalitarian in legal terms but deprives individuals of self-confidence and a vocal and confident awareness of their value and dignity gives with one hand what it takes away with the other. That is why the moral lesson of the humanity of men, respect for men and human fraternity is so essential upstream from law: it is

1. Jeannie Oakes, *Keeping Tracks: How Schools Structure Inequality*, New Haven: Yale University Press, 1985.

designed to shape and sustain a certain idea of self and others that is based upon their respective independence, common dignity and necessary social interdependence.

Attaining self-confidence, or teaching it, is a difficult process that is never fully achieved. It is a matter of fostering a positive, or at least serene, idea of one's history, origin, roots and parental filiation. This further presupposes that we enjoy the benefits of the education and instruction that allow us to acquire the knowledge necessary to protect our own social and intellectual independence. Every society must encourage developments that allow us to achieve the necessary maturity that demonstrates the individual's ability to express an informed choice. The individual is then regarded as a social being, and a socially responsible being. Linguistic competence, a minimal understanding of the law and the ability to identify institutions are so many objective preconditions for the enjoyment of the rule of law and for the hope of receiving potential equal treatment. That process must, however, be taken to its logical conclusion, and we must acquire the ability to master communications and the complexity of the symbolic apparatus that is (although this is not always obvious) the driving force behind social representations, our common culture (both active and passive) and the mysteries of collective psychology.

It is of course impossible for all members of society to develop this critical awareness, to enjoy the benefits of that training and to acquire that knowledge. Even so, a society that seeks equality must think about the real, ideological and symbolic content of what it officially teaches, about the equitable distribution of knowledge, and about its consistency when it comes to applying the law and granting access to positions that are representative in official and institutional terms. If the rule of law does not guarantee the distribution of knowledge and equal access to symbolic representations, it is a sham and can therefore become an object that can be manipulated in dangerous ways, either directly or indirectly, and deliberately or otherwise. Equality is a fragile right, and one that must be demanded constantly, at more than one level and in more than one sphere: we must have confidence in ourselves and in our rights, confidence in our ability to communicate and to be heard, and also confidence in the legitimacy of resistance, or even in the constructive nature of opposition and protest.

That confidence must go hand in hand with great lucidity: a discourse of equality that fails to take into account the multiplicity of power is at best naive and at worst Machiavellian in that it can, without his realizing it, turn the subject into a toy. Confidence and lucidity on the part of all are preconditions for equality of rights for all. The *state* of law is therefore closely bound up with the *state* of personal and collective psychologies.

Being self-confident is the surest way of learning to trust others and to recognize their place as subjects and brothers in humanity. We have already spoken of how imperative this is to promoting equality between individuals and citizens. The whole of that philosophical, religious, social, political and psychological construct may, of course, be undermined by fear and mistrust. Fear can work in two different spheres and at several levels. The individual, for his part, may develop a fear about his status (because he is poor, because he is not the same colour as the majority, because he belongs to a culture or religion that is publicly stigmatized . . .) and become trapped in a sort of mental ghetto where he finally determines for himself the logic of his own isolation. This fear and this anxiety about being exposed to one's own limitations, to rejection or to psychological pressure has a perverse effect and can lead to a passive, and above all psychological, acceptance of unequal treatment. Society is not immediately responsible for this phenomenon, as it is indeed the individual who shuts himself away and experiences a self-imposed segregation by adopting the attitude of a victim, but the general social climate is still a determining factor that influences individual attitudes, and must be taken into account when we analyse the phenomena of self-marginalization and resigned self-exclusion.

Nurturing collective fears can also directly affect the right of individuals and equality of treatment. Centres of power (political, economic, military-industrial or media-based) sometimes decide to fuel, or even create, threats and dangers for national, international, economic and/or geostrategic reasons. The climate of fear and insecurity makes citizens accept measures that restrict the rights they have won, or even differential forms of treatment that are justified by the threat itself. There is nothing new about this strategy, but its strength is amplified by the power of modern means of communication. An enemy is created, his ability to do harm is demonized and the public is encouraged to draw the logical consequences from the situation: 'You are afraid. We will guarantee your security, but in order to do that we must take exceptional measures – keep you under surveillance, keep the enemy under surveillance – and may sometimes have to encroach upon your rights, dignity or equality.' The exceptional nature of the threat justifies the suspension of existing laws: fear is indeed the enemy of law. All dictators have, to varying degrees, used – and use – this method to justify their policies. Hitler stigmatized the 'Jewish enemy's power of infiltration', but so did other forms of fascism, certain communist regimes and dictatorships in South America, Africa and Asia. Democratic and liberal societies can be manipulated in similar ways, though the effects and consequences may seem less far-reaching. In the United States, Senator McCarthy launched a campaign against the 'communist threat' in the 1950s and used that threat to justify lies, surveillance, arrests, the infringement of basic rights and the freedom of expression, and even torture. The internal 'threat' (which was related to the external threat posed by the Soviet Empire) was so great as to justify the most dubious and excessive political practices and intelligence-gathering methods. What we are witnessing today with the 'war on terrorism' is of a similar nature and produces similar consequences: when fear rules and when security is under threat, rules no longer apply and rights can be reconsidered, personal integrity can be violated. Equality becomes a matter of wishful thinking, and the majority of the population, which is subjected to psychological and media brainwashing, gradually comes to accept the implications of the threat.

Phobias are fuelled from within, and they produce and justify forms of racism which undermine any hope of any *de jure* or de facto equality, especially in political terms. The dangers are legion: the other, with his supposed identity, culture, religion and intentions, is within the gates. And then there are all the potential immigrants on the border who threaten to colonize us and take advantage of our wealth. All rich societies nurture the same fears, in Europe, America, Asia and the emerging countries, but also in the 'petromonarchies', where curtailing immigrant rights is becoming more widely accepted, and immigrants are being turned into downright 'criminals' or new slaves.

Everyone is talking about security, the fear is spreading, and the emotions are colonizing minds. We are no longer capable of thinking calmly, rationally and in human terms. We are witnessing collective movements that are under the disturbing sway of real social phobias, and they are beginning to affect the most highly industrialized and educated societies. Exclusive identities are being asserted, singular affiliations are being stressed, and it is becoming increasingly difficult to recognize the other in the mirror of one's own quest. The reduction of the other to the mere expression of his 'difference' is one of the stages of dehumanization and law alone – and still less the right to equality – cannot suffice to remedy the situation. Here comes the time of the new 'barbarians', as Rimbaud might have put it.

Therefore, ethics must be revived upstream from law. There can be equality without education: we must learn to observe, listen and decentre ourselves. We must learn to empathize in both intellectual and emotional terms, and try, first of all, to discover the meaning of respect, dignity and human fraternity. It is important to remember that equality before the law does not mean that competences must be standardized. It does, however, mean that everyone must have the same right to fulfil their intellectual and human potential. This brings us back to the point we made earlier. In the mirror of this encounter, we must take the positive and constructive path that leads to self-knowledge and to an inner confidence that is ready to face up to and deal with a feeling of insecurity that is real and/or instrumentalized. We must admit to our fears and commit ourselves to overcoming and managing them. A being who is under the sway and domination of his phobias cannot be free, and cannot hope to achieve equality with his fellow human beings. Such a being is an object and not a subject. The road is long, and it obliges us to make a conscious and voluntary choice. We have to choose human fraternity, confidence in ourselves and others, vigilance and resistance. This involves loving and respecting men. And sometimes we must learn, constructively and without any naivety, to distrust them. Naive and blind sincerity, humanist and/or religious, has all too often provoked terror and oppression. Like phobias, naive sincerity can become the negative mirror of equality. What is involved is fraternity, but this is a fraternity with no illusions or naivety.

7

Female, Male

How did it all begin? What was the first cause? Did it have to do with the essence of things, or was it an accident of human history? How is it that, as far back as anyone can remember, all human cultures and societies have always established relations of power that almost systematically work to the disadvantage of women? We can obviously cite odd examples of matriarchal societies or of women who enjoy freedom and power, but, like it or not, they are notable exceptions rather than the rule. Some conclude from this, on the basis of their interpretations of the teachings of their own tradition or religion, that this is the law of nature, or even of the essence of things. Others try to understand the social dynamics and logics which, at a very early stage, inscribed relations between men and women within the logic of a relationship of power and domination. Between these philosophical, ideological and sometimes religious extremes, most men and women have changed as they respond to their social history and environment. It is clear that women have gained some rights. It is equally clear that men have lost their traditional points of reference, and there is no denying that great changes have taken place. But certain questions remain unresolved, as do certain inequalities, tensions and doubts: the situation is far from perfect whatever the societies, irrespective of whether they are in the North or the South, rich or poor, secularized or not.

The trauma is long-standing. Most Creation stories describe how man was created first, and how woman was then created to be his companion or helpmeet. The stories or texts are sometimes clear, but in some cases these truths were established by male interpretations. We find the same constant in the social and political realm. Although there was a multitude of pharaohs and kings, only ten or so were women, and in most cases the public role they played amongst their people was quite secondary, or even non-existent. Women's fate was the same amongst the Incas, Mayas and Aztecs: they were wives, mothers or servants, cooks and housekeepers, though some were held in high esteem because they were weavers. Amongst the Aztecs, midwives also enjoyed special status: they helped in giving life, and took in and protected women and girls and then released them from the throes of childbirth. The real relationships and symbolic representations are always the same: female roles relate to service (and are usually, though not always, seen as secondary or inferior) and other specific functions relating to life and the sacred. The latter confer upon women a distinction or particular power within a social and cultural order that is highly masculine and very patriarchal.

It will be recalled that there was no female presence in the philosophical circles of ancient Greece. Socrates' wife was at his side when he was condemned to death and drank the hemlock, but that was the exception to the rule. In those circles, they spoke about women, they philosophized about love, which, as in *The Symposium*, was seen as a form of sublimation that transformed the attractions of the body into the beauty of Ideas, but the ambiguous image of femininity remains: for the philosopher-hunter who was in love with truth and absolute beauty, woman was at once a stage, a quest and a symbol. She represented a stage within the transcendence of the body, a quest for a love that had to become more profound and a symbol of human experience and initiation. But in terms of their being and personal aspirations, women were still 'absent'. It goes without saying that women were acknowledged as having a certain power, but men did not trust that power and tried to control it as best they could: women's bodies were the source of life and were therefore indispensable, but those same bodies also had the power to seduce, to subjugate reason and to bind men to their animal destiny. Greek and Roman mythologies depicted this type of ambiguous figure with the goddess Artemis, also known as Diana and Hecate. Having witnessed the pain of childbirth, she never wanted to marry, remained a virgin and represented the huntress – surrounded, strangely enough, by the animals that were her natural prey. By day, she protected fertility, virgin purity and life; by night and by the light of the moon, she took her revenge, inflicted death and turned into a witch. She had two faces, but one unfathomable and fascinating power.

In his quest for truth, Socrates likens his dialectical method to childbirth. Maieutics allows the philosopher to become a midwife of the mind who can help his interlocutor give birth to ideas he did not know he had. The philosopher was to ideas what the midwife was to children, plus the lofty spiritual elevation and minus the pain. The corporal essence of life could thus be reappropriated through access to its higher intellectual and spiritual meaning: woman belonged to the body, but the philosopher belonged to the mind. But that very comparison reveals something about the mysterious power of women, which is at the origin and heart of life. And besides, the supposed nobility of the midwife who brought life into being could not exist without the prior acceptance of women, their bodies and the desire and sexuality that gave life. Women's other power – that of seduction, passion and instinct – revealed man's fate and unveiled the nature of his tensions and contradictions, together with the implacable pain that still he had to endure. On Mount Olympus, the three Morae (fates) spin, or more accurately *weave*, the destiny of men by the light of the moon – night, once more – and have a power that is at once invisible and yet so obvious.

Earlier, the Hindu and Buddhist traditions had already reached the shore of these paradoxes. Although present throughout the Hindu pantheon, woman remains a mystery. She is at once the path and an obstacle, and woman's primary qualities in everyday life are her fidelity and abnegation. The pain of childbirth that is associated with giving life (and living) is also the most explicit parable for the cycles of bondage and suffering that have to be overcome in the Buddhist tradition. Recurrent motifs and symbols appear in one tradition after another, in one culture after another: life, the body, instinct, fate, purity, seduction, desire and suffering. The stories told in the Torah and the Bible are no exception: Eve is associated with temptation and the forbidden fruit. She seduces and is seduced, experiences cycles of impurity and gives life. She is so noble but suffers so much when she completes the sexual act through organs that convey both the intensity of desire and the shame of natural needs. We see once again the power of darkness; it is disturbing and, ultimately, stronger than all orders and all rules. In his historical novel *The Sorceress* the French writer and historian Jules Michelet describes the stages of the woman-sorceress's ascent to the heart of the night, 'by the light of the moon': black masses, counter-power and real power. Man owns the day, but she owns the night. Man sustains an apparent order that is historical and fragile; she possesses the invisible desire that is essential and invisible. Man has the power of the master who is nothing without his slave; she has the power of the slave who is a free being without the master. Thanks to this inversion of realms, woman acquires a knowledge that brings her close to the devil. Nietzsche shared this intuition when he asked in the preface to *Beyond Good and Evil*: 'Supposing truth to be a woman – what?'[1] and speculated that she represented both the mysteries and the dangers of knowledge. The forbidden fruit belonged to the tree of knowledge, and it was the devil who tempted the woman to taste it. This is a terrifying revelation: woman is life, suffering and knowledge or, more precisely, she is the suffering, seduction and knowledge that are the essence of life. The social body may well subjugate her, but everything suggests that she possesses its heart. She has two faces, and is the paradox of a contradiction, just like the two Quranic characters: Bilquis, Queen of Sheba, with her noble and exemplary wisdom, who wields political power over men, and the passionately mad wife of the master of Joseph (Yusuf), who is seduced and possessed but still remains the mistress of all wiles. This is a difficult relationship, and these relations of power and fear are as old as the humanity of Men. It is a matter of understanding, controlling and sometimes dominating, in the full knowledge that the essential secret remains intact: the secret of woman's indomitable power and inalienable freedom. And then what life actually offers her must be organized in society.

EDUCATION

We could spend a lot of time glossing the terms and qualifications men have used to describe women, and the terms that the texts of spiritual and religious traditions have applied to them for so long.

1. Friedrich Nietzsche, *Beyond Good and Evil*, trans. R. J. Hollingdale, Harmondsworth: Penguin, 1990, p. 32.

What emerges is a somewhat paradoxical constant. Beyond such matters as biological differences, physical strength, menstrual cycles or emotional reactivity, what emerges is the power and the real strength of the so-called 'weaker sex'. The relationship with life inherent in giving birth, the experience of the physical pain that had to be borne and overcome (until the discovery of the benefits of epidurals) and the injunctions to dress modestly that we find in everything from Hinduism to Buddhism, the Epistles of St Paul to Islam, all these reveal the fragility and vulnerability of men, their doubts as to their real powers and above all their weakness in the face of their instincts, bodies and needs. Both what men say about women and male interpretations of spiritual or religious scriptural sources (which have sometimes been applied to the family and social order) are highly revealing – in the sense that a mirror is revealing – and tell us a lot about men's self-image. The terminology they use, the order and the system they impose and the roles they prescribe are as much expressions of a need for protection as any real will to power.

We have to begin at the beginning. The intuitions of the women's liberation and feminist movements all over the world from the nineteenth century onwards and throughout the twentieth were highly pertinent: autonomy is central to the 'woman question'. In order to protect themselves from the strength, power, freedom, and sometimes the domination, of women, men organized and systematized their ontological, physical, social and financial dependency, and sometimes their intellectual dependency. The movements that fought against women's slavery in the United States (Female Anti-Slavery Society) and the Suffragettes who, from 1865 onwards, fought for civil equality, first in Great Britain and then in the United States, wanted recognition of women's autonomy in terms of being and status as much as in terms of the enjoyment of rights. The three ages of feminism in the West were a slow and difficult ascent from the periphery to being: access to rights, a critique of the system of domination and, finally, access to discourse and recognition of women's being. Irrespective of whether or not one recognizes militant feminism as legitimate, the one thing that all these approaches and theories have in common is education and, more importantly, speech. It is true that the things that first shape a mind and construct its relationship with reality have to do with the words, concepts and terminology that are used. What runs through all the traditions, cultures and (male) religious interpretations is the focus on the function of women rather than their being. Such is the male vision of women and the male discourse on women: men 'naturally' organize, control and determine 'their functions'. Their status as men makes it impossible, by definition, for them to elaborate any discourse about the 'female subject', or about the being and femininity of women. This approach to being through the medium of the word is the first stage on the road to autonomy.

When Simone de Beauvoir asserts in *The Second Sex* that 'Women are beings in their own right, as distinct from men', she is trying to establish the principle of autonomy and independence as the first foundations of discourse and education. That autonomy and independence must be founded at the ontological level and must be protected (or demanded) at the social, political and economic level. That, in her view, is the best way to resist the logic of alienation that produces the stereotype of the socially dependent woman who constructs her own secondary status: 'One is not born, but rather becomes, a woman.' Debates over this issue have been lively and sometimes violent, even when they were debates between feminists themselves. Is there or is there not a difference between men and women? Are their differences inherent in their respective natures, or are they products of social conditioning? Some feminist milieus, both Catholic and secular, assert (like the supporters of 'difference feminism' and Carol Gilligan in the United States) that there are indeed differences, whilst other groups are critical of women's social conditioning, but they are all agreed as to the importance of education, and see it both as a vector for representation and a liberating instrument.

There are many different female and/or feminist views as to the nature and real extent of the possible conditioning of women, the degree to which it influences the way they see themselves, their choice of profession, their role in the family and in society, and so on. But all the critiques are in agreement about three basic themes: 1. the importance of a discourse about the feminine being that is the product of women themselves, without any mediation from men; 2. the critique of all discourses and all projections that maintain that women's dependency is a *sine qua non* for access to self-recognition and autonomy; 3. the emergence of an autonomous and independent woman-subject must lead to a new definition of the feminine and a new representation of femininity. We therefore need a systematic analysis of how girls and boys are educated within the family, of how/ what they learn at school, and of the representations associated with the roles that are ascribed to girls and boys from infancy. We may well, depending on the theory or school of thought we endorse, think that girls will naturally make different choices from boys, but the important thing is to facilitate the assertion of woman's being and to protect her independence and the choices she makes.

Women's movements have emerged within Hinduism, Buddhism, Judaism, Christianity and Islam, and they represent a reaction to the ancient male imagery that associates women with life, suffering, the body, desire or temptation (or even, in certain Catholic circles, that raised the issue of whether or not women have a soul). Similar movements have emerged in the agnostic or atheist circles that assert, in both North and South, women's autonomy, their right to education and to be both present and active in social life. In historical terms, these movements started out from a very different place: demanding the right to vote, like the feminist Clara Zetkin, meant demanding a social maturity that implied recognition of the female subject's freedom (and access to the education that was its precondition). It became apparent from that commitment and struggle that a new awareness had to be developed, and that individuals had to be taught to understand the meaning of what they were asserting, or rather the meaning of their reappropriation of their individual and social identity. Education is, for both women and men, a precondition for being, and the substance of what they are taught can either reproduce schemas of alienation, marginalization or domination, or reform them. The need to recognize women's rights and their demands for autonomy and liberation necessarily involves a determined commitment to education: in terms of the 'woman question', this is a constant in all human communities because education produces knowledge, and because knowledge has the power to undermine established and self-contained systems of power that reproduce their own logics, and therefore inequalities.

These approaches are multidimensional and require particularly demanding preliminary critical work upstream. In terms of spiritual and religious traditions, we have to undertake a rigorous evaluation of male appropriations of the meaning and objectives of the scriptural sources. As there can be no spirituality or religion without culture, we must at the same time study cultures, their logics and the way real and symbolic powers are distributed between men and women. In the light of those superstructures, to borrow the vocabulary of Marxism, it is possible to understand what subtends and legitimates the social system, the organization of private and public space, relations with authority and power, and even the philosophical, religious or cultural representations that justify the distribution of roles and functions. A female rereading and analysis of historical legacies and memories, of hermeneutical exegeses and of the management of power will make an important contribution to our understanding of their logics and to changing the mentality of society as a whole.

Many women said it in the twentieth century, and we now have to say it again – and emphatically – in the light of what we said earlier about the quest for meaning and the universal: women's commitment to the recognition of their female identity, autonomy and equal access to both spiritual experience and social involvement was and is a demand of their share in the universal in the elaboration of human thought and values. Irrespective of whether we think that women and men are intrinsically different, or whether we think that a distinction should be made between 'sex' and 'gender', so as to try to circumscribe the real impact of social conditioning, or whether we base our arguments on contemporary psychoanalytic theories, our primary and fundamental goal is the same: we must determine and identify the feminine universal's role in constructing the universal common to all human beings. The new critical readings of religious texts produced by women (an imperative commitment for all religions) as well as men – from Hinduism to Islam, and from Buddhism to Judaism and Christianity – basically express the same ambition to integrate female being, the female gaze, her quest, status, and her differences from and similarities to the 'masculine'. Education is the guide we need for that fundamental quest.

EQUAL AND THE IDENTICAL

Not all ancient cosmologies give men and women the same status at the ontological level. Some interpretations of spiritual and religious traditions, both ancient and contemporary, come close to asserting that women's 'ontological' difference (in terms of their nature, rationality and/or purity) justifies the transhistorical and transcultural inferiority of their status. The comments of the philosophers are no less essentialist. Even though men and women partake of the same being (the men and women who make up *The Symposium*'s androgyne are complementary), the male is the nobler of the two according to Socrates and Plato. Aristotle considers women to be 'naturally defective' and essentially inferior, and we find similar comments in some of Hume's asides about the relationship between women and power in his essay *Of Love and Marriage*. Kant took a similar view and avoided philosophical discussions with women, whom he liked to be witty but better disposed for kitchen matters: 'That is the way it is,' he is reported to have said to a woman seeking intellectual recognition, 'and it will not change.'

Things changed, and reflection became clearer or more diversified over the centuries. Religious discourse began to place more and more emphasis on the basic equality of men and women in terms of their spiritual initiation and before God. Their natural equality finds expression in their functional complementarity at the family and social level, as the 'biological differences' and the specific nature of the spiritual and religious (and sometimes philosophical, ideological and political) teachings addressed to women have to be taken into account. Many women, both inside and outside religious and cultural communities and feminist movements, have developed critiques of theories of the 'natural and functional complementarity' of men and women. In their view, the recognition granted to women by discourses on equality in essence or before God is negated by the way theories of complementarity justify their confinement within roles that make them dependent in familial and social terms (and then justified actual discrimination). In the name of the complementary nature of the so-called 'strong sex' and the 'weaker sex', or the public man in society and the private woman at home, a hierarchy was established. It prevented women from achieving any autonomy in terms of their social being, and confined them to functions that were always dependent and always viewed as secondary.

The feminist literature of the nineteenth and twentieth centuries criticized and denounced these instrumentalizations and alienations. As early as the second half of the nineteenth century, there were calls, including those from the Christian activist (and feminist) Catherine Booth, the co-founder of the Salvation Army, for women to have equal access to the public sphere, recognition and upward social mobility. The critique was to become increasingly sophisticated, and sometimes radical. In an attempt to close any loophole that might lead to discrimination, some women recognized 'no difference' between men and women: both were human beings, and there was no need to take their biology into consideration. Others took quite the opposite view, and argued that women were fundamentally different from men. Women were, as 'cultural feminism' asserts, the 'other', had nothing in common with men, had to fight for a recognition of what they were and had to resist men and their system of domination. There were lively and contradictory debates in America between Carol Gilligan, who argued that there was an ontological difference between men and women and that the gender polarity had to be reversed, and Christina Hoff Sommers, who argued the case for getting back to basics and advocated an equity feminism, as opposed to gender feminism. These debates demonstrate the difficulty of the problematic, and above all the blind alleys in which some currents found themselves trapped. By laying claim to either an ontological difference or an absolute essential similarity, feminists, wittingly or otherwise, established a permanent relationship – and an inverted relationship of dependency – with men and the way they saw men. There were a lot of exaggerations and a great deal of reductionism, and they were criticized by the many women intellectuals and/or activists who denounced the lack of any discourse based upon the core of women's experience, which, whilst it could demand legitimate rights (to work, a wage, autonomy, and so on), was not afraid of either the biological specificity or the singularity of certain of women's attributes (going so far as to accept the specificity of certain social functions such as teaching or nursing). On the basis of a very different reading, Black feminists, like Angela Davis in her famous *Women, Race and Class*, and then the promoters of post-colonial feminism, extended the critique to the relationship between race, gender and social class.

The pendulum then swung the other way. The reaction to theories that, either explicitly or implicitly, justified the social and political discrimination that denies women access to autonomy has seen the emergence of stances and ideologies, some of them exclusivist or radical, that either deny the differences between the sexes or exaggerate them in the name of the idea of absolute equality. In Susan Bolotin's article 'Voices of the Post-Feminist Generation' (*New York Times Magazine*, 17 October 1982), women voiced their support for theses and struggles supporting autonomy, social recognition and equal rights, but did not identify (or no longer identified) with feminism and some of its ideological positions. Like them, many women want to be free and independent, to have access to work and to earn the same wages as men, but they also want to assume their status as women, their femininity and motherhood and even a family role. They expect more from men, but they are not men and recognize the differences between men and women. They want to be 'equal', but have no desire to be 'identical'.

Achieving a balance is very difficult. All spiritual and religious traditions, all philosophical systems and all social struggles have always found it difficult to find a nuanced, balanced and rational approach to relations between men and women. Contemporary scientific discoveries (the neurosciences and neurobiology) confirm that there are biological differences between them, and that it would be insane to deny their existence. Scientists do not deny that our relationship with the social and cultural environment has a determining influence (epigenesis), but they have found some basic differences: the left hemisphere of the brain is more highly developed in women, who are actually less emotional than men but tend to be better at expressing their emotions because of their greater need to verbalize and communicate. Women have a more highly developed sense of hearing and touch, whereas men's sight is more highly developed and means that they have a different relationship with visual spatial abilities. An analysis of hormonal functions shows that men and women relate differently to the environment and have different needs in terms of safety, no matter what culture they live in: women have a greater need for protection, and men a greater need for adventure. We are free to reject these scientific discoveries, or to regard them as irrelevant, but we have to admit that we must not confuse 'equality' with 'identity' in the sense of similarity. Some psychologists have tried to account for these obvious differences. The psychotherapist John Gray's bestseller *Men Are from Mars, Women Are from Venus* expresses the same idea, with the stated intent of promoting a better understanding between men and women.

We have to negotiate a path between traditional and religious teachings, philosophical postulates and scientific discoveries in such a way that we can recognize beings and their identities (in terms of race and class as well as gender), their differences and similarities, and the way they contradict and complement one another without denying the need for ontological and social equality, and for the recognition of the legitimacy of women's right to autonomy, work and equal treatment as both citizens and wage-earners. This requires a complex and multidimensional approach. We must keep a critical eye open for invisible and unspoken logics, for power relations and for theoretical arguments that justify their existence in philosophical, religious or ideological terms. This also presupposes a continued awareness of the subtleties and paradoxes involved: for indeed, treating what is not identical in the same way can produce inequality. We therefore have to adopt a global and diversified approach and avoid both the spirit of dogmatism and blind radicalism. We have to hope for a meeting between men and women who can come to terms with their being freely and autonomously. They must be aware of their respective rights and determined to defend them ... but they must always be reasonable.

FEMALE, MALE

No human society has ever succeeded in promoting complete equality between women and men. We still have a long way to go. Even though the old representations that associated women with the body, seduction and impurity have been done away with – albeit not entirely in certain traditional societies or in some fundamentalist or literalist circles – the fact remains that we have yet to achieve the objectives of justice, the absence of social discrimination and the right to autonomy and equal pay. We find in all societies – without exception – social and cultural behaviours that encourage the ill treatment of women, domestic violence and the stigmatization and marginalization of girls. The situation remains alarming in all societies, albeit to different degrees: in the most closed and dogmatic religious circles, in traditional (and sometimes male chauvinist) cultures that perpetuate an exclusive patriarchy that is quite unfair to women (and which sometimes practise genital mutilation, forced marriages or honour killings) and in the richest societies, where women have made some gains but where there are obvious inconsistencies and where new forms of slavery have emerged: unequal pay for men and women with the same qualifications, discrimination because of the fear of pregnancy (or because women over the age of forty-five no longer conform to the canons of youth), the commodification of bodies, a new trade in prostitute-slaves, sex tourism on the part of rich men that dehumanizes the poor, women, girls and children, and so on.

Women turned to the law in order to overcome the male-chauvinist and negative representations of the past. At a time when the means of communication are becoming globalized and when we are bombarded with images, new representations force themselves upon us with even greater power and impact, and they are even more effective. What Umberto Eco calls the 'carnivalization' of life, the colonizing power of fashion, the imposition of a uniform aesthetics in terms of facial features and physical weight, the obsession with youth and the instantaneous, and the feminization of symbols and ideals, all so many phenomena that influence minds and psychologies with the force of oppression. There are so many illusory freedoms! And so many forms of alienation! The social gains we have made have not allowed us to achieve well-being and inner peace. It begins at a very young age . . . because they have been colonized by 'models of beauty', two-thirds of sixteen-year-old girls are unhappy with their bodies and experience a profound lack of well-being in the richest societies on the planet. The new representations and consumerist dictates of the modern era and neo-liberal societies are indeed tyrannical, and they now affect every society in our globalized world.

The serious crisis that is affecting men in the modern era must also be taken into account. Their points of reference have been called into question, their traditional roles within the family and society have become obsolete, relations of authority have been undermined, public spaces and everything to do with aesthetics and the body have been feminized, and the old – and reassuring – form of paternity is a thing of the past. How can anyone now be a man who is autonomous and balanced, who is a woman's companion and a father, reconcile presence, love and some idea of authority? No matter whether we come from Mars or Venus, the upheavals have been so great that they affect men and women in the same way, and they give rise to doubts, a lack of well-being and an inability to find our way. What does it matter if the other – man or woman – does come from another planet, if she/he is like us or basically different from us? What do such considerations matter if we cannot define for ourselves the meaning of our being, our dignity, our freedom, our choices and our hopes? Whether we live on Venus or on Mars, being under the domination of a man or a woman, of a cultural system, of dogmatic norms, of money or an image means that we have lost our freedom and our autonomy. When we are, or feel ourselves to be, less than ourselves, the other always looks like a threat, a danger or a rival . . . and rarely like a partner.

And yet neither women nor men can make it on their own. They must walk together along the road of the quest for meaning as they assert the existence of a shared universal (in both the feminine and the masculine) and as they demand freedom, dignity, autonomy and justice. They are equal but not the same, and both men and women must allow the other to bring their distinctive outlook towards the resolution of common problems. Women are determined when it comes to their rights and justice, but have to come to terms with their femininity and with the different way they see the world, politics and human relationships. What we now require is a certain feminization, but not that of the cult of youth, fashion or aesthetics, but one that promotes a more feminine relationship with communications, the preservation of life and the resolution of conflicts. Within this partnership, both men and women will be able to take a new look at the basic questions of meaning, freedom, masculinity, paternity and authority by coming to terms with what they are. In the ocean . . . a woman and a man are both beings who are on a quest for the same justice, the same truth and the same peace. Once they have got beyond naive talk of equality and made a critical analysis of the logics and structures of powers, they will reach – together – the shore of philosophical, spiritual or religious questions. The ocean will teach them that their difference is both a necessity and a blessing. The eyes and hearts of their children will teach them the same thing . . . and their bodies, intellects and loves will confirm it. The threat posed by their difference will then be dispelled by the masculine or feminine echo of their shared humanity. Their beings and their paths may well be distinct, but their destinations and their hopes are surely the same.

8

The Ethics of Independence
and the Independence of Ethics

He seemed destined for success. He had passed the examinations that would allow him to become a mandarin and could expect both spiritual and political recognition. And yet the Chinese philosopher Wang Yangming (1457–1529) resolved to remain true to himself and to defend his principles to the end. In 1506, he defended a civil servant by challenging a eunuch who had unjustly sent a police officer to jail while the officer was investigating corruption at the highest level of the administration. Wang Yangming then had to go into exile, leave his position and forgo his potential privileges in order to remain true to his own morality. He was to find himself in the same position on more than one occasion, and systematically chose to act ethically rather than to make the political decision to compromise. Wang Yangming had a vision that led him to abandon the classical values of official Confucianism and always tried to remain true to himself, his values and his goals. In his study of what it is that makes a man a saint, he sought the path that would allow men to understand the principle of all things and to live in sympathy with the essence of the universe. He discovered that the key to initiation was to be found in the mind – hence the need to go back to the mind and to rediscover its original purity so as to dispel the illusions of the ego and desires. Men would then be able to discover the essence of morality and reconcile themselves with their innate understanding of the existence of good and evil. If they could see through the veil of deceptive illusions, human beings could learn that the moral basis of all things lay within them. They only had to look within themselves.

Greatly influenced by Buddhism, Yangming's Neo-Confucianism was a positive answer to the age-old philosophical question of whether morality is innate rather than acquired. In line with the great spiritual traditions and monotheistic religions, the Chinese philosopher asserted that, in the purity of the state of *nature*, the mind could find an inner peace based upon and congruent with a *natural* attraction towards good. By no means do all philosophers share that vision, and the one thing that even Rousseau's thesis of the natural goodness of men and Hobbes' very different claim that men are basically aggressive predators have in common is that they both claim that the birth of morality is an a posteriori product of the law or the social contract. The moral law is therefore not so much a basic a priori principle as a tool that is developed a posteriori in order to regulate how human beings behave towards one another (according to Hobbes' theory) or their dealings with the law (according to Rousseau's social contract). The question is of fundamental importance and the answer is no less essential. In spiritual terms, Wang Yangming turns the moral law into a principle, and stipulates that moral action ensures the union, the fusion, of two dimensions in the mind. The mind is both a principle and something active, and it allows us to live in harmony and peace with the cosmos, the elements, and men. This is the principle of faith and love associated with moral injunctions found in the fundamental teachings of Judaism, Christianity and Islam. In strictly rational terms, the moral law is not a liberation, but a regulating, and therefore constraining, factor that is often useful and positive. It does not lie at the core of the mind; its place and functions lie between minds and allow the harmonization of interpersonal relations.

This is not, however, the only rationally based philosophical attitude. In his *Critique of Practical Reason*, Kant establishes the principle of the autonomy of morals. It certainly requires establishing consistency postulates (freedom, God, the immortality of the soul), but it also means that this principle of the moral autonomy is based solely upon its own necessity. To tell the individual consciousness that a 'person should never be used as a means except when he is at the same time treated as an end'[1] is to enjoin it to accept a 'categorical imperative' that has a universal import. The principle of morality that

1. Immanuel Kant, *Critique of Practical Reason*, trans. Lewis White Beck, Upper Saddle River, NJ: Prentice Hall, 1993, p. 91.

spirituality and religion establish in the hearts of men in the name of the meaning of the Whole and/or faith Kant establishes on rational grounds, and as a universal maxim that exists both in itself and in relations between individuals. And yet, even in the rigorous meanderings of the *Critique* and the *Groundwork for the Metaphysics of Morals*, he regains mystical aspirations and states: 'Two things fill the mind with ever new and increasing wonder and awe ... the starry heavens above me and the moral law within me.'[2]

Kant spoke of the moral law; the rationalist Spinoza, who wrote before him, referred to ethics. For Spinoza, ethics was the means that allowed man to become an active agent, and to subordinate the imperfect illusions of the imagination to the reasoned and rational controls of the human understanding. The tension between the two faculties is permanent, and ethics gives the conscience the power to transform a being into a subject. Contemporary debates about the distinction between morality and ethics are located between the two poles represented by Kant's universal morality that commands and Spinoza's ethics of the individual conscience that masters. The French philosopher Paul Ricœur admits that his own distinction between the two is purely conventional: he uses 'ethics' to describe the individual aspiration towards the good (at the level of action) – a description that follows the Aristotelean tradition – and 'morality' to refer to a universal norm which has, as Kant suggests, a constraining power and that is incumbent upon men. The German philosopher Jürgen Habermas, who is also influenced by Kant, makes the same distinction by relating ethics to the material principles of the sensibility and determinants of the individual's quest of the good, and the moral law to formal principles that have universal implications. Habermas does, however, want to make the universality of the moral principles of rightness and justice the subject of critical study and discussion. He does not simply wish to state, like Kant, the universal basis of the categorical imperative and to stipulate the rule: 'Act as though the maxim of your action were to become by your will a universal law of nature.'[3] A debate

2. Ibid., p. 169.
3. Immanuel Kant, *Groundwork for the Metaphysics of Morals*, trans. Thomas E. Hill Jr, ed. Thomas E. Hill Jr and Arnulf Zweig, Oxford: Oxford University Press, 2002, p. 222.

must be opened, and the universality of morality and of its fundamentals must be grounded in 'what everyone can recognise as a universal norm'.[4]

It is as though, from sixteenth-century China to age-old religious traditions, rationalism in the Age of Enlightenment and then the twentieth century, we had been going around in circles and encountering the same three questions about morality and ethics, albeit in different forms: do we all have an innate sense (that exists in our minds, as Yangming would put it) of morality that is in fact universal? Is morality a fundamental principle for actions, or is it a circumstantial instrument of interpersonal relationships (which is used to protect or control)? Is there a difference (or must we introduce one) between the individual and collective quest for the good through action (ethics) and a shared universal norm that applies to all (morality)? Questions about the origins, function and objectives of the moral law have sometimes given rise to a distinction between the Latin (morality) and the Greek (ethics), but the one constant in these endless debates is the need for rules and norms that determine goodness, justice and what is right, and which, whatever their origin, exist within all of us and regulate relations between us. Irrespective of whether the moral law is inscribed in my innermost being or whether it is born of the peregrinations of my reason, it must be impersonal. It must be depersonalized and transformed into a collective ethics the universality of which may or may not be challenged, but whose benevolent, protective and regulatory function is collectively recognized. The modern era is afraid of morality and enamoured of ethics. True, but that may be nothing more than a 'conventional' distinction designed to reassure us about authority, since it seems that morality is imposed while ethics is negotiated. It remains that action needs limits and society needs norms, whether relative or universal, negotiated or imposed. There can be no human societies without ethics. Ideally, ethics should apply to all: they should be everyone's ideal, and no one's property. Theocracies and dictatorships, for example, pervert the meaning of that ideal, whilst democracies, because of the contradictions between their stated ideals

4. See Jürgen Habermas, *Justification and Application: Remarks on Discourse Ethics*, trans. Ciaran Cronin, Cambridge: Polity, 1993.

and actual practices, often (and insidiously) make ethics the exclusive property and instrument that allows some (a social class, race, gender, and so on) to wield a certain power.

THE SCIENCES AND ETHICS

It is in the field of the experimental sciences that we can best understand the need for ethics to be autonomous in both senses. Ethics is inevitably bound up with the subject who refers to it or produces it (in the case of religious or rational ethics) or with the object to which it has to be applied (the life science, medicine: the realms of bioethics), but must remain distinct from both the subject and the object. The subject, in other words, puts forward his ethics as, on the one hand, a norm (or corpus of norms) that he would like to be shared by all and, on the other, as a norm that must never be confused with the free practice of a science as it establishes ethical and juridical limits (whose goal is to prevent the abuse of science). No matter whether we are speaking from within a philosophical or religious tradition, or from the point where they interact, imposing one's own norm is an expression of the spirit of dogmatism and exclusivism, whereas interfering with the twofold autonomy of science and ethics (by confusing the two realms of knowledge) can muzzle the sciences and can let the inquisitorial spirit emerge once more.

It also has to be said that the contemporary sciences remind us every day of the need for ethics. Scientific knowledge is now so complex and efficient that men have the power to transform nature and the Creation, to manipulate genes and to produce the means of their own destruction. The experiments that have been carried out, the technologies that have been developed and the constant scientific advances that are being made have implications for life, the intellect, collective psychology, social relations, the natural order, the climate and, of course, the future of humanity. Expert and scientific commissions have been established, and the number of committees on ethics has increased dramatically: their goal is to open up a space for collective negotiations between the agents of scientific progress and the guardians of the human conscience who wish to prevent abuses of knowledge that might turn against its human authors and destroy them.

There are numerous and contradictory interests involved here. Science is indeed concerned with knowledge, but its interdependent relations with the world of the economy make its decision-making procedures more complex. The knowledge and progress that the sciences allow generate skills, interests and wealth. The contemporary sciences, for instance, produce both knowledge and money, and economic operators (who are rarely invited to sit on scientific commissions and ethics committees) often play the part of the omnipresent but absent agent who bears upon the atmosphere of the place and influences the direction taken by the debates and the nature of the decisions that are taken. When so many millions of dollars and so many private and/or public interests are at stake, realism demands that we put into perspective the competence and powers of the committees on ethics and the calls for collective responsibility. Declarations of good intent, scientific studies and expert opinions notwithstanding, we have seen how little effect ethical and ecological recommendations have when the economy and the multinationals bring all their influence to bear on political decision-making processes. The United States' failure to ratify the Kyoto protocol on cutting emissions of greenhouse gases (even though it is the most polluting country on earth) is only one of the many examples of how a conflict of interests can arise between the domains of ethics, the sciences, the economy and politics.

The world of the experimental sciences means that we have to think about ethics in terms that concentrate upon its concrete application and which, to that extent, prevent us from getting lost in nebulous and relatively unproductive preliminary philosophical debates. Moreover, an inductive approach – one which works backwards from the question of the practical applications of ethical norms to their source – allows us to clarify the status of ethics at the core of the pluralism of spiritualities, religions and philosophies on the one hand, and with respect to the object or activity to which it is applied on the other. The principles of ethics can be derived from what is considered to be a universal moral law (to use Kant's terminology), but we must all be aware that there are many different philosophies and spiritual and religious traditions, and that we must therefore debate and exchange different points of view and determine the status and nature of the values we share. Those values do not belong to us alone, and nor are they the property of a religion or philosophy that can be imposed on others. They are the common property of the social or human community (depending on whether the question is discussed in national or international terms). Some basic challenges call into question our ability to produce, together, a shared universal ethics that can and must be applied, because they are global, transnational and transcultural. That is what the theologian Hans Küng wishes to achieve with his project for a 'planetary ethics' that is in keeping with interfaith initiatives and transversal and very concrete forms of cooperation between different traditions and religions.

Ethics is born of itself, but is independent of itself. Once it becomes a product that is shared collectively it must also, as we have already said, become distinct from its object if it is to ensure that, rather than forcing itself upon scientific methods, it concentrates on the limits to their applications (whilst obviously concerning itself with their meaning). It is imperative for it to maintain its independence from all other domains of human activity, and above all from politics and economics. And that independence is both its strength and its weakness. Because it is not subordinate to any order, it can claim to be the objective norm we can use to evaluate the accurary of human choices, be they scientific, political or economic. And yet its independence does not give ethics any leverage that allows it to have a practical influence on the real world or to transform behaviours. Theologians, philosophers, scientists and ecological activists may well discuss meanings, limitations, human responsibility and the destruction of the planet, but they often look like ineffectual dreamers. They sometimes speak loudly, but they do not really have the means to change anything. The power of ethics is no longer religious, philosophical or political; it lies simply – and unfortunately – in its awareness of the imminent catastrophes that men are about to unleash because they are so irresponsible. The power of a rational ethics stems from the fact that it is, objectively, the last defence against human madness. Because of their actions, men find themselves under an obligation to summon their conscience in one way or another in both the North and South. The destruction of the planet, global warming, corruption and new forms of slavery leave them no alternative. We are now approaching the limits of survival, and ethics now is invested with the power of the collective consciousness that must teach us how to survive. We are witnessing, as the philosopher Michel Serres has said, the return of morality. It is no longer the universality of its principles that allows us to call it 'the moral law', as the Kantians would have it, but the nature of the global catastrophes that threaten the whole planet and each and every one of us. The return of morality 'forces' us to take stock and to accept that we have an individual responsibility as to how we behave in our day-to-day lives. A personal ethics obliges us to take another look at our behaviour, our habits, the amount we consume and our whole way of life. We have come a long way from philosophical debates and conventional distinctions, and we are witnessing the marriage or fusion of morality and ethics: we no longer have any real choice between obligatory universals and individual choices. When we lose our freedom, morality and ethics are essential.

THE ETHICS OF INDEPENDENCE

Ethics is born in a thousand ways; it comes from different universes and finds its true realization in its independence from both the subject who elaborates it and the object to which it is applied. And yet, in the name of that very independence, its full rigour must be applied – independently – to both its subject and its object. We have seen how ethics must be applied in the domain of the sciences (its object), and how it must give them a meaning, guide their orientation and establish the limits beyond which they must not go. This is now a matter of urgency in the fields that pertain to our continued survival, including the climate, genetic engineering, discoveries and advances in the arms industry, and, more insidiously, the systems that keep individuals under surveillance. The field is vast, the challenges are many, and the demands are very strict.

It is not, however, stating the obvious to recall that ethics also applies to the individual. Scientists must, for their own sakes and in their professional lives, respect a strict code of ethics. Objectivity, transparency and intellectual probity are minimal requirements, and the demand for them will increase as the sciences in question and their fields of study become more complex. These requirements inevitably affect the sciences, both experimental and human: scientists, specialists and thinkers are expected to respect their sources by citing them, faithfully translating the objects of their observations and trying to remain as objective as possible (or, failing that, to state clearly where their subjectivity, or ideological and political prejudices, begins to intrude). The ethics of the scientist or researcher consists in trying to make their object of study as objective, transparent and honest as possible. What is disturbing, for instance, in the conclusions Sigmund Freud claims to have drawn from his scientific practice obviously has to do with the inexactness of his accounts, which were written a posteriori. Despite what we are told in the *Studies on Hysteria* and then in *Five Lectures on Psycho-Analysis*, the case histories, Dr Breuer's patient Anna O. (Bertha Pappenheim) was never really cured of her illness (her long-standing hydrophobia) by the psychoanalytic sessions she herself described as a 'talking cure'. She sought refuge in crises, anxiety and alcohol, even though she was, as Freud reports, able to identify the origin of her traumas. This example, like many others from the domain of the experimental and human sciences, does a lot to discredit the conclusions that have been drawn and casts a shadow of a doubt over scientists' intellectual probity and capacity for objectivity.

This rigorous ethical attitude towards scientists allows us to go further and to try to circumscribe the conditions under which it applies to the subject, and to each one of us in our day-to-day lives. The question is at once explicit and difficult: what can be said of ethics in relation to the subject when the subject becomes its own object? In other words, what role does ethics play in my relationship with myself, or in the relationship between my conscience and my actions? This question and this first stage (I as an ethical object) are determinant because they influence every other field of human action. A rapid survey of all the teachings of ethics – from the oldest African, Amerindian, Asian or Australian (Aboriginal) traditions to Hindu or Buddhist spiritualities, from the monotheistic religions to philosophy from Socrates to Heidegger, and from Descartes to

Schopenhauer – reveals one constant: ethics is always, and basically, simply a matter of an appeal to the individual conscience to ensure that the values and principles we have chosen (for reasons of faith, reason or imagination) coincide with the actions we are about to perform, or for which we have to assume responsibility. The same is, as it happens, true if we regard the action in question as immoral; if, as Nietzsche suggests, there is no reason to grant 'truth' any greater value than 'lies', we have to conclude that someone who lies is, basically, acting in accordance with the pre-established principle that lies have a value that must be respected. Even the immoral or amoral Nietzsche therefore asks of the superman-artist that he respects the principles he himself has established 'beyond good and evil'. We can never escape the principle of consistency.

Between me and myself, the critical mind develops. It is simply a matter of evaluating our actions by the standards of the principles we have adopted. As Kant notes in his necessary postulate, the first precondition is that we must be free in terms of our choices and actions. The conscience then has to move, in a constant dialectic, between values and actions: I then become my own object of study, and the principles of my ethics allow me to evaluate my being and my actions. I can neither evaluate the state I am in nor commit myself to reshaping my being or harmonizing my values and my actions unless I become as independent as possible of myself. The appeal to conscience, be it a moral conscience or not, is a constant feature of all religions, spiritualities and philosophies, and it calls upon the critical consciousness to distance itself. Such work on oneself, such critical work – even though it involves liberating ourselves from ourselves, and in ourselves setting free the forces of the unconscious imaginary or of art – is a precondition for the quest for meaning that is incumbent on all of us, whatever choices we may make. We must distance ourselves, observe ourselves independently, carefully examine our values and our daily lives, draw up a balance sheet of our hopes and commitments, and draw, for ourselves, a somewhat externalized self-portrait that has at least some objectivity. Once again, there is no escaping the few universal principles of the common ethics that belongs to no one, probity, transparency and justice – the paradox is merely apparent – if we are to be able to evaluate the extent to which our choices are consistent with our ability to choose dissimulation and injustice. Indeed, we have to go even further, as we saw in the case of Nietzsche: the man or woman who has chosen disorder and incoherence as a principle and a way of life must still refer to the principle of consistency to discover if he or she is being consistent with his or her ideal of inconsistency.

This independence, this distancing ourselves from ourselves (which is the key to personal development), must be extended to all our affiliations. In our families, our religious or spiritual communities, our schools of thought or our political parties, we have to keep alive the critical mind that allows us to measure the discrepancy between the values we claim to uphold and our actual practices. We must not confuse a self-aware sense of belonging with compromising partisanship. Being able to say 'no' to our mothers or fathers when they go against our principles or rights, rebelling against our own society when the nationalist spirit blinds the masses and justifies the annihilation of the other, demanding that democratic principles must apply equally to all when racism and exclusion set in, speaking up against the excesses and betrayals of our own co-religionists in the name of our religious principles, opposing the exclusivist logics that may emerge within our political party and betray its ideals from within . . . these are the natural and obvious implications of a mind concerned about ethics and consistency and the ability to remain independent. Human history provides many examples of men and women who have refused to compromise and who have, in the name of their principles, their duty to remain consistent and even their religious or philosophical affiliations, acted against their own people, their society and/or community at the risk of being considered traitors. Wang Yangming defended his colleague, Voltaire defended Calas, and Zola defended Dreyfus. Russell came to Einstein's rescue, intellectuals criticized colonialism, whilst French, German, Swiss and other citizens disobeyed their governments and hierarchies by saving Jews from extermination. Jewish, Christian, Muslim and atheist American soldiers refused to go to fight in Vietnam and are now refusing to fight in Iraq. These men and women were and are the conscience of their countries and the personification of the ethics of independence. This appeal to the critical mind and to the founding principle of consistency runs through all spiritualities and religions. There are no exceptions. A Muslim prophetic tradition sums up a feature common to all affiliation: the best way to help an unjust brother is to make him stop being unjust. That is why Gandhi went on hunger strike: my conscience and principles have nothing to do with my affiliations (be they religious, cultural or intellectual) and I will embrace my independence by having the courage to be critical of those who constitute my community of affiliation. This is a matter of belonging to one's principles rather than blindly belonging to a community that might betray them, or which might allow betraying these principles.

Defending one's principles, exercising a duty of conscience or consistency, and asserting one's independence in the face of all blind loyalties (be they ideological, religious or nationalist) certainly demands an ethics, but it also takes will power and courage. We have to face the criticisms from within, from men and women who regard this attitude as an act of desertion or betrayal that plays into the hands of the 'other' or the 'enemy'. In the new fictitious relationships between 'civilizations' that are 'clashing', emotions run high and blindness runs deep: Jews who denounce Israeli policies or the silence of their co-religionists, Muslims who denounce the attitudes of countries with a Muslim majority or the behaviour of certain extremists and the Americans and Europeans who denounce the inconsistencies and lies of Western politicians are seen as men and women who, respectively, nurture self-hatred, act against the interests of the *umma* or have a guilt complex and outdated 'leftist' ideals that lead them to declare their guilt endlessly, and dangerously. The virulence of rejection from within, by one's own community of affiliation, is proportional to its lack of self-confidence and sense of insecurity: a critical attitude is seen as a betrayal from within, and as marking the emergence of a 'fifth column' that is working and plotting on behalf of the 'enemy'. When we are faced with this fear and hyper-emotionalism, it is difficult to argue rationally that this independence is based upon a rational ethics, and that it is not a mater of 'playing into the other's hands', but of 'being reconciled with oneself' and one's ideals. It is a matter of conscience and dignity.

CRITICAL LOYALTY

The modern era is one of confusion and insecurity. The globalization of communications has globalized attitudes that were once mostly encountered at the local or national level. Simplistic and monolithic representations of the 'other' or the 'foreigner', who may well be a neighbour, once sustained certainties and a more or less conscious racism towards 'him' and 'them' that were reassuring to oneself ('me', 'we') and one's own doubt. The phenomenon has spread and become more pronounced, and the twin phenomena of globalization and migration have, by increasing insecurity and fears proportionally, helped to foster attitudes that are often irrational, or at least unreasonable. Conversely, the circles to which we belong have become proportionally smaller and increasingly exclusivist: we must have an identity, belong to a community or group, and our loyalty to it must be absolute.

Contemporary obsession with the question of 'identity' appears to be a neutral way of asking questions about our affiliations and loyalties. Just as we should have 'an identity', our loyalties should be absolute: if that loyalty is not our prime consideration, or if it is critical of the group to which we belong, doubts begin to arise as to our intentions, loyalties and, ultimately, the nature of loyalty itself. The constructive and positive approaches to diversity outlined by philosophers and thinkers like the Canadian Charles Taylor, the Lebanese Amin Maalouf, the Indian Amartya Sen and the British sociologist Tariq Modood are both welcome and of fundamental importance. It is important to recall that our identities are multiple and fluid, and that our societies will not survive unless they can find positive ways of managing the wealth of their religious and cultural pluralism, and of celebrating it as it should be celebrated. These philosophical and sociological contributions are decisive, but we have to add a political dimension, and that dimension is, ultimately, tied up with the question of loyalty and power. The spectre of the identity we display masks, I repeat, the lingering, and important, question of which loyalty we are defending, and of which power we are defending it from.

It is not a question of denying our identities or betraying our loyalties. That would be strictly impossible, and probably dangerous. The important thing is knowing how to manage them, and how to situate ourselves in relation to ourselves and to the groups that are constituted, or which we constitute, around us. By using 'I' to refer to his identity and 'we' to identify his affiliations, the individual establishes spheres of judgement and power, and each person must imperatively ask himself about his relationship and the nature of his loyalty to this power and this judgement. What we have just said about the independence of ethics and the ethics of independence shows that only critical loyalty respects the principle of consistency that no individual and no society can escape. Being loyal to ourselves and loyal to our community requires us, at the ethical level, to be self-critical and to criticize our communities in the name of the values we – we and our community – have determined both individually and collectively. This approach is philosophical, but it is also eminently political: individuals, groups and societies determine the field of power, and the ethical and critical approach clearly consists in judging the exercise of that power reasonably and limiting its potential abuses.

We must be able to at once respect individuals and criticize their behaviours within our families and in the face of the power of our parents, siblings or clan. Critical respect has to be combined with respectful criticism. This is never very easy in traditional families or in the cultures of the South. The same attitude should prevail in our spiritual and religious communities: we should be able to trust in a community's ideals and ability to remain true to them, and at the same time be objectively critical of the behaviour of certain individuals that the collective comprises. More broadly still, critical loyalty is an imperative in any human society: whilst we must recognize the need for identity and belonging, all the resulting powers must be subject to the 'arms of criticism', to use the language of Marx, who, quite rightly, wanted men to be under no illusions as to the nature of relations of power and domination (both economic and political). We should, however, be aware of their existence, even within our clans and amongst our own people. Under a dictatorship, the logic of resistance is inescapable, but the same principle should apply to the consciousness of the citizens of democracies: we must be able to challenge the decisions made by elected politicians, the injustices we accept, the instrumentalization of populism, dubious international alliances, support for dictatorships, inconsistencies with respect to human rights, structural discrimination and racism, abuses of police power in the name of security, the acceptance of torture, and so on. The list is long, very long, but if loyalty to one's country and to the principles of democracy means anything, it begins with the use of our critical faculties and respect for the principle of consistency. That is the role of civil society in general and of intellectuals in particular. Whilst it is natural for peoples and nations to have an identity, their need for a conscience is an imperative. If the appeal to identity and to the sense of belonging leads to a loss of lucidity and consciousness, men lose both their ethics and their independence . . . and part of their humanity. Bergson intuitively sensed this when he was writing his last book, *The Two Sources of Morality and Religion*. He recognized the existence of stages, and wanted things to evolve. The distinction he makes between the two types of morality and religion contains the idea that the primary function of religions is to allow the constitution of the group or society, and then to guarantee its protection. 'Closed societies' such as this determine 'belonging' in terms of security and protection. And yet we have to go beyond these dispositions, open ourselves up to universal values and turn our societies into 'open societies'. It is, therefore, our awareness of universal values (which transcend our affiliations) that allows us to transcend ourselves because it encourages an openness that is at once rational and critical. Bergson thought that it was exceptional men like Christ who showed us the path that leads to transcendence. The final stage of this path is love, beyond oneself and one's own, which combines confidence at the origin, ethical and critical conscience along the way and the recognition of similarity with the other beyond differences at the end of the quest. Spiritualities, philosophies and religions assert this, Wang Yangming exemplifies it and Bergson repeats it: ethics is a matter of the conscience as well as the heart.

9

Emotion and Spirituality

We have been robbed of our poetry, and of much of our imagination. We used to think that our emotions came from within, from our hearts and from our guts. They seemed to express our feelings, our nature, our spontaneity, and therefore our sincerity: my emotions are my freedom, I am what my feelings say about me. Reality is much less romantic than that. Contemporary studies of the workings of the human brain give us a very different idea of the 'production' of the emotions and of their 'nature'. The vocabulary used by specialists in the neurosciences is unsettling: in the new geography of the brain, there is no question of a landscape that gives our inner life and our imagination free rein; it is much more like a railway station or even a military camp in which every movement is tightly controlled and fits into a clearly defined hierarchy. Signals are emitted by our sensory receptors and sent to the thalamus, which analyses the content of the information it has received. That information is then passed to the neo-cortex (once known as the 'thinking brain') where it is recorded and sorted before decisions are taken. Emotion-related data is sent to the limbic brain, where the amygdala (which is located at the top of the cerebral trunk) reacts on the basis of the information it receives and 'produces emotion'. It triggers the secretion of hormones, stimulates the cardio-vascular system and mobilizes the nerve-centres that control movement. The amygdala is the 'seat of the emotions' and sends out signals to the rest of the brain. As norepinephrine is secreted, the reactivity of the brain increases, and the senses are sharpened. The information sent to the cerebral trunk increases the heart rate, raises blood pressure, slows down breathing and produces facial expressions (joy, fear, etc.). Not long ago, American neurologist Joseph LeDoux discovered the existence of a bundle of neurones which connect the thalamus directly to the amygdala, bypassing the neo-cortex. A certain number of the signals that produce emotional reactions therefore do not pass through the centre of the 'thinking brain' and take a shorter route through a single synapse to the amygdala, which triggers immediate reactions. According to LeDoux, the system that controls the emotions can act independently of the neo-cortex. This, he argues, explains why our emotions can sometimes take over our reason and cause us to act in uncontrolled, exaggerated or seemingly insane ways. At such times, we are under the sway of our emotions because the neo-cortex has been taken unawares: its power has been short-circuited by the immediate reactivity of the amygdala.

This is the vocabulary of an army camp in which all ranks are subject to orders and directives, and in which information and power centres can lose control of the whole system (when certain signals – data – no longer go through the chief executive office, namely the neo-cortex or thinking brain). So our emotions are nothing more than that: they are physical reactions to signals, stimuli or the secretion of hormones, and their intensity depends upon which pathway of clusters of neurones a signal takes to reach the limbic brain. So what has become of the heart's impulses, the depth of our sincerity, to which our obvious joy or continuous floods of tears so obviously bear witness? What has become of the beauty of our spontaneous and freely expressed emotions? All that would appear to be merely a matter of neurones, synapses and hormones inside a brain where the administration experiences great tensions and where two agencies compete for power. The neo-cortex tries to control the data and to allow the subject to control how it reacts to the signals received by the senses, whilst the amygdala produces immediate secretions that can take possession of the brain and make it lose control of the situation. The American psychologist Daniel Goleman actually uses the phrase 'an emotional coup d'état' to describe how the authority of the neo-cortex can be overthrown, and how the balance of power can be completely inverted when the amygdala takes control of the greater part of the brain. The subject loses all self-control and is completely under the sway of the emotions. The subject can no longer take any decisions ... the emotions are in control of the subject's reason and ability to take decisions. A real coup d'état has indeed taken place in the army camp that was designed to maintain a strict internal order so as to prevent it from coming under attack from outside. It transpires that the potential enemy or real danger comes from within the system itself and from conflicting internal authorities.

We are a long way from the poetry of the emotions and the spontaneous impulses of the free imagination. Our emotions are primarily responses to signals and stimuli. Struggles for influence and tensions are always there in the amygdala, which is the seat of the emotions. Depending on the intensity of the signals that are carried by the respective neuronal bundles, we may even see palace revolutions. When that happens, the individual becomes a slave to her or his affects. Neurology tells us about physiological characteristics that are of great interest in psychological and philosophical terms: emotion is the result of a relationship, sometimes controlled and sometimes quite conflicted, between the seat of thought and the seat of affectivity. It is the speed or immediacy of the reaction that allows the emotions to be expressed with such speed and intensity. Tension, reactivity, intensity and immediacy: these are some of the characteristics of emotion. What we have lost in terms of poetry, we have gained in objective knowledge, and we have to make the best of it. The paradox – and the illusion – of the affects has to do with the fact that we thought that we used them to freely express the spontaneity of our being, but neurology reminds us that it is quite the opposite: the emotions, which can vary in intensity, are always products of a reactivity over which we have little or no control, and which determines the modalities of our actions at the very moment when we are least free.

PASSIONS

Socrates, Plato and Aristotle were not neurologists, and knew nothing about the role of the amygdala or hormones. They did not know that there were such things as synapses. The same was true of the oldest Asian, African, Hindu and Buddhist traditions. The monotheistic religions did not base their teachings on the sciences, and the psychologists and psychoanalysts of the late nineteenth century and the first half of the twentieth tried to formulate theories and establish method-ologies on the basis of experiments they were able to analyse by exam-ining the behaviour of their patients. And yet all these approaches make the same observations and strive to achieve a similar objective: no matter whether their message is based upon moral principles, the aspiration to inner freedom or even the desire to achieve a psycho-logical equilibrium, the goal is always to achieve and maintain mas-tery and control over one's emotions and passions. They are beyond our control, and the task of the philosopher, initiate, believer or patient is to become aware of the indeterminate element within himself or herself and to understand, insofar as that is possible, how that ele-ment functions in an attempt to control it and thereby attain an inner harmony. Socrates' 'temperance' requires a determined commitment on the part of reason which, through introspection and asceticism ('know thyself'), gains the ability to win the fight over the passions that bind us. Even Aristotle's catharsis serves the same function: drama attempts to work upon the non-rational (affective and emotional) ele-ment in the spectator in order to influence the free and sometimes untamed dimension that escapes the control of his conscious reason. No matter whether we agree with the Greek dualists who contrast the soul (or mind) with the body, or whether we support the very differ-ent monist theses of contemporary physicalism and argue, like Otto Neurath, that 'the language of physics is the universal language' (he is referring to the theories of the philosopher and logician William Van Orman Quine), empirical and day-to-day experience always reveals the same truth: it is as though some indeterminate, non-conscious and uncontrolled element (which may be physical, unconscious or mental) has to be kept under control and surveillance if we are to find inner peace and a degree of well-being. This is an age-old insight: both the oldest teachings of philosophy, spirituality and religion and modern scientific knowledge reveal the same truth: our nature, bodies and brains are subject to tensions and ruled by conflicting powers and authorities, and we are torn between a limited consciousness that senses its freedom and the free and spontaneous emotions to which we are bound.

Our emotions are often beautiful, but they can also be dangerous. They represent our spontaneity and seem to speak to us of our freedom. And yet all contemporary studies – from neurology and psychology to marketing – prove that our emotions are the form of self-expression over which we have least control, that they are highly vulnerable and, basically, easily manipulated. Advertising, music, atmospheres, subliminal messages and films can have an impact on our emotional life, and we cannot control it because we are not even conscious of it. The 'army camp' that coordinates the agencies of our brain is vulnerable, both in itself and from within. In effect, he who can know and master its functioning and psychology from outside can become twice its master. The era of global communications is also the era of global emotions: from the death of Princess Diana to sporting events and even the devastating tsunami that struck Asia in December 2004, we have witnessed massive ritual gatherings in which millions of individuals were overwhelmed by tears, joy or communion of mourning. Such planetary phenomena are unpredictable and uncontrolled and sweep away and colonize our consciousness and our hearts: no one can predict which direction such popular tumult will take, or which gods the impassioned crowds will worship. We try to assess the risks posed by these new 'ritual rallies' of the uncontrolled at both the individual and the collective level: how can we control the emotions? Can we be spontaneous whilst still remaining rational?

SPIRITUALITY

Intimate tensions and inner conflicts (which oppose the mind and the body or, more prosaically, the amygdala and the neo-cortex) can result in a dangerous loss of self-control, or to a feeling of imbalance and unease. We find the same aspiration at the heart of the basic teachings of Hinduism, Taoism and Buddhism: we must overcome the inner conflicts and imbalances that cause us to suffer and that bind both us and our humanity. The natural state of the individual is to be 'in tension', to be torn between the demands of the conscious mind that strives to be in control and the emotions and passions that take possession of the mind, the body and the heart. Spiritual healing involves a quest for inner harmony, introspection and self-liberation. This immersion in the 'self' has several objectives. It involves introspection, attempting to distance ourselves from our immediate emotional reactions by trying to identify, observe and contemplate them so as to gain control over them. This 'entry into oneself' also reveals the essence of things, of presence in the world, and of the presence of the world. Distancing ourselves from our selves whilst at the same time striving to achieve deep insight is therefore associated with elevating consciousness above the physical dimension of the elements with a view to understanding their metaphysical meaning and their inscription within the cosmos. This dialogue between the intimate microcosm and the infinite cosmos reveals a third dimension that sheds light on the essence of the soul, the intelligence of the heart and the meaning of death. The initiation can be long and difficult, and the stages of these teachings are bound up with the understanding of the self and control over the emotions. That understanding and control represent a stage in the journey towards inner mastery and then ultimate transcendence (which brings both harmony and peace as the self fuses with the Whole). This final stage may have the substance and form of an emotional disposition, but that disposition has been oriented by the conscious mind, educated by reason and mastered and transcended during this initiation into being. Our era appears to have deceived us by confusing certain emotional states with spiritual states: there can indeed be no spirituality without emotion but, whilst our emotions can turn us into 'purely reactive objects' or even slaves devoid of will power and freedom, spirituality requires us to become conscious subjects once more, and to seek the meaning of both the instant moment of impulse and the infinite cycles of fate. Emotion is that dimension of the subject that is expressed in the being's immediate reactivity; spirituality is what the subject discovers and expresses through mastered education of that being.

Ancient philosophy had the same ambitions. The mind–body dualism of the Greeks posited the apparently objective existence of two agencies, but the rationale behind the entire philosophical experience was the attempt to reconcile and harmonize them. The soul, the spirit or reason had to take control of the body and our inner machine or animal in order to give our being access to the higher level of its humanity. The being who was a slave to its passions becomes a 'lover of wisdom' (which is the etymological meaning of 'philosopher'), and is then attracted to and called by Beauty. Both the physical 'beauty' that can subdue the instincts, emotion and the body, and the metaphysical Beauty that appeals to the mind, the inner inspiration and the soul teach us a philosophical lesson that is akin to giving birth or breaking one's chains. This individual experience is as profound as that of the individual who, in the 'cave allegory', turns his gaze away from the flickering pictures he can see and understands the nature of the illusion that binds him. He resolves to free himself, to seek the light, the fire and then the sun. He enters into himself, and then emerges from himself. He was a prisoner, but now he is free . . . even though all the prisoners, who are drowning in the illusion of the spontaneous emotions that bind them, judge his wisdom to be his madness and his prison.

Judaism, Christianity and Islam have also codified the meaning of this shared spiritual experience. Their rites are the means or educational exercises that initiate us into this return to the self, this reconciliation and this quest for harmony. Many of their teachings are the same, but there are also significant differences between them. The Christian tradition's 'original sin' reveals something about the nature of human beings that is not very far removed from the traditional teachings of Hinduism and Buddhism, even though they start out from very different premises. The state of natural tension and the suffering that is both primal and consubstantial with being and consciousness in the Eastern traditions appears to correspond to the meaning of the intrinsically sinful nature of man in the Christian tradition. Suffering and evil are both states from which man must deliver himself either through the extinction of the ego or through salvation, but in both cases man is expected to consciously choose introspection or self-mastery (no matter whether grace is sufficient or efficacious). Socratic philosophy makes the same demand; it identifies the emotions with the body, and the body with the world of the senses, with relative truths, and especially with the chains of the passions. The Islamic tradition is somewhat different and takes the view that the body and the 'soul in the body' (*an-nafs*) have no intrinsic qualities, and that their qualities depend on how the human consciousness uses both the body and the soul: the body that exults in sexuality whilst remaining true to ethics can express a prayer, just as the soul that betrays the principles of ethics can express the most extreme evil.

What is more, man's original state is that of the harmony of a being that is naturally drawn to the divine element that will grant it peace. It is the veiling of that state of nature that distracts the heart from the initial call by creating tension and unease, and by making the heart 'ill' and in search of a cure. There is no mention here of a 'fall' or of the need for a Saviour in the Christian sense. The Islamic tradition speaks of a veil that envelops the heart and requires a consciousness. As Asian spiritualities teach us, consciousness has the ability to free itself. The conception of man is very different, but the spiritual teachings and objectives of initiation are ultimately the same: we must become self-aware, identify and master the nature and power of the emotions, and thus find harmony and a higher form of freedom. Despite what we may think when we experience emotions, freedom does not lie in the spontaneous expression of affects, but in the mastery that sets free the conscious and rational part of our being. As we saw when we were discussing music, freedom is the product of discipline and mastery.

The contemporary psychological sciences – from psychoanalysis, ethno-psychoanalysis and behaviourism – are attempting to achieve similar objectives: self-knowledge, an inner equilibrium, autonomy and an awareness of being confident and assured 'subjects' (despite the uncontrollable elements that have been with us for generations and/or since early childhood). Spirituality is not, however, just a quest for equilibrium and freedom: this entry into oneself, this handling of inner conflicts, this initiation into rational and reasonable management of emotions is determined by the 'quest for meaning' we have already mentioned. Emotion is a programmed response to the meaning of signals and stimuli, whilst the characteristic feature of spirituality is that it is a choice, a free decision to determine for oneself the meaning of our existence, of life and of our friendships and loves as well as the cosmos. Contemporary thinkers such as André Comte-Sponville suggest that there may be such a thing as a godless (or secular) spirituality that refers to no spiritual tradition and no religion, and that may be absolutely atheist.[1] The inspiration behind that theory would

1. André Comte-Sponville, *The Book of Atheist Spirituality*, trans. Nancy Huston, London: Bantam, 2008.

appear to be the humanist rationality that produces meaning. Once again, the goals are the same: being oneself, being reasonable, being free and choosing one's own path.

FEAR AND TRUST

We have seen how the mind can suddenly be overpowered by the amygdala and can trigger completely uncontrolled emotional reactions in the individual. Those reactions can range from joy and daring to fear or violence. In an era of globalized communications, it is as though the millions of images and pieces of information that circulate and endlessly appear on our television and computer screens were producing signals that can take over the nerve centres of whole societies and communities. The heavy psychological (but not always conscious) burden of the information that reaches us through so many different channels all over the world on the one hand, combined with the stress of everyday life, the lack of time to think, read and try to understand, the feeling of insecurity and the frustrations on the other, make the 'social body' fragile, and, to pursue the comparison and to be more specific, weaken the 'social brain' and make it quite febrile.

Depending on the sensitive issues and controversies of the day (which are in some cases global phenomena) we observe collective reactions in various societies; the symptoms we observe in an individual who is overwhelmed by emotion are the same as those we observe in the social community. Uncontrollable phenomena can spread like wildfire as a result of some news item, a controversy (which may or may not have been orchestrated), a statement, an accident or a mere rumour. Society and the public debate suddenly seem to fall under the sway of the passions. The resulting turmoil can sometimes take the form of collective hysteria. Reactions become unpredictable, and people lose their ability to listen and to understand. There is no logic to either the arguments or the conclusions, which are used piecemeal, and collective emotions take over thanks to the force of numbers and the power of the instantaneous. The amplified democratization of the emotions often defeats the need to democratize both our collective rationality and intellectual debate. We live in dangerous times in which global technologies are instruments whose power escapes our control, and they can exert a terrible influence over individuals. A generalized loss of control can lead to a real collective 'emotional coup d'état' that may result in a dictatorship of the emotions. As we have already said, what the neurologists tell us about the workings of the brain can also be observed at the collective level: the parallels are disturbing, and sometimes frightening. News-stimuli provoke a sort of shock, and immediate reactions of doubt, fear and insecurity. The passions take over, and may influence the nature of popular decisions. The American armed forces staged the 'incubators affair' in Kuwait during the first Gulf War of 1990 (Saddam Hussein's soldiers had supposedly ripped babies out of their incubators and sadistically left them to die) in order to sway the emotions of the American people and to convince them of the need to go to war. Unfortunately, the operation was crowned with success, and hundreds of thousands died as a result. We saw similar displays of emotion after the terrorist attacks of 11 September 2001 on the United States, and with the political upheaval that followed the attack on Madrid on 11 March 2004 (the left won the elections, despite all the predictions that had been made a few days earlier). The same phenomena of emotional amplification provoked passionate (and sometimes violent) reactions in predominantly Muslim countries at the time of the 'Danish cartoons' affair at the beginning of 2006.

Like a brain with multiple agencies, and parallel and sometimes contradictory centres of power, the global world is experiencing repeated crises and controversies, some national and others international. They are reactions to signal-events, sometimes random but sometimes instrumentalized, that systematically produce more or less uncontrolled mass phenomena. This power of emotion over communities (and the control of its 'means of production' in the richest countries, with their armies of communications specialists) is an open invitation to political populism. Voters are no longer interested in the power of ideas and convictions (or the vision of a shared ideology); they are mobilized by their fears, their need for security, reassurance, comfort and clearly defined points of reference and identities. Because of the pressures brought to bear by communications and the media, and the need for an immediate political reaction, what matters is to reassure, to calm or, at the opposite extreme, to excite fears. Reassure, calm, excite . . . the words relate to the emotions. We have entered the realm of emotional politics or, to be more specific, of the politics of emotions. The technique is familiar, and has long been used by far-right populist parties that stir up fears, stigmatize the other and glorify the pure identity of the race or nation. We are now seeing the normalization of that technique, and the normalization of the very substance of a populist politics that is designed to seduce rather than convince voters. This political attitude, which is more interested in the individual and collective amygdala than in the neo-cortex, certainly makes it possible to win elections, but in the long term it has devastating effects on the future of societies and democracies.

These perversions have long been criticized by thinkers and politicians representing the full spectrum of philosophical and political positions, but not always for the same reasons. Elitist circles, be they aristocratic, bourgeois or conservative, fear, like Socrates, Kant, Nietzsche, Tolstoy and so many other thinkers (with very different sensibilities), that the people will be swayed by blind passion rather than the wisdom of the learned; safeguards are needed to protect the good political decisions of the elite and the 'wise men' from uncontrollable popular movements. The ultimate expression of this fear of the people is the ideal of the 'enlightened despot' who can act for the good of the people without yielding to their sometimes contradictory wishes and their passionate impulses. This is the philanthropic Chigalevism described by Albert Camus in *The Rebel*: the people must be enslaved for the good of the people! Others, from the early humanists of the Renaissance to Saint-Just and then socialist thinkers from Marx, Proudhon, Bakunin and Spencer to Marcuse, Noam Chomsky and Naomi Klein (who also have very different sensibilities), are more inclined to trust the people. But even in those circles, we find the same fear that the power of the people might be instrumentalized by economic and political powers, and nowadays by the means of communications and lobbies. The recent *Shock Doctrine* described by Naomi Klein is based upon this manipulative use of power (including the people's power that democracies recognize) in order to protect private and undeclared interests and, in the long term, to go against the interests of the people.

As we can see, the threat is many-sided. And yet the greatest danger of modern times lies in the implications of the new supremacy of the emotions, emotional politics and instantaneous popular reactions. We are dealing with populations that are kept in a state of alert, with emotional reactivity and with the irrationality and fear that come in their wake. Just as the subject feels that he is acting under the sway of his emotions, communities see themselves as the 'victims' of whatever disturbs them or seems to threaten them. The era of popular emotionality is also an era in which there is a mass feeling of victimization. In a climate of permanent insecurity, the presence of the 'other', and the other's visibility, demands and struggles for justice and respect are unsettling, and produce a feeling of unease that can be used to justify a refusal to listen and differential treatment. The perceived threat of terrorism is now so great that ignoring the requirement to respect the human rights and dignity of individuals has become acceptable: the outcome is discrimination, the imprisonment of individuals without trial, summary or extraordinary renditions and even torture, which is now deemed to be legitimate because the threat is so great. Emotions give those who think of themselves as victims the right to act outside the law when dealing with those they identify as their dehumanized potential killers.

The feeling of being a victim naturally erodes all sense of responsibility. Because they are reacting to external threats, the victims of these attacks feel justified in blaming an aggressor who loves neither them, the very fact of their existence, their civilization nor their values. The fear of the victim of aggression projects on to the other the only justification for their 'essentialist' hatred. We are therefore dealing with a purely emotional conflict in which fear is the answer to hatred, and we need to be able to 'clarify' the terms of the opposition and the polarization in intellectual terms. The politics of the emotional uses recurrent campaigns to convince people that the need for security measures arises because of the external (and internal) threats posed by a dangerous 'other' who is at once so far away, so close at hand and even among us that we no longer know who 'we' are. The third effect of the supremacy of emotion is the obsession with identity. Because we are victims and have no particular responsibility for the disorder that surrounds us, it is no longer in our interest to speak of justice or politics, of the economic order or of the redistribution of wealth: it is all about the conflict of civilizations and values, and of cultural and religious identity. Social justice and politics are nothing: cultural and religious differences are everything!

It will be recalled that the hierarchy of authorities in the brain fears attacks from within as well as from without: both are capable of overturning its order and allowing the emotions that make us both impassioned and deaf. Societies and peoples are also in danger of being paralysed with fear, insecurity, the obsession with protection and isolationism, and the rejection of the other. The problem is as intellectual as it is psychological. Then how are we to rediscover the path to trust and self-confidence? Doing so involves knowledge, self-knowledge, self-mastery and a critical mind. We have to give a new meaning to things rather than merely responding to signals and stimuli. Our emotions need spirituality, and our affects need to be spiritualized. We need to find, collectively, ways to celebrate the union between emotion and reasonable reason, because, ultimately, that is what it is all about. There can be no spirituality without emotion . . . but spirituality finds the emotions acceptable when it can successfully embrace all that is good and noble in human beings.

THE AESTHETICS OF MEANING

Our emotions imprison us, but spirituality is both an inspiration and a quest for freedom. The teachings of ancient spiritualities, modern psychologies, philosophies and religions are always the same; we have to become aware of how we function as individuals and communities, establish a critical distance between both ourselves and the world around us, learn to listen and learn to speak and to communicate, and to understand at last our own complexity and that of the other. It may seem strange and paradoxical to say so, but the first act of spiritual liberation lies in the initial attitude adopted by the subject. The lived experience of spirituality demands of the human subject three things that are implicit in all the traditions: the autonomy of the subject (as opposed to dependency on that which affects the subject), the conscious acceptance of responsibility (as opposed to the victim mentality), and a hopeful and constructive attitude (as opposed to despair, defeatism or the nihilism that does not believe in the possibility of change). Whilst emotion can be something we undergo, spirituality requires an initial (and determined) act of the will to assert our ontological freedom, no matter where the individual finds himself. The individual must also assume a basic responsibility for his own transformation, and sustain the profound conviction that everything is possible . . . always, and for the better.

These are, as should be obvious, the three preconditions for self-confidence. How can we acquire this individual and collective self-confidence in an age characterized by fear and the obsession with security? Spirituality liberates and gives things meaning: it is based upon an initiation into, and education in, self-awareness, maturation, the acceptance of responsibility and gradual transformations. Jewish, Christian and Muslim mysticisms constantly remind us of the archetypal stages of this spiritual awakening: for the initiate, they are basically expressions of the most natural and banal experience of common mortals. When we are faced with external signals and stimuli that threaten to seize power inside our brains and/or hearts (and consciousness), we must be forearmed if we wish to remain in control of our reactions. If we can do that, we remain free and human. Education therefore begins at what appears to be the periphery. It begins with the individual's senses and perceptions, because they are the channels through which the first stimuli reach us, and the paths of emotional reactivity. Both children and adults have to be taught to see, touch, listen, smell and taste: we must take the time to reflect and meditate upon the feelings that invade us when we see certain landscapes, or the people we love (or hate). We must study the meaning of listening, and of ways of hearing . . . learn to touch, taste and smell the material world, scents, nature and human beings. But that is not all. We have to breathe meaning into our senses and so spiritualize our perceptions that we are not overwhelmed by our immediate emotional reflexes, but greet them with the confidence of an awareness that has been enriched, that has succeeded in taming itself and that has therefore set itself free.

In a world of global communications and culture, educating our perceptions – at the periphery – entails returning to fundamental teachings. It in fact seems that every consciousness must acquire some knowledge of the principles and histories of spiritualities and religions, master some philosophical notions and have an elementary understanding of the arts and their evolution. Religions and spiritualities, philosophies, and the arts are the three disciplines that should be on the core curriculum of every intellect if we wish to give it the wherewithal to become autonomous, free and responsible. No matter whether we are believers or not, it is vitally important to understand the basic principles of the world's spiritualities and religions. Spiritualities and religions can sometimes allow human beings to blossom and can sometimes protect them from their fears, but they always make sense and confer meaning. We are all free to choose our own path, but we must do so with full knowledge of the facts. If we state that we are giving an individual the freedom to choose when we have deprived that individual of knowledge, we are dishonest: freedom in a state of ignorance is an illusion. Philosophy shapes the critical consciousness and the critical mind: it forces the intellect to observe, to know how to ask questions and to take its time. Nothing is simple, and even simple things are complex: studying philosophy should be a lesson in detachment and humility that teaches individuals to suspend their judgement. Arrogant philosophies that 'know' the ultimate truth and judge or despise the truths of others are not philosophies: they are ideologies. We would all benefit from observing a philosopher just before he reaches his conclusions and certainties: the intellectual exercise consists in recalling that philosophy is indeed a quest in the course of which we put forward a series of hypotheses and postulates. Such is man's intellectual destiny: without critical questioning, he falls short of his humanity; when he asserts that his truths are 'the truth', he arrogantly oversteps the limits of his humanity. We have to be initiated into art, creativity and the human ability to explore the paths of beauty. Beauty imparts meaning, and aesthetics is in effect a twofold quest: it is both a quest for meaning and a quest for beauty. Socrates thought that there was a continuum – or a generic unity – between the physical beauty of bodies and the metaphysical Beauty of essences and ideas. The applied exercise of philosophy allows us to rise above ourselves: Beauty is the marriage of philosophy, spirituality and art. All spiritualities associate the encounter with the sacred or the divine with the proximity of beauty and with the transcendence that, thanks to the aesthetics of form, recalls the meaning of its substance. 'God is beautiful and loves beauty,' says an Islamic prophetic tradition that synthesizes the import of all these teachings. The arts, with or without the sacred, call upon man to discover within himself the resources that allow him to transcend himself through an imaginary that can give him meaning and inspiration. The Romantic poet John Keats, who wanted his epitaph to describe him as one 'whose name was written in water', was the bard of self-transcendence in the proximity of Beauty: 'Beauty is Truth, Truth Beauty.' Our life on earth is brief, and 'that is all we know'. As he encounters Beauty, the poet speaks the meaning of the eternity on whose shores his morality has cast him up. The poet will pass away like a wave, and all artists will pass away with him . . . the ocean, works of art, Beauty and Meaning will remain. It is as though the beautiful Moon goddess (Selene) had bathed in the ocean and then, as she watched over the beauty of the shepherd (Endymion), opened up the path that leads to eternity and the divine. 'Truth is Beauty', and Beauty is the proximity of the Sacred.

Educating the heart, the mind and the imagination in order to train ourselves to see better, hear better, smell better, taste better and touch better is one of the requirements of the autonomy and freedom that lie at the heart of modernity, of advanced technologies and of the globalization of the means of communication. In an age of global communications, anyone who has not been trained to be critical of information is a vulnerable, fragile mind who is open to all kinds of potential manipulations. We also need the time to distance ourselves, to analyse situations and to evaluate critically what we perceive. Nothing is easy. This spiritual exercise is crucially important because it gives meaning to the most elementary actions in life: seeing, hearing, touching . . . and thinking, praying and creating. Spirituality consists in the added meaning that is inherent in even the simplest human actions. It may take the form of faith, thought, art or love, but it always involves a choice, an act of the free will, as opposed to emotion which is a passive reaction, imposed and sometimes uncontrolled: an ocean of difference between the two. Emotion is to spirituality what physical attraction is to love.

10

Education

Education means 'drawing' or 'guiding' individuals out of themselves so that they can establish a conscious relationship with themselves and their physical and social environment. When we are born, we are all physically dependent on our parents or carers. We need to be welcomed into the world, fed, protected and looked after if we are to survive, live and reach the first stages of learning. This dependency in itself requires education, and it is only then that the individual begins to evolve naturally. Being a human being means, first of all, 'becoming a human being' . . . and it is only through education that we become human beings. That is why education is a basic, inalienable right that must be guaranteed in all human societies. Education has as much to do with the transmission of a value-system, behavioural norms and elements of culture as with the transmission of pure knowledge and the skills pertaining to what is usually called training. If there is one universal principle common to all spiritualities, religions, philosophies, civilizations and cultures, it is education. Education is a precondition for man's humanity, and it is an immutable and inalienable right.

The content of education obviously varies from one culture, society or place to another, and from one historical period to another. But even before those differences become apparent, conceptions of education differ in their very ideas of what it means to be a human being, and of what education means to human beings. The many theories we find in the educational sciences and studies of pedagogy put forward very different, and sometimes contradictory, assumptions, approaches and methodologies. Piaget's studies, which are influenced and inspired by Herbert Spencer's evolutionary theories, and James Baldwin's genetic psychology place the emphasis on stages of psychological development, from the sensori-motor stage to the stage of formal operations, and relate them to the cognitive relationship between subject and environment. As the intellect develops through contact with the external world, children develop 'basic units of intellectual activity' ('schemata') which enable them to learn, evolve and develop a more complex relationship with both the world and ideas as they gain access to formal logics, begin to advance hypotheses and to make deductions from the real world. The schemata then become more organized, take on their final form and gradually allow children to develop an autonomous intellect between the ages of eleven and sixteen.

All this is of course far removed from some of the theories to be found in modern psychology, and especially psychoanalysis. For Freud, his successors, disciples and critics, and for Freudian dissidents from Jung to Lacan, it is not the intellect or cognitive element that determines the individual's evolution and relationship with himself, the world, knowledge and education; it is the affective dimension that is present in the psyche in both an essentialist and a determinant sense. The three agencies of the psychic apparatus operate through relationships of tension and mutual regulation that relate, either directly or indirectly, to the affects. The 'id' or unconscious contains the drives and responds primarily to the pleasure principle. The stages of the individual's evolution follow the evolution of her or his sexuality, which is defined by Freud in very broad terms as anything to do with pleasure. The stages of infantile sexuality, and then the evolution towards adolescence and adulthood, play a crucial role in enabling the individual to become autonomous. What is at stake here is not the ability to acquire schemata, but the ability to handle repression, and the relationship with desire, morality and society that will determine the individual's psychic equilibrium, freedom and relationship with knowledge, others and the world. Jung's contribution introduces the historical depth of the unconscious (the collective unconscious), which transcends individual history and relates to more complex symbolisms. The structuralist perspective introduced by Lacan integrates development with the processes of identification ('I' and 'me', 'I, me' and 'the other') inaugurated by the 'mirror phase'. Neither of these contributions denies the centrality of the relationship with the drives and affects that determine the shaping of the individual (on the contrary), irrespective of whether or not they are accepted by the adult (Lacan) or by society and its moral imperatives (as described by Freud and all post-Freudian schools of psychoanalysis).

Some schools of psychology, in contrast, put forward analyses that go beyond the realm of the observable. Some concentrate upon the evolution of the cognitive relationship, and others on states of the unconscious and stages of sexuality, but all involve projections that do not rely upon strict scientific observation alone. That is the opinion of behaviourists such as the American psychologist John Watson who contend that only observable behaviour should be taken into consideration: the study of human psychology and modes of learning should avoid all introspective extrapolations and restrict itself to the subject's experiential relationship with the environment. The environment sends out stimuli, and the individual responds by behaving in specific ways. Psychologists should focus primarily and essentially on the observable twofold relationship between stimulus and subject, and then between subject and response, and then deduce from their observations the typology of possible relationships that can be established between stimulus and response. From this process, they can arrive at the nature of the determining factors. There is, they argue, nothing that is specifically human about these relationships: Tavris and Wade argue in their *Psychology in Perspective* that the basic principles of learning are the same 'for all species' from worms to human beings. The notion of 'operative conditioning' is then introduced to supplement the classic 'conditioned response' observed by Pavlov in the immediate relationship between the stimulus and the behavioural response. This makes the relationship more complex by introducing the way the environment mediates various forms of what Thorndike and Skinner call 'reinforcement' or 'punishment'. That is how morality, 'superstitions' and social norms operate; they then determine behaviour and modes of learning. Education therefore consists in studying the nature of the relationship between stimuli and reflex or conditioned responses (in either the 'operative' or 'response' mode) in order to understand how they operate at various stages of intellectual and emotional maturation. As we can see here, the individual or subject is of secondary importance in the analysis of the learning process; this is the antithesis of the theories of Piaget and Freud, which are already quite different from one another.

It is obvious that these theoretical and scientific disagreements between the three schools we have discussed (which prioritize, respectively, the cognitive agent, the affective agent and the agent of the genetic or physical reaction) derive from very different conceptions of the human being. In every case, the focus adopted in the approach to the experimental and observational sciences on the one hand and methods of analysis on the other reveals a distinct philosophy of being and of education, each with its own postulates and objectives. Ultimately, what is at stake is at once a conception of man, a theory of learning and a philosophy of the sciences. When it comes to studying modes of learning and ways of educating individuals, epistemology comes close (in the sense of 'inductive proximity') to being a metaphysics. It is interesting to note that African and Asian traditions, Hindu and Buddhist spiritualities, like religions and the various general (or educational) philosophies, have often outlined a very different approach for their members or followers: metaphysics, cosmology and the meaning of the created world already determine a conception of man, though the existence, essence and finalities of human beings have yet to be defined. Here then, whatever forms of learning are involved, education must make it possible – in the best way possible – to achieve the objectives that promote the good and welfare of human beings. This approach is by definition holistic, and cannot be content with either the strictly cognitive theories or purely affective or behavioural analyses. All those dimensions should be considered together and educated concurrently.

Further reflection indicates that, although there are contradictions between these theories and although their views as to the source and modalities differ, they do have something in common. There are areas where they overlap, and they have similar aspirations. We should therefore invert our perspective and approach the issue in terms of ends rather than fundamentals. Rather than arguing (or quarrelling) about different conceptions of men, we should, that is, be asking what these different traditions or schools of thought have to offer and how they can help human beings to develop their full potential. We have by no means reached a consensus, but the differences are minor and the goals are the same. There is something universal about all these traditions, no matter which dimension they emphasize. They all express the hope that education will produce individuals who are confident, autonomous, dignified, curious, critical, constructive, creative and caring. Such individuals may well be audacious, but they remain basically optimistic despite all life's difficulties and sufferings.

Every age faces its own challenges and, as we have said again and again, the age of globalization is one of upheaval. It is difficult to be confident, autonomous and critically aware in a world where our old points of reference have disappeared, where fear and unease appear to be the dominant emotions, and where the constant hype of instant communications and advertising leaves too little room for deep, subtle and critical debates. We have already said that it is important for our age to reconcile itself to the need to teach individuals about spiritualities, religions, philosophies and art. They all represent 'distancing' skills that, because they objectify the object of study and its complexity, restore the subject's autonomy, outlook and complexity. Education means acquiring knowledge and skills, but it also means learning to keep our spiritual, intellectual and aesthetic distance (from ourselves, the objects and judgements).

EDUCATION AND TEACHING

Bringing up children has always been a difficult challenge. How can we love and protect our children, and pass something on to them, and at the same time grant them their freedom, help them to develop a critical mind and sometimes accept that they will reject our received values and even what we pass on to them? How can we help them to become self-confident, dignified and curious? How can we instil into them both courage and a sense of solidarity? These questions have always been there, but in a global age in which traditions no longer provide reassuring points of reference and religious teachings play a dwindling role in structuring relationships between individuals and between the generations, it seems hard to rely upon a definite frame of reference and to refer to collectively accepted norms. We know and sense that our children need communications, limits, references and a sense of direction, but we no longer know just how to set about listening to them, offering them guidance or exerting an authority that gives advice without being oppressive.

The task is even more difficult for families with a spiritual or religious heritage and concerns. How can we transmit meaning, a relationship with one's being, a relationship with God, a morality and an ethics, and a taste for introspection when the culture of entertainment and mass communications seems to be sweeping everything away? Hindu, Buddhist, Jewish, Christian and Muslim parents all share the same haunting concerns with the depositaries of age-old African and Asian traditions: how can we transmit to and how can we educate the children? How can we live out the meaning we have chosen without imposing it upon children who have chosen nothing, and how can we love them without smothering them? The challenge is tremendous, and no model seems to be readily available. Time is short, the danger is growing, and we no longer know just how to handle our authority as parents in contemporary societies.

The pendulum seems to swing from one extreme to the other, and all parents feel their way and experiment, usually with the best of intentions. Some want to listen to their children, understand their needs, meet their expectations and believe that it is important to negotiate with them as to how to meet their requirements, as to how to exercise their authority, and to what purpose. In our day, spaces and demands for freedom have to be managed. That is the argument behind Simon Soloveychik's famous book *Parenting for Everyone* (1977), which insists on the need for a 'negotiation pedagogy' if we wish to train 'free people'. The interesting and paradoxical thing about his approach is his preliminary postulate: the essence of pedagogy is not psychology but ethics. He is attempting to get away from the many psychology-based schools of thought that have become lost in the maze of interiority. We should indeed listen to our children, support them and negotiate with them, but Soloveychich also argues that establishing goals and limits is also essential: a pedagogical ethics. Traditional milieus, in contrast, wish to resist and to be stricter about maintaining a conventional sense of respect and authority.

Frames of reference are established, norms are known, and children should understand both the rules and the expectations of their parents and teachers. One should *Dare to Discipline*, to use the title of a book by the American evangelist James Dobson, who associates the breakdown of marriages with a loss of moral sense and of respect for rules and parental authority. In Southern societies and cultures, as in immigrant families in the West and in families with a spiritual and religious heritage, authority looks like a weapon that can provide protection against the excesses of an age that is increasingly seen as having lost its values and principles. Rules are often imposed, and 'respect' is what is expected of children: there is little room for freedom and critical thinking. One of the references used by Muslim communities in the West is *Meeting the Challenge of Parenting in the West* by Ekram and Muhammad Beshir. The authors argue for the need to resist the authoritarian trend and outline a more balanced approach that encourages dialogue and discussion. Others react against this view and argue, often in the name of an exclusive love, that children should be protected from themselves by an authority relationship that in effect denies them any autonomy. Once again, a balance has to be struck between respect and critical awareness: genuine respect should be critical, and criticism should remain respectful.

Education is a matter of establishing both a distance and a balance. As we have seen, teachers and psychologists may well argue over priorities, methods and sometimes objectives, but they are all agreed that parenting is very difficult. It is all the more difficult in that our life rhythms, and the choices made by governments, public services and the social organization as a whole do not prioritize 'education'. Educating children does not make money and is not an immediately profitable investment. And when the logic of economics does take charge of family affairs, the outcome is often disastrous. In the West, lifestyles change very quickly, time is short and finding institutional support for families is a problem. As a result, people are having fewer and fewer children. The demographic statistics for the richer and more industrialized countries tell us a great deal about how people's relationships with themselves, children and education are changing in a world where day-to-day life seems increasingly merciless.

According to the traditional distribution of roles, parents transmit meaning, values and good behaviour, whilst schools and teachers transmit learning and skills (though in actuality, their respective functions are not, fortunately, quite so clear-cut). The same disaffection can be observed in the realm of teaching and parenting: schoolteachers and educationalists seem to have lost their former prestige. Teachers once possessed both knowledge and authority, and were the guardians of the norm. They are no longer acknowledged to have any specific status or real moral authority. People joke that they are 'over-paid' and enjoy 'long holidays'. Their value no longer lies in the noble function of transmitting knowledge, but in economic parameters (or league tables such as in the UK) calculated in terms of labour power and the jobs market. The complaint that teachers are very often over-paid is still heard, but the whole educational system is now being re-evaluated in terms of economic competitiveness. Schools are no longer seen as the exclusive preserve of public service or as a state-funded *investment* priority. Private investors, multinationals, big companies and financial groups are invited to make up for the state's shortcomings. The issue is not simply that of the (dangerous) privatization of education. The very function of a public sector that was once responsible for providing universal education and, more important, protecting equality of opportunity is coming under challenge. The decision to prioritize economic logic can have only one outcome: the aim will always be to encourage competition, to fund the elite and to identify the 'best' students . . . or in other words those who do best in the job market. Such is the spirit behind the conclusions of the Lisbon Special European Council of March 2000. The phrasing is quite explicit: the aim was to promote, by 2010, 'the most competitive and dynamic knowledge-based economy in the world capable of sustainable economic growth and with more and better jobs and greater social cohesion'. The economic logic and terminology are quite obvious. Campaigns to resist this trend have been launched in the United States, Europe and Africa. Sharp debates and protest campaigns brought together teachers, parents and educationalists in New York when it was proposed to put some state schools under the control of the public management firm Edison (the American system is already highly privatized). French teachers went on strike in 2003 for similar reasons, and rejected a decentralization that would have paved the way for the growing privatization of schools and education. In Nigeria, there were mass political, trade union and popular protests when the government tried to privatize the country's 'Unity Schools'. The privatization plan was dropped in 2007. Similar protests greeted the World Bank's proposals everywhere from South America to Africa and Asia. Education has become a commercial venture, even in those disadvantaged societies where the best elements will benefit from the 'positive discrimination' that allows the North to select the South's best minds or those it needs most in various fields. The South will continue to produce minds at a loss. The South used to be exploited and despoiled of its raw materials; the ageing societies of the North now need its grey matter. Teachers' loss of status and state disinvestment policies with respect to education both reveal the depth of the crisis affecting educational systems all over the world, East and West, North and South. We have to choose: *Schools or Markets?* to use the apt title of the collective volume edited by Deron R. Boyles (2004) on the effects of privatization in the United States.

And yet we are all aware of the importance of both education and teaching. Family breakdown, violence on the streets and in schools, the lack of norms and the flouting or rejection of authority are all phenomena that transform teachers into improvised educators who sometimes take the place of parents. Each group makes the other take responsibility for its own shortcomings. Parents are no longer doing their job! Teachers are lazy! In the meantime, politicians make grand speeches, and there is a plethora of 'structural' educational reforms. Our societies, on the other hand, are caught in a deadlock and cannot escape the vicious circle: teachers have a poor image, parents feel guilty, there is a lack of state investment in schools, vast numbers of young people seem to be drifting away, and the social divide is widening. Everything that is said is increasingly contradictory. Everyone wants 'egalitarian' state schools for all, but there are already two or three tiers within the state system. Despite the devoted efforts of so many teachers, some schools are second-class institutions, and their pupils already know that the future holds little for them. It is not surprising that secular, faith-based and private community schools are being established in an attempt to compensate for inequalities: we cannot both introduce the market logic of competition into the state system and reject, or denounce, the privatization of education on philosophical, religious or cultural grounds. States no longer offer their citizens much of a choice.

Our relationship with parenting and education reveals the deep contradictions that lie at the heart of the global economy and culture. We speak of protecting families and democratizing schools, but the logics of productivity and competition in fact force us to adopt family and social policies that have precisely the opposite effect. We tend to disparage stay-at-home fathers or mothers who devote their time to educating their children and teachers who do transmit knowledge. Children from richer and better-protected families have little difficulty in acquiring the self-confidence, autonomy, critical minds and curiosity they need if they are to make progress and find fulfilment. They may well have little sense of solidarity, but that has never been a prerequisite for climbing the ladder to social success. Children from more modest families find that their status poses problems both at school and in society. Injustice is piled upon injustice.

Contemporary societies cannot hope to solve the problems of our age unless they face up to the crises that are inherent within them. A necessary and complementary approach to education and training means first of all that we must take the role of families seriously and begin to value the status of teachers. The obsession with reforming educational methods and structures must be resisted as a matter of urgency: modern times challenge us to redefine the content of what is taught in our schools and the priorities of what children learn within the family. Teaching, which is both a public domain and a product of public service, must be discussed in terms of those objectives, and in the light of social justice and equality of opportunity. Everyone has the right to be self-confident and autonomous, to think critically and to be creative. That is what allows an individual to become a free citizen: an autonomous conscience as his parents want, a responsible being as society wishes. The choice could not be more political. Surrendering to the logic of economics (and of the advantages offered by the big multinationals) will not produce the desired results. Education 'under pressure'and 'efficient' teaching will 'produce' money-making machines, and not human beings with a propensity to share.

MODELS

The doubts and crises we are experiencing with regard to education-and teaching-related issues mean that we have to look for new solutions. Some experts, such as psychologists, educationalists and theorists, concentrate on techniques, structures and methodologies. They study the nature of the difficulties and suggest new directions. Observing the gaps between parents and children, parents and school, teachers and students, and schools and the social environment, they outline methods of communication and relational strategies that should make it possible to 'connect' spaces, parties and institutions facing similar difficulties. Numerous books, studies and reports have been published in both the North and the South in an attempt to face up to the crises of authority (both within the family and at school), communication and transmission. They attempt to outline a new approach to a system that is being forced upon us by the imperatives of globalization, the attractions of a hypertrophied individualism, the pressure to produce results and the dominance of mass communications that provide no opportunity for any real dialogue. Institutions are being created to support and counsel struggling parents, psychologists are sent to listen, advise, support and, ultimately, 'communicate'. Teaching methods are being revised, curricula are being reformed and selection procedures are being reorganized in an attempt to get better results, or least limit the damage that has been done. A deep and widespread feeling of unease has set in. Precisely the same situation can be observed in the countries of the South, at the heart of the more traditional societies of Hinduism, Buddhism and the three monotheisms. They may not have the resources that are needed to rethink the whole system or to reform the family and the educational system, but they often hide behind a veneer of 'preserved' traditions or the ideals of their spiritual and religious teachings, which they repeatedly evoke to avoid the need to contemplate the deep crisis affecting both the family and the educational system. It is the same from South America to Asia: the ideals of 'the family', 'education', 'knowledge' and 'equality' are celebrated in the abstract, but the reality is much more bleak: families are breaking up, heritages are being lost, and memories are fading away. Knowledge (which should, it is to be hoped, include meaning, ideas and critical thinking) is increasingly reduced to know-how, and equality through education and schooling is no more than wishful thinking.

Our relationship with memory and history is one index of the depth and scale of the crisis in education. This will be the subject of the next chapter, and we will simply note here that globalization seems to produce one constant: we are living in a new world culture, and it is a culture of speed and the instantaneous. Our world's younger generations are cruelly lacking in historical knowledge and have a very uncertain relationship with 'memory'. No matter whether we refer to memories of past events, of repetitions and cycles, or to traditions and roots, our relationship with the heritage and teachings of the past has undergone a revolution. We are being swept away by the 'novelty' of the present and engulfed by the 'progress of the future'. Our families and schools, which have a responsibility to pass on the heritage of the past, are, of course, the first victims. The crisis affecting them has to do with the fact that our memories lack any sense of history.

In our search for solutions, we often go back to the basics that have been common to all spiritualities for so long. If we turn to the old African and Asian traditions, we can always find Creation 'stories' and other narratives that often use symbolic human figures to personify the meanings of the rites and teachings they describe. The gods of Olympus and ancient Rome served the same function and acted as archetypes with which both men and women could identify. The Hindu, Taoist and Buddhist traditions abound in gods and spiritual guides who, like Siddhârta, act as mirrors and reflect or serve as living examples of what we are and give us a sense of what we could or should be. Judaism, Christianity and Islam use and extend the same educational model: their prophets and saints are role-models who, through their lives, experiences and example, teach the principles of life and good behaviour, and the meanings of personal and social success. The 'model' function is a central part of all spiritual and religious traditions: it allows us to identify, and instils values through experience. The model and the values it conveys also indicate that we really can achieve our goals, and give the fundamentally positive message: 'It is possible.' The gratitude and praise shown to the prophet, saint or guide by his fellows, community and society adds an essential dimension to his exemplary function: even though he must suffer rejection, criticism or exile, his being, values and experience grant him a special status amongst his fellows. The possibility of identification, the actual experience of values, the realistic humanization of goals and social recognition are key aspects of the model's function.

Both modern and more traditional societies are now returning to the idea of *the model* regarding relations between adults or teachers and children. Children should, it is argued, be provided with role-models in the form of men and women with whom they can identify, who can teach them values in a practical way, and who can convince them that success is within their reach and that, in the long run, they can earn the esteem and respect of their families and society. In Africa, Asia and the West, role-models are now being used in problem areas, schools and neighbourhoods, as well as in the media, sports and popular culture, in an attempt to influence young people in a positive sense, and to show that they can succeed and that there is hope for the future. The use that is made of role-models is interesting and often positive, but it can be dangerous unless certain basic issues are addressed. Identification on the basis of colour, culture or social status has become more important than identification with our common humanity and with the quest for meaning and values. There is nothing trivial about this change of emphasis: 'success' stories are publicized, but the nature and substance of 'success' is rarely questioned. What kind of success is involved, and what system of recognition and what values are being promoted? Are we talking about upward social mobility or well-being? About the ability to make money or solidarity? Wealth or human dignity? Are we promoting a functional system that is adapted to the structure and logic of the economic system, or a human model that can challenge and fight the power of that logic? The voices of the philosophers, thinkers, mystics, moralists and educationalists who speak to us across the ages have always been critical of educational systems and of the content of education and teaching. From Confucius and Socrates, through Rousseau, Kant, Nietzsche, Pestalozzi, down to Maria Montessori, all the 'new education' theorists and many others throughout history and in all societies all say the same thing. Their criticisms of parenting and of educational systems, which have always resulted in reforms, have often been associated with social and political criticisms. If we look at them in historical terms, we find that, no matter how far back we go, they have always defended a certain conception of man and outlined ideals worth striving for. The humanist Montaigne makes it quite explicit in his *Essays* that he sees a link between his conception of man and his ideas about education. In his *Some Thoughts Concerning Education* John Locke concentrates on the aristocratic elite and argues that man is not just a mind, but also a body that must be properly trained and educated. *Emile; or, On Education* tells us about Rousseau's views on man and wisdom. The same is true of the sharp and incisive criticisms made by Nietzsche in his lectures on *The Future of Our Educational Institutions*. One senses the impact of his philosophy when he argues that the surest way to corrupt minds is to have educational institutions that teach us 'to value those who think in the same way more highly than those who think differently'.

In an age of globalization and mass communications, we need to think seriously about the role of the family in both traditional, modern and postmodern societies. We should opt for priorities and systems that relate the philosophical, spiritual or religious conceptions of humanity. We must know what we are transmitting, how we are transmitting it and why we are transmitting it.

SYSTEMS AND FINALITIES

What kind of people do we want to be? What kind of children do we want to educate and train? We are trapped into our systems. Time is short, and we have to perform. Selection begins at a very early age, and parents no longer have any real choice. Some opt for home-schooling, but they do so with the knowledge that one day they will have to face society, its order, its requirements and its system. The alternatives are very difficult. It seems to be a long time since both parental roles and the classical education that was officially provided by schools were determined by a certain human ideal, a spiritual path, a philosophical conception or a religious hope. Education used to be something of a rite, and there was something 'sacred' about followings its stages, which were initiatory rather than critical. Greek and Eastern traditions are very similar, contrary to what has often been suggested: the quest for truth, asceticism, renunciation and meditation require teaching techniques that have been established with reference to the philosophical and spiritual objectives that are being pursued.

That stage is conspicuously absent today, given the frenzy for structural reforms in every area of education. At the primary-school level, we argue about age groups, repeating years, the need for grading, the curriculum and the role of teachers, but discussions of the underlying philosophy of educating children have been marginalized. They are regarded as no more than pointless philosophical discussions; the important things are, we are told, efficiency and 'performance'. Children are given more and more information, and the new technologies are influencing both their minds and their behaviour. The means of communications constantly reveal the diversity of cultures and societies, but it is also visible in the reality of the classroom, where children of different colours and from different backgrounds mingle. We need a philosophy of education that can meet contemporary challenges at the local level, in our relationship with the environment and with the world. Now that we live in an age of globalization, education requires a new philosophical debate involving as many sensibilities and schools of thought as possible. Philosophers seem to have lost interest, whilst theologians hide behind the ideals of religion and educationalists focus exclusively on techniques. And yet a school system that does not discuss its conception of man collectively is a system that has no ideals and no soul. By definition, it will turn out 'standardized' individuals and citizens who adapt to society but who have not been taught to reform and transform anything. They may well enjoy their freedom and be able to think critically, but they will use their abilities only to promote their individual well-being and/or personal success. Kant's maxim has some truth here: even at the very earliest stages of education, when ends are transformed into means, alienation is complete. A system that worships performance, selection and competitiveness has nothing to fear from the critical mind of the individualist: its pupils have already been shaped into its mould.

Some protagonists in the world of economics, mainly at the UN, have reconsidered the nature of the Assessment Indices that are used, but their work has been somewhat marginalized. They have suggested replacing GNP (Gross National Product) and GDP (Gross Domestic Product) with the Human Development Index (HDI), which takes into account well-being, standards of living and sometimes our relationship with the environment. Similar reforms are essential in education, where the notion of and criteria for 'success at school' have to be redefined and reassessed. If freedom, autonomy and responsibility are to mean anything, and if they really are the ideals we value, we must provide children with the means to achieve those ideals. They must have a capacity for criticism, especially where information is concerned, a civic sense and a sense of critical loyalty. We live in pluralistic societies and in a global world that is alive with diversity, and it is essential to stimulate children's curiosity and creativity. The cult of consumerism means that an understanding of taste, ethics and sports (real sports) is also important. Socrates stressed the importance of a healthy body, as did Montaigne and Locke. Many modern educational theorists, from Pestalozzi to Montessori, associate teaching and training minds with the realms of psychology (affectivity and well-being) and the body (physical balance, relations with physical space and hygiene).

The ideal of the 'man of breeding' that sustained the critique of religion during the Renaissance is still of interest. It involved the acquisition of knowledge but also liberation from any imposed ideals. We now seem to have gone to the opposite extreme: we impose knowledge, but have no ideals. We have to strike a balance, but that is difficult because the logic of performance is overwhelming, and the competition never ends. There is no way back. There is no room or time for philosophy, or for rational, spiritual and religious discussions about the meaning and purpose of education. And yet we can all see that we have to take the time to have these basic discussions. We will get nowhere without them. Today's 'man of breeding' must be lucid and must, as he acquires knowledge, be able to determine his goals and priorities. He has to be a protester and must criticize an educational system in the name of a human ideal and an applied ethics that can resist economic, financial and even cultural logics that dehumanize. The Spanish liberation theologian Castillo once said that 'dehumanity' is a dimension of man, and that dimension cannot be overlooked. Knowledge cannot be divided up into sectors, and we require a holistic approach that can integrate a conception of man, ethics and ends on the one hand, and philosophies, religions and the arts on the other. That is the approach that should govern and direct our thinking about both education and teaching. We have to break out of the infernal logic we are trapped into. 'Let us free ourselves!', as Siddhârta would say in the East, as Aristotle would say in the West, and as al-Ghazâli would say somewhere in between the two. Perhaps we need the educational equivalent of 'liberation theology' – an education of liberation – and perhaps we can have it if we think in terms of ends. We need to challenge the substance and purpose of skills, the relationship between school and society, between the universities and civic life, and between knowledge and solidarity. This is not a utopia. It is a necessity.

I I

Tradition and Modernity

Time exists, and time passes. Our lives are passing. Our lives are passing more quickly than the human community to which we belong. From time immemorial, the human intellect has been challenged, and basically shaped, by an awareness of both my personal time, which was born together with me and which will carry me off, and the collective time of the human community to which I belong, which came before me, which runs through me and which will outlive me. Who am I in time? Who am I in relation to my forefathers? Who am I in relation to my children? Am I the temporary guardian of a memory and values that might justify my presence here on earth, or am I rather the expression of a historical singularity that I accept because no one but me will ever be me?

We have reached the parting of the ways. Let us go back to the heart of the twentieth century that has just left us midway between the African storyteller Amadou Hampâté Bâ and the French poet André Breton. When the time came for him to write his memoirs, Amadou Hampâté Bâ brought together his scattered writings, reconstructed the story of his origins and integrated the 'Fulani child' he once was into a cycle of successive generations, of families with countless relationships, transversal oral traditions, values and norms that were both spoken and unspoken, received, repeated and transmitted from age to age and from person to person. *Amkoullel, l'enfant peul*, which is the title of the first volume of this 'Fulani child's' autobiography, comes from that world. His consciousness and memory are full of those human relations, of the never-ending cycles that are reflected in the landscapes of Africa. Those landscapes transmit that sense of the infinite, of power and vulnerability, and of the return of the same, which is of the essence, and of the vanishing of singularity, which is a matter of contingency. Poetic, realist and surrealist, André Breton's novel *Nadja* is the complete antithesis of the Fulani child. The two universes could not be more different, and nor could the writers or their characters, who are, in both cases, direct or indirect incarnations of their authors. The poet asks himself about the 'significant events' in his life, about his subjectivity and his obsessions, and about the 'me' (*moi*) that exists inside the 'I' (*je*). He seems to have no past, to live completely in the present and to be looking for a future he can decide, shape and create. His memories are of random events, of the unpredictable and of chance encounters. He quite naturally asks himself what it is that justifies his presence on earth and concludes that it is his singularity and difference: the 'I' that no one else has ever inhabited, that no one else will ever inhabit, and that will never inhabit any consciousness but his. His heroine Nadja comes from nowhere. She is the incarnation of the subject that exists in the fleeting moment, in the evanescent. She has no memories and is attached to no norms: she is 'the heart of a flower that has no heart', and she is free. She leads the poet into an uncertain future that comes close to madness and knows only creative but fleeting intuitions that know no past and no tradition. The scale of the cycles of time and of millenary affiliations says something about time and maturation, and about the old and the wise who bear and convey a memory and meaning. When an old man dies, said Hampâté Bâ, 'a library burns'. The carefree youth Nadja could not be more different. She draws the poet not into an awareness of an extensible time, but into the dense energy of a fleeting moment. André Breton wanted the hereafter to exist here in this life, in the eternal instant of the 'I' that exists . . . Amadou Hampâté Bâ watches himself in the cycles of the infinite and thinks of himself as an instant within an eternity in which everything returns, but the hereafter is far away, way beyond that.

Tradition and modernity. This is, of course, a matter of our relationship with time, and of our relationship to ourselves in history. And at a much deeper level, it is a matter of power and authority. The old traditions, and especially those inscribed within the oral tradition, stress the importance of the past and the meaning of the cycles that bind us to that past and give a meaning to the present. Nature, the seasons, life and death and agriculture teach us about the perpetual return of things and about repetition. We have to meditate on them and give them a meaning. Orality is to tradition what cycles are to time: we must speak, transmit, repeat and inscribe in our memories the history of our origins, our sources, our line of descent and the path that leads us to ourselves. Traditions speak of meaning and iden-tity: we know where we come from. Memory transmits a meaning to us and inscribes us in a history that both repeats itself and moves on because it always includes the younger generations. A tradition is, by definition, never static or closed. Traditions constantly evolve, in par-ticular through transition to the next generation, which becomes part of them and that will in its turn pass them on. Along with memory and a concept of 'meaningful time', a tradition transmits values, norms, a culture and a way of life. Whether we like it or not, our indi-vidual consciousness accepts (or rejects) them, and those values and norms have a natural authority: they are what bind the tradition together, give it substance, organize its internal system and determine its priorities and hierarchy. Human beings therefore discover that change is based upon a collective memory rather than individual rea-son when it comes to determining meaning and values: maintaining a tradition implies an act of trust on the part of the faithful.

Whilst traditions are never static, modernity is not without a sense of its origins, references and traditions. It is always conceived and conceptualized in terms of a particular history and memory: in the West, modernity is bound up with a process that began before the Renaissance and climaxed in the age of the Enlightenment. The Euro-pean cultural tradition and the power of the Church had the effect of producing the stages of the modern 'resistance', and art and love were its first vectors. Italian painting, drama and sculpture were expres-sions of transgression and dissidence (sometimes mediated by Ancient Greece and Rome); the courtly love of which the troubadours and trouvères sang was also a literature of resistance that contested the norms and values of Christianity, its conception of the body and pleasure, and, of course, of paradise, where carnality became spirit-ualized. In certain medieval love songs, the hereafter, with its pure springs and emancipated bodies, is already of this world. It is already 'here on earth' and anticipates Breton's 'surrealist' wish. Reason then joined the senses' resistance, and demanded its share of autonomy and freedom both in the quest for truth and in the organization of society and the political realm. Modernity, or what we understand by modernity in the West, derives from that history and that tradition, and bears the mark of both its resistance and its emancipation. When philosophers, writers, sociologists and researchers from Byron to Chateaubriand, Weber, Rawls, Habermas, Touraine, Gauchet or Wolton speak, either directly or indirectly, of modernity, they find that the universe of the Christian (and sometimes Jewish) tradition is omnipresent, and that it has been read through the prisms of both the heritage of antiquity and post-Enlightenment developments. Modernity is in effect an affirmation of reason, of the autonomy of the individual, and of the demand for progress, the sciences, secularization (which is what made the process possible) and democracy, which is its legitimate Western daughter. The political power of religion recedes, and religious tradition loosens its hold over minds and memories in terms of points of reference and heritage. The world becomes 'disenchanted' and becomes an object of study for a newly liberated analytic and scientific reason. Time becomes linear, and the mind projects itself into an indeterminate future that is always new, always open and always there to be conquered.

This modernity is not the modernity of all civilizations and all cultures. It is the modernity of the West, and it is very much in the minority if we look at all the world's memories. It has become the terminological norm thanks to developments and advances in industry and the sciences, and of course the economic and political hegemony of European societies (and now that of the United States). Modernity was therefore the product of resistance to a tradition that had failed to allow its members to fulfil their human potential because it was beholden to a religious hierarchy and moral norms that finally smothered them. Modernity is, in historical terms, the other name for that process of liberation. Elsewhere in the world, other civilizations, such as African and Asian cultures and traditions, did not experience the same intense conflict, and power relations are never so pronounced, mainly because the religious hierarchy and the upholders of tradition never had such exclusive or absolute power. In historical terms, Native Americans, South Americans, Africans and Asians had to face the consequences of the emancipation of the West and the revolution that took place there: colonization, the mastery of technology, economic power and political domination overturned their ancestral traditions and undermined their certainties. Some thought that the West's dominance was proof that its civilization was superior and wanted to imitate it. Others saw it as nothing more than an expression of its arrogance and dehumanization and were determined to resist it, whilst still others tried to be more selective and to strike a balance between the benefits that might be derived from a painful historical experience, and their potential harmful effects. Quite apart from the complexity of relations between the West and other civilizations, the products of Western modernity were to entail serious consequences, whether to positive or negative effect, for every society in the world. All traditions and religions had to ask themselves new questions about the status of reason, the individual, progress and how to deal with pluralism. These questions were in themselves both basic and positive: it was often the way in which they were asked and imposed that created the problem. And to put it in negative terms, the problem was the imposed postulate that there was only one legitimate answer and that it was provided by the dominant civilization.

The West's scientific understanding of the elements forced the African, Amerindian and Asiatic traditions to reconsider the role of 'spirits'. Hinduism, Taoism, Buddhism and many other ancestral traditions in the South had to reconcile their conception of cyclical time with the proven efficiency of the postulate that time is linear. The freedom of reason, the primacy of the individual and equality challenged ancient orders, from Hinduism's castes to the traditional powers of communities, of memory and of its depositaries. A lot of certainties were undermined, a lot of habits were disrupted, and a lot of orders were thrown into disorder! Did the accession to the conditions of an exogenous modernity mean casting aside the roots of tradition and millenary endogenous points of reference? With the exception of a few minority voices within them, most civilizations and cultures have always chosen to remain true to their past, whilst agreeing to compromise, should the need to do so arise, without losing a sense of their own identity. In some case, the balance of power meant that cultures could not survive, and in others the compromise resulted in adulteration and alienation, but resistance sometimes allowed endangered civilizations to renew themselves from within. Ibn Khaldûn, who was the precursor of sociology, made an interesting study of these relationships and these cycles of emergence, paroxysm, resistance, tension and decline. Our recent history often proves him right. The civilizations of South America, Africa and Asia, like Hinduism, Confucianism, Buddhism, Islam and so many other spiritualities and cultures, are in a state of crisis and are asking themselves questions about the meaning of their traditions: how can they preserve their memories, values and norms, and their feeling of belonging to a world of pre-given points of reference?

Modernity and its at times excessive effects have their critics inside Western civilization itself. There have, of course, been political criticisms of the attitude of the colonizers and the use they made of their power. Like Montaigne, the early humanists intuitively sensed that the way they judged and treated 'savages' and 'cannibals' implied the possibility of abuse. Those criticisms were to grow louder, and they went hand in hand with comments on some basic philosophical, political and economic issues. Nietzsche saw the so-called democratization of the intellect and rights as a dangerous inversion of the old order and, like Schopenhauer, opted for a return to the cyclical conception of time and the idea of selection (through the agency of the Eternal Return). The linear nature of time not only implied, in his view, a reference to Christianity associated with morality; it also established a dangerous link between rationality and the illusion of progress. Schopenhauer defended an oriental conception of temporal cycles, whilst Nietzsche turned to art, where the idea of a cycle had the twofold advantage of allowing him to use form to avoid the question of meaning. The 'last metaphysician', as Heidegger called him, was a true critic of modernity, even though, or perhaps because, he was its most perfect exemplar. Heidegger was also critical of modernity, as was Bergson, who rejected the reductionism of rationality, albeit for very different reasons. Other thinkers and intellectuals, such as the political theorist Hannah Arendt, saw Stalin's purges, the extermination of the Jews and the enslavement of whole peoples as the logical outcome of modernity's premises. Others were to adopt the same position, and many ecologists, such as René Dumont, associate the destruction of the planet with the economic order and behaviours promoted by the 'ideology of modernity'.

The critical theory of the 'Frankfurt School' is of interest in that it attempts to discuss both the founding assumptions of modernity and its implications. Its studies of the 'mass culture' produced by the combination of rationalization, individualism and scientific and technological progress reach the conclusion that what was originally a process of liberation has turned on itself and produced a new alienation. Without roots, without memory, without belonging to a group, man is left prey to economic logic that offers for consumption the plural illusion of standardization. Herbert Marcuse's *One-Dimensional Man* makes a critique of this illusion of freedom and diversity by revealing the underlying trend towards the standardization of terminologies, behaviours and consumerism. The power to influence minds has changed its form, but it is as effective as ever: we have to begin by deconstructing power relations (this was the thesis of Foucault and Bourdieu). Modernity, it would seem, does no more to set us free than tradition, whilst mass culture traps individuals into a relationship of stimulus and response that is anything but rational. The culture of mass consumerism is killing cultures and their diversity: the former caters to the instincts while the latter cultivate taste. Both the excesses of modernity and the prisons of tradition are bringing about a crisis in the quest for a balance.

MEMORIES

There can be no humanity without memory. In times of doubt, crisis or conflict, memory is a refuge, a remedy, even a hope. The same is true at both the individual and the collective levels, and this phenomenon is a constant in both the most traditional and the most modern societies. Rousseau sensed this intuitively, and psychoanalysis proves him right: our identity is the product of a memory that is full of joys, sorrows, encounters, wounds and the aftermath of life's ups and downs. The marginalized philosopher experienced a crisis and wanted to understand, to understand himself and to be understood, which is why he wrote his *Confessions*. The title refers to a well-known

Christian practice that is also found, in different forms, in all spiritual and religious traditions. The intellect pauses for a moment, turns its attention to itself and its recent or distant past and waits for the conscience to draw up a balance sheet of what it remembers in a bid to understand, change and grow. It tries to reveal the intentions and meaning of the past, to trace the path that led us to where we are now and the events that nurtured and shaped us. Memory reveals, often explains things and sometimes clarifies things. According to modern psychology and especially psychoanalysis, being cured requires an act of memory. It means going back to our parents, reliving things that we may never have done or understood, and identifying the repressions, the trauma and the blocks. The unconscious accumulates memories, and is a particularly active passive memory, and the Jungian school insists that it transcends the individual. Because of the way it reorganizes our relationship with ourselves and the primacy it gives to the individual, modernity is primarily interested in the 'memory that dwells within me'. The old traditions had a very different relationship with both time and communities and society: what was meaningful was 'the memory that carries me'. Memory is, however, basic and determinant for both because it shapes the identity of individuals. It does not, however, have the same relationship with the self, the world or meaning.

As we have already said more than once, globalization has paradoxical effects. As we shall see in the next chapter, the loss of points of reference and the greater cultural diversity of our societies encourage individuals to adopt individual, social and communitarian attitudes based upon identities and communal loyalties. The reference to memory is an essential part of this process, as it appears to be one of the things that legitimate our identity and singularity. There can be no identity without memory. Memory allows us to plunge into history, to give our presence a meaning, to justify our affiliations and, in times of crisis and confusion, to distinguish ourselves from others. The one thing that matters in an era of globalization is the ability to lay claim to a heritage, an origin and roots. This is a curious inversion: modernity seemed to have set us free from traditions that were forced upon us, from an authority that was never negotiated and from the lack of any recognition of the individual and his critical freedom. Yet, our fears, our lack of self-confidence and the fear of the other that is undermining our certainties now force us to turn to our memories to justify our differences and affiliations. Fearful memories recreate, or rather reinvent, their traditions.

And yet those traditions are no longer quite the same. The old traditions had an inspiration of their own, and an intrinsic power and energy that inscribed us in both an order and a project. They may well have restricted the exercise of reason, but they offered prospects for the future: their scientific or social legitimacy was open to criticism, and the moderns did criticize it, but it has to be acknowledged that they did have their uses, and that they did help to foster a cultural and social cohesion. The new traditions are reconstructions: their primary function is to establish lines of demarcation rather than any intrinsic cohesion. Traditions once shaped identities; identities now reconstruct traditions. Traditions are no longer a source of inspiration. They are frames of reference. They now define frontiers rather than the horizons that bound landscapes. Civilizations, culture, nations, regions, native-born citizens, immigrants, former slaves and colonial subjects and natives all demand origins, a history and a memory that justify the way they specify their differences and, should the need arise, resist the way the other's memory instrumentalizes history. Memory is a banner and a weapon in conflicts over representations and power that are meant to guarantee our survival. This economy of memories is very unhealthy, and the very opposite of what the rationalism that gave birth to modernity wanted: it is no longer a critical analysis, and it no longer integrates many different points of view into a historical study. Memories are produced to suit the purposes of those who need or instrumentalize them; memory has become a functional reconstruction, and an ideological product.

The sources of modernity lay in a desire to find a universal. Descartes' project was to use a rigorous method to arrive at a truth that applied to all men, and Kant hoped to give his maxims the same universal status. Philosophy had to break free from culture and religions in order to formulate a rationality that was common to all men. We have achieved a phenomenal emancipation and industry and the sciences have made revolutionary advances: the economy is now becoming planetary, communication is instantaneous, and culture is global.

As we reach the end of this process and approach the threshold of a postmodernity which may or may not actually exist (not all philosophers and sociologists are in agreement about this), modernity finds that its order has been inverted. Although it exists on a global scale, it produces singular memories and claims to particularity rather than shared universals. What began with reason seems to have been torn apart by the passions; our memories are emotive and do not identify with 'history'. And our shared history is certainly not the sum total of our memories.

HISTORY

As we have said, the minds – young and not so young – of our era need to study history. It would therefore be a good idea if they rediscovered and reconciled themselves to the early achievements of modernity and reconsidered their opinion of the nature and human function of 'tradition'. We need to get away from impassioned and fearful effusions and keep a reasonable distance between ourselves and the 'deconstruction', 'postmodernity' and 'post-structuralism' (which adds to our era's emotional feverishness by making the assumption that rationality and truth are quite relative), reformulate new simple principles and establish the conditions for an elementary objectivity. The humanism of the Renaissance used art and philosophy to launch intellectual resistance movements that demanded the autonomy of the individual, reason and the sciences. It had to put a critical distance between itself and the Catholic Church and the power it wielded at that time. Love, reason, autonomy and freedom were both means and ends in a struggle for emancipation that was waged in the name of the status of man, science and progress. The origins of the process go back a long way: when Dante (1265–1321) invites us to follow him in Virgil's footsteps on the initiatory journey of a *Commedia* that was later described as *divina*, he takes us to the gates of hell and heaven, where we meet representatives of an ancient and pagan philosophy who were neither recognized nor celebrated by the Christian tradition. At the gates of paradise, his beloved muse Beatrice becomes the guide who reveals the delights of success to the

Dante figure: the female motif takes us a long way from the Catholic references that are still central to the *Divine Comedy*. The love that was celebrated in the courtly tradition (which aptly termed it *fol'amor* or *fin d'amor*) from the twelfth century onwards is associated here – at the heart of a Christian-inspired epic – with a certain recognition of the value of the Greek and Roman heritage, and especially of philosophical reason. The same phenomenon is even clearer in the work of Petrarch (1304–74), who was undoubtedly one of the most important representatives of Italian humanism. When he met Laura, it was love at first sight, and the encounter was to determine both his life and his work. Petrarch was an erudite scholar best known for his poetry. His initial project could not have been more explicit. He wished to 'rediscover the very rich lessons of classical authors in all disciplines', and never stopped reading, studying and compiling – and having his friends and family compile – ancient Latin texts. He left Italy and settled in France, first in Avignon and then in Carpentras. In Avignon, he fell foul of the clerical hierarchy but, in poetic terms, living in the Vaucluse and the south of France gave him direct access to the work of the troubadours who sang the praises of courtly love. In intellectual and philosophical terms, the humanist Petrarch was the link with the Greek and Roman heritage he wanted to rediscover, rehabilitate and set free. Rather than opposing the Church, he sought possible reconciliation. When Laura died, his poetry broke free and sang out, borrowing from all the sources he found around him and especially from the literature of courtly love. In his *Canzoniere* ('Songs') and especially the allegorical *Trionfi* ('Triumphs'), Petrarch celebrates his physical and spiritual love for Laura, a woman who is at once physical, real, spiritual and ideal. The *Canzoniere* ended with a prayer to the Virgin Mary, but the *Trionfi* invoke Laura, the beloved woman who is carnal and highly sensual. This is a significant development that recalls the status of the 'Lady' in the literature of courtly love. The lover is the servant of a Lady who gradually takes the place of God.

We have here a double marriage that is highly significant. On the one hand, the 'pagan' heritage of Greece and Rome is reclaimed and associated with the faculty of reason, and, on the other, art and poetry are reconciled with a spiritualized celebration of earthly and physical love. The Graeco-Roman heritage, reason, art and love appear to be the wellsprings of humanism, the Renaissance and then of a modernity that owes a great deal to this history. If we analyse in greater depth the historical developments and the nature of the tensions involved, we find that this intellectual and cultural revolution is marked by an interplay between power and resistance. The humanists, and then the philosophers of the Enlightenment, had no qualms about using 'a tradition', namely the Graeco-Roman tradition, to free themselves from what they saw as the exclusive grip of a 'Christian (and primarily Catholic) tradition'. The process was endogenous and emerged from within Western culture itself, but still contrasted the two traditions and used one to free itself from the other. Courtly love and the celebration of carnal love, which came into conflict with the Christian frame of reference, came from a different tradition. That tradition was exogenous, but it produced the same upheaval. In his *Love in the Western World*,[1] Denis de Rougemont reveals the Arab and Muslim influence on courtly literature, and shows how Arab and Muslim artistic motifs were reappropriated by the oral traditions of the troubadours of southern France. Anyone who is familiar with medieval Arab literature can easily recognize its influence. Unlike Catholicism, the Arab tradition does not demonize the body and physical love, and has no qualms about celebrating love. Once again, the resort to a tradition that is both artistic and religious (the reference to the divine and to ethics is still present) allows an escape from the limitations of the dominant tradition. Once again, transgression is a form of liberation. Humanism, the Renaissance and modernity have a history: traditions that were in tension and sometimes in conflict and quite distinct are either reconciled or contrasted, contradictory memories in a quest for legitimacy, freedom and power.

If we recognize the objectivity of these intense and long-standing tensions (within the West's relationship with itself), we are in a position to understand how the same tensions set in and played a determinant role with respect to neighbouring civilizations and traditions. The same logic and the same relationship of tension, potential conflict and power set in. Access to rationality, freedom, science and progress

---

1. Denis de Rougemont, *Love in the Western World*, trans. Montgomery Belgion, Princeton: Princeton University Press, 1983.

did not prevent men from privileging their own tradition and memories, no matter how humanist and enlightened they may have been. The phenomenon is at once disturbing in intellectual terms and very human. After the French Revolution, which was born of the demand for rights and freedom, the country experienced the cult of Reason and a devastating Terror. It was as though everything had been forgotten. As it happens, noble values had not been forgotten, so far as the French were concerned, but the attractions of power and the drive to have power over others never disappeared. Emancipatory movements that demand freedom for us neither prefigure nor guarantee equality and freedom for all. We always think on the basis of the state we are in, of our status and of our own tradition. Communism told us that the oppressed proletariat would have its revolution and establish a 'dictatorship of the proletariat'. That dictatorship was supposedly a step towards freedom for all. History, and especially the history of power relations, teaches us that it was a real dictatorship, a point of arrival and not a stage, and a mere, if unfortunate, substitution of one autocratic and absolute power for another. The supporters of human rights, equality and freedom may well have resisted by brandishing those ideals, but that did not prevent them from forgetting about them when it came to dominating and colonizing America, Africa or Asia. The advocates of a 'civilizing' colonization may well have been, or have seemed to be, staunch supporters of the right to education for all and of respect for individual freedom where their own society was concerned, but some of them, such as Jules Ferry in France and Lord Cromer in Great Britain, had very few 'humanistic' scruples when it came to 'civilizing' natives (some critics note that, in the case of Jules Ferry, there was no real contradiction: the mission of the free and compulsory education he advocated was also to 'civilize' the interior of France and eradicate regionalisms and any other counter-powers). Political and economic domination and colonization, with the terror, torture and summary executions they brought in their wake, were suddenly justified . . . in the name of the meaning of history, which is always defined by the victors. We find the same phenomenon in the United States with the idea that America had been entrusted by Providence with a mission and had a 'manifest destiny', to cite O'Sullivan, that justified the genocide and deportation of the Native Americans.

History, and the memories and traditions that fight over how events, values and references should be interpreted, have always been battle-fields and the focus of power struggles. It is unlikely that this will ever change.

Things now seem to be crystallizing in two polarizing trends. They appear to be contradictory, but are in fact the same. In the globalized world and in societies that are becoming more and more pluralistic, we find both demands concerning 'the universal' and demands for the recognition of 'memories', of the legitimacy of specific cultures and traditions and of specific historical experiences. We quarrel over who has the monopoly on the universal, and on the 'truth' of memories when it comes to the objectification of history. Further analysis reveals that it is always the same demand, put forward for the same reason: recognition of the legitimate status of our being, affiliation, tradition and truths. Passion gains the upper hand and leads to a flawed reduc-tionism that has nothing to do with the heritage of humanism and the critical spirit. Because we are afraid and because our identity is in danger, we reconstruct our pasts, reduce, ideologize and purify them when, that is, we simply exclude anything that is 'impure' or alien. When, in his academic lecture of 12 September 2006, the Pope spoke of Europe's Greek and Christian roots, he did not give an objective account of history. Whilst Europe obviously does have Greek and Christian roots, the fact remains that they are far from being its only roots and that Judaism and Islam have also long played a part in shaping Europe's identity. Our analysis also has to take into account other comments from Cardinal Ratzinger, who subsequently became Pope Benedict XVI: he has often said that Europe would be under threat if it forgot its Christian roots, and that, in religious and cultural terms, it is now 'in danger'. Fears about the present (the fear of secu-larization, dechristianization, of the presence of Islam or other spiritu-alities such as Buddhism) and the need to come to terms with new relations of influence (in terms of numbers and strength) that seem to be undermining a hitherto homogeneous tradition lead to selective and reductive reconstructions of the past. We are no longer talking about a common history but about a singular memory that is both discriminatory and selective. This can herald a future of passionate conflicts over roots as well as identities.

A DUTY TO REMEMBER

If we listen to men and women living in the societies of the South, from Latin America to India and Indonesia or the African continent or the Middle East, we find that globalization is perceived mainly as a form of Westernization. If we listen to African-Americans, Latinos and new citizens of the United States, or the citizens of Canada, Europe or Australia, we find that they are uneasy about their culture, values and memories. Relations of power do exist, and debates about universals and specific identities obviously reflect the tensions between tradition and modernity, but they are really debates about 'self' and 'other'. They are about defining ourselves, giving our history a dignity, our memory a legitimacy and our tradition (defined as cultural and/or religious) a meaning. They are about our presence and our hopes.

Officially, pluralist societies must take into account the diversity of the culture and historical experience of their citizens and residents. Values, symbols and language shape our consciousness, psychology and worldview, and so too does the memory of colonization, migration, exile and settlement (and sometimes of rejection and racism). Rather than allowing our memories to be torn apart by squabbles over universals or the higher truths of rival points of view, contemporary societies, both rich and poor and in both the North and the South, should be doing more to institutionalize the teaching of a common history of memories. They should be combining the wealth of all our memories, explaining different points of view, and trying to understand collective consciousnesses and collective hopes as well as historical wounds and traumas. We have already said that, as a matter of urgency, modern man must reconcile himself with a sense of history, and rediscover the essence of the cultural and religious traditions in an age of globalization. It cannot be said too often that globalization itself is producing a culture that exists on a world scale. That culture has a tendency to make other traditions and cultures, with their symbols, rites, arts and food, look 'exotic' or peripheral, though some of their artistic and culinary products can of course be integrated into the logic of its economy because they hold out the promise of substantial profits.

From India to Africa, a new consciousness is awakening in a quest for spirituality and meaning. The same is true of Western societies: it is therefore important to produce a better understanding of these different traditions in order to ensure that they do not become fantasy 'refuges' from materialism and/or the consumer society. There is a certain enthusiasm, sometime joyous and sometimes naive, for Buddhism and Jewish, Christian and Muslim mysticism, but it tends to adulterate the very essence of the teachings of these traditions. 'Reincarnation' has come to mean a reassuring story about 'coming back', whereas it actually refers to the fact that we are bound by cycles of suffering. Sufism has been turned into ethereal flights of fancy that make no ritual demands, whereas the Sufi tradition itself has always been very demanding in terms of its practices and disciplines towards the initiate than towards the ordinary faithful.

Languages, cultures and traditions should also be explained and promoted in our schools, just as they should be celebrated and encouraged by local cultural policies. Given the dominance of English, fast food and stereotypical consumerism, it is important to teach children more than one language, to introduce them to new intellectual worlds with different terminological points of reference, and thus to multiple sensibilities, tastes and points of view. Languages convey and transmit sensibilities; they have and *are* particular sensibilities. Studying the meaning of symbols, practices and customs calls into question the legitimacy of our own symbols, practices and customs and relativizes our certainties and pretensions. Drinking tea in China is a ceremonial affair that reveals a way of life, a conception of time, conviviality and dialogue. That ceremony now has to compete with – or resist – the standardized consumerism offered by the big multinationals, which are now introducing, and gradually imposing, a different view of life.

We live in an era in which it seems imperative to come to terms with the multiplicity of our memories, and to defend the equal right to be, to express ourselves and to speak out. Memories introduce us to different views of history, language and the many traditions we have to understand for what they are. When modernity laid claim to a truth, it was the truth of autonomy, of the freedom that is its precondition, and of the diversity that results from it. The ideologues of modernity have (with modernism) turned it into a particular and

exclusive tradition that has to prevail because it is superior. It therefore comes as no surprise to see some women and men in both the
South and the North resisting a dangerous standardization. They eat
'slow food' whereas the majority eat 'fast food', and prefer healthy
produce, fair trade and local produce, and food and drink that is en-
vironmentally friendly. They are beginning to resist and are keeping a
watchful eye on the surprises that might go with the economic – and
perhaps cultural – rise of China and India at a time when the United
States appears to have been so weakened and when Europe seems to
have lost all sense of direction. They are, then, beginning to resist and
in that sense they are profoundly modern. The paradox is that they
are now demanding, in and through their cultural and religious traditions, precisely what the humanists, who were the precursors of
modernity, were demanding when they rebelled against tradition,
namely autonomy, freedom and diversity. This is a disturbing reversal
... unless it is precisely the same process and involves precisely the
same relations or force. Perhaps we have to admit that modernity is
basically nothing more than one tradition amongst others. Depending
on the historical circumstances and the endogenous and exogenous
relations of domination and power, 'modernity' does not necessarily
do more than any other tradition to guarantee us autonomy, freedom
and diversity. Tradition or modernity? This is a terminological illusion
or a tautology: despite all the differences and the gains that have been
made, both modernity and tradition are indirect expressions of power
relations. 'One must be absolutely modern!' cried Rimbaud because
he felt, deep down, that there was no way – modern or otherwise – of
escaping his tradition.

12

The Sense of Belonging

We have to come from somewhere. We may try to forget, regret or try to erase that fact or we may, on the contrary, make an effort to reclaim our origins, homeland or traditions, but our personal or family past will always be an important part of our being and our identity. Whether we like it or not, we belong to our memories. Origins, surroundings, smells, parents or no parents, perhaps a house and perhaps a street, peace or family rows, war, smiles, tears, presences and absences: we are inhabited by what we have inhabited, what we still inhabit, and what we will always inhabit. Life is short, and none of the important events we remember will ever disappear: images return or fade away, echo and mirror one another, speak with one voice or clash in the midst of our joys, pain, doubts or hopes. We are always looking for 'something' in the light of our past-belonging, because we want to rediscover certain joys, a few habits and a friendly or loving presence, or because we want to avoid suffering, abandonment, disappointment, pain or violence. We are sometimes surprised to find a likeness between the people who were once with us and those who are with us now, and sometimes we are surprised to find that they are quite different in terms of their character and temperament. It is as though we spent our lives looking for similarities or hoping to find something very different. Our past shapes our present and colours our future. Every encounter, every smile, every tear and every mirror reminds us that we really do belong to the past.

What are we looking for? What are we looking for as we wander the world, with its countries and its horizons, as we look into the eyes and hearts of those who love us and those we love, and in our moments of solitude and introspection? What are we looking for? Probably for

well-being, peace, reassurance, harmony and love. Our past sometimes helps us and sometimes hinders us. We always have to revisit the
past, understand it, disentangle it, tame it and forget it, but we can
never really flee from it. We have to live with it and come to terms
with it. When we turn to the future, it is our present: we are always
looking for the places, the loves and the meanings to which we belong.
We know that we have to seek and, basically, to find. Sometimes we
do not even know what we are looking for, and at other times we
know exactly what we have to find, but cannot find it. And sometimes
we have already found what we are still looking for. This is disturbing, and difficult. And as we wander, we really want to belong to
ourselves, to be ourselves and to feel that we possess ourselves.

There is nothing new about this. This search for a sense of belonging can be seen in the world's oldest traditions and philosophies, and
we find it in the torments of the most modern minds and the most
recent psychological theories. Something dwells within me, and I must
succeed in dwelling within it if I am to find harmony, experience equilibrium and set myself free. My past reminds me, and so do my heart
and my consciousness: I come from somewhere, and I have to choose
a destination. I am bound and free ... and I am also free to remain
bound and not to look for anything. Lao Tzu said, 'I do not act, the
Tao (Way) acts me,' in order to emphasize that the force that led him
on his quest for freedom was already that of the object of his quest.
What he was seeking made him seek: the liberation of the 'self' consisted in reconciling the direction in which we must go with the destination we have chosen, and reconciling the Way with the destination.
We must belong to our path if the path is to belong to its goal, and if
we are to belong to ourselves fully and freely. Socrates says exactly the
same thing at the beginning of the *Symposium*, when he talks about
love and remarks that we can only seek that which we know must be
sought. He is pointing out that there is a close connection between
what has made us, what is making us, and what we are trying to do
and experience. Love, like the quest for spiritual liberation, is very
revealing: much of the self is in its object. The paradoxical words of
Christ, the 'hidden God' to whom Blaise Pascal refers, reveal the same
essential truth: 'You would not seek me if you had not found me'
(*Pensées* #919) God obviously already dwells within those who seek

Him. Once again, the encounter is a reconciliation: it then becomes possible to dwell with our hearts in that which naturally dwells within us. Finding, consciously and freely, what drove us from ourselves, either unwittingly or as a matter of urgency, actually means, in other words, retaking possession of ourselves, belonging to ourselves and finding peace. Here, the words of Christ indicate that this really is about God, and the revelation we find in all three monotheisms echoes Psalm XVI, in which David, according to the Jewish tradition 'finds refuge in' the God who dwells within him. This experience of *devequt* (clinging to) allows David to find a refuge and a dwelling place. He finds peace and can link his destiny to his fate: 'The Lord is the portion of mine inheritance and of my cup; thou maintainest my lot.' The Muslim tradition confirms the meaning of these teachings: the Revelation calls upon the faithful to raise '[his] face [devote himself to] towards the religion, a sincere monotheist, according to the natural aspiration (*fitra*) in which God has created Man' (Quran, 30:30). The faithful must turn their faces toward God, fight against the veil of illusion and forgetfulness and return, through their will power and memory, to His truth: 'Surely in the remembrance of God are hearts comforted' (Quran, 13:28).

The object of the quest may not be the liberation of the 'self', as in the Eastern and Asian traditions, or love or God, but the various schools of modern psychology formulate the same goal when it comes to defining the meaning of therapy. It has to do with getting back to ourselves, trying to understand what drives us, the way we function, our blocks, needs, expectations and wounds, and analysing them so that we may master them. We want to stop 'putting up with ourselves'. We want to be able to 'belong to ourselves' and, whilst it may be a matter of 'giving ourselves', as in friendship or love, we would like it to mean not 'being dispossessed of ourselves' (willingly or otherwise), but on the contrary to give ourselves fully and consciously. There is a great difference between the feelings that life seems to steal from us and those our being can master and offer like so many gifts. Retracing our past, attempting to gain access to the tensions within our unconscious (assuming that we believe in it and that it exists) and analysing our behaviours and reactions is indeed an attempt to identify what dwells in our psyche, to understand what causes us to act and react in one way or another. It is going into ourselves, going home, understanding and giving our conscience and will the power and means to decide how we behave and what we expect from ourselves and others.

The natural quest for belonging is a quest for well-being. Those men and women who decide to forget themselves and to lose possession of themselves, by drinking alcohol or using drugs for example, are seeking a well-being that their lucid consciousness seems to deny them. It is as though they had decided to lose possession of themselves at a superficial level because they feel at some deeper level that they are run through with a feeling of self-dispossession, with a void. We find other complex behaviours in certain adolescents and adults who seem to be always on the lookout for confrontation and conflict. They give the impression that they are never at peace and are not in search of 'peace', rather as though aggression and tensions were the states that made them feel at their best. We are dealing with a two-fold phenomenon that has been studied in some depth: they look for trouble because doing so masks their deep unease about themselves. The individual is also under the impression that his hostility towards others allows him to assert his well-being and to feel at ease with himself. In most cases, aggression and looking for trouble hide expectations and demands of a different kind: they are a way of pushing the other to his limits, forcing him to demonstrate his attachment, love, and to express recognition and gratitude in spite of everything. Although they are complicated and complex, these modes of behaviour do not, however, call into question the elements we were discussing earlier. Human beings who behave like this are trying to regain possession of themselves in the eyes of others; they need the mediation, recognition, love and trust of others. Their aggression is often a form of communication, and looking for trouble is a way of looking for love. The other or others – those they love or with whom they live – determine the world to which they belong, and their real or symbolic violence is their way of entering that world and living in it in order to be seen and recognized and of ensuring that they have a place in it, 'their place'. The relationship with the self and the group is especially important, at both the psychological and the normative level.

Spirituality, psychology and the law allow us to approach the question of belonging in holistic terms. As we have just seen, the psychological dimension is of fundamental importance and relates to many different orders that are always interacting: the quest for the truth in which we wish to dwell, the inner balance that allows us to belong, and our presence within the family, group and society to which we actually belong. Belonging always obeys certain rules: the truths of Eastern spiritualities and religions demand, without exception, discipline, effort and a scrupulous respect for what are often very precise rites. Introspection, psychotherapy and psychoanalysis are exacting, and require a framework, norms and stages: without them, they will not work. Belonging to a community means obeying laws that define obligations and rights, a typology of degrees of belonging (citizens, residents, immigrants and so on) and a normative framework for their interaction. In contemporary pluralistic societies, we can see that the law is necessary because it regulates and protects, but it is not enough in itself: we also have to take into account the psychological dimension that completes (or undermines) our sense of belonging to a group. Cultural and religious diversity promotes that sense of belonging, provided that beliefs and sensibilities are collectively recognized and respected even before the law intervenes. The individual then feels that he belongs to a community that 'comprehends' him in both senses of the term: it comprehends his values in intellectual terms and 'takes him in' as a full and legitimate member of its organization. This is not a legal issue; it is a matter of collective psychology and sensibilities. And we live in troubled times in which dominant and legitimate sensibilities can exclude what the law has already integrated.

CITIZENSHIPS

The notion of 'citizenship' has been analysed and debated in greater depth, and for much longer, in the French tradition than in the various traditions of the English-speaking world. And yet things appear to have changed over the last ten years or so. The growing number of immigrants and the security threats to Western societies have brought new notions and new debates to the fore. The question of 'citizenship' is being raised in both Europe and the United States. This is a way of asking, 'Is she or he one of us?', and of asking what requirements she or he must meet in order to become one of us. This approach is not fundamentally constructive, generous or positive because it is a response to the many fears we have already described, and to the difficulty of managing cultural and religious diversity despite the existence of a common legal framework. The early theoreticians of the social contract, such as Hobbes, Locke, Rousseau and Tocqueville (who was in fact more concerned with equality of social and political condition), did not share these preoccupations and were more interested in the legal basis of 'belonging', the preservation of equality and the use of the law to regulate interpersonal relations or the relations that had to be established between individuals and the State. Cultural homogeneity was taken for granted, and there were no grounds for thinking that either the letter or the spirit of the law would be broken. Their goal was to use the social contract in order to manage political powers in such a way as to limit the prerogatives of the State, to restrict the influence of the rich and powerful and to protect the rights of the most vulnerable members of society.

The celebration and defence of democratic principles had a very positive effect and allowed European and then American societies to make the rule of law more effective. But, as we have already said, one insistent question had long been recurrent, and it was difficult to find a coherent, if not clear, answer to it. At the level of philosophical conceptions and basic rights was the idea of equality and the social contract something to be defended in the name of a certain idea of man (in which case everyone should benefit from it), or did it apply only to our society and its members, and did it imply that others must be excluded or simply ignored? The question is neither trivial nor new: like Athenian democracy, which was enjoyed by a minority at the expense of everyone else (and especially the foreigners known as 'barbarians'), the ideal society described by Plato in *The Republic* appears to concern an elite. The contribution made by al-Fârâbi (870–950), who was described by Ibn Rushd (Averroes) as 'the second Aristotle', reveals the same set of problems. In his reflections and propositions on the relationship between politics, philosophy and ethics, and especially in his *The Perfect City*, he asks what is to become of those who are not members of the virtuous or perfect city, or of those who, for one reason or another, cannot be regarded as full members? The positive principle of the rule of law and of equality between 'us' does not exhaust the question of justice for those who are described or represented as 'them'. They are 'others', barbarians and 'foreigners', but their number also includes individuals in our society whose status is despised, as was and is the case with India's *dalit* (oppressed *pariahs*). The fact that we are democratic and fair when we are amongst our own does not necessarily mean that we cannot be autocratic colonists who treat others unfairly. The finest philosophies have not been able to avoid these contradictions, and history is full of examples of how attitudes towards the 'other' can be contradictory and of how others can be treated unfairly.

Although they are to a greater or lesser extent democratic and wealthy, our contemporary societies have by no means resolved these difficulties. The problems are piling up. 'Citizen' status, of course, supposedly gives everyone the same rights and the same obligations. The social contract is quite clear on this point, and members of society know their duties and prerogatives. But not everyone has the same status: residents have a different status from immigrants (whose status is, in most countries, defined in terms of temporal criteria such as 'long-term', 'temporary' or 'seasonal'). The status of refugees is different again, as there is an indeterminate category of 'illegal' and 'undocumented'. The law makes a distinction between them, and yet the principle of equality is by definition dependent on them. The disturbing, and highly embarrassing, thing is that such differences in status are used to justify differential treatment that can contradict the principle of respect for human dignity. The ways in which the law is interpreted and applied (rather than the letter of the law, though it can create problems in itself) legitimate unacceptable forms of treatment that completely contradict what we regard as fair when it comes to 'us' and our own people. 'National preference' can marginalize perfectly competent residents, and immigrants are sometimes treated despicably in many countries in the West, in Asia, all over Africa, and in oil-rich monarchies. Refugees and undocumented immigrants are criminalized and humiliated daily: they are exploited, arrested and sent back to their 'countries of origin', either individually or on mass charter flights. Can we, like the ancient philosophers who could both sing the praises of Athens and despise 'foreigners', simply enjoy our noble status as citizens and be so shortsighted as to despise the unenviable status of immigrant or illegal 'barbarians'? When we accept these categories and labels, are we not creating, or accepting the existence of, new castes and defining status in terms of origins, colour and wealth? Does the existence of our protected democracies justify the fact that so many women and men are living in what amounts to slavery? Whilst our democracies are obviously not directly responsible 'as such', is not our silent acceptance of these hierarchies and this discriminatory treatment a moral failing in itself? That is what was being implied when the countries of Latin America protested about the European Union's adoption of immigration laws and a 'return directive' that encouraged 'voluntary repatriation', and allowed undocumented immigrants to be imprisoned and minors to be deported. Amidst a deafening silence from Africa, and especially North African countries, the countries of Latin America denounced this 'shameful directive' and reminded Europeans that it is not so long ago that they migrated to America, where they received a very different reception. They also argued that a direct link had to be established between migrations and human rights: human rights also applied to immigrants and refugees whose economic conditions, usually meaning poverty, forced them to look for a way out in order to survive. It is as though human rights had become a discourse and an instrument for the benefit of the rich, or a discourse that celebrated their ideals and a variable-geometry instrument for protecting their interests. That is how millions of men and women from South America to Asia see the idea of human rights; their living conditions are such that human rights are just wishful thinking.

We have to pursue the argument still further, as these categories are now being applied to citizens too. There are, it would appear, 'citizens' and 'citizens'. On the one hand, there are those who were, in ways that can be either real, idealized or fantasized, involved in the original social contract, who share the same culture and who are, in terms of its collective psychology, full members of society. Those seem to be naturally entitled to the same rights. And then there are the 'new citizens', whose culture and religion are perceived as different. They may well be citizens, but they do not have the same status. They are still 'them'. They come from outside and are a 'minority', even though the category of 'minority citizenship' does not exist in any legal sense. This is a psychological status: these 'citizens' still have to prove that they can integrate and can really be part of 'us' (even though many of them have been here for generations). We have thus created a new type of citizenship for those we do not entirely trust (or whom we openly distrust), and mere respect for the law is not in itself enough. Indeed, these 'new' citizens would be in the wrong to demand equal implementation of the law, as it is 'natural' for further demands to be made of those whose 'integration' and 'loyalty' has yet to be demonstrated. This is what the young Dutch sociologist Willem Schinkel calls 'moral citizenship'. There is nothing legal, and not even anything formal, about it, but a sort of list is drawn up of what is expected of citizens who are, in religious or cultural terms, 'different' before they can become 'full citizens'. Society demands of them that they respect the law and learn the language, but goes beyond that and has no qualms about intruding into their private lives by asking about their customs, the way they dress, the way they educate their children and so on. This is rarely spelled out, and everything is very informal, but the informality of 'moral citizenship' or 'psychological citizenship' has very concrete implications for the individuals concerned. They are not really part of the collective psyche and can be subjected to a discrimination that does not really offend the 'majority'. The fact that these new citizens have been here for generations and have succeeded in integrating in legal and psychological terms should have put an end to talk of 'integration', but the reverse is true. After two, three or even four generations, 'they' are still 'of immigrant stock'. It should perhaps be recalled – and this was the implicit message behind South America's protests about Europe's 'immigration policy' – that the only difference between immigrants, 'new' citizens and 'native citizens' is that the latter simply immigrated earlier. We are no longer talking about the law, but about psychology, informality, time and trust (in ourselves and others), and it would be a mistake to minimize the implications of this.

DISCRIMINATION

These endless debates about values and laws may well be interesting, but they do not help us to resolve the real problems of everyday life. Theoretical – and idealist – philosophies can, with the best intentions in the world, become real diversionary tactics. Core issues, practices and real life are avoided. We therefore have to promote a 'philosophy of everyday life', or in other words an applied philosophy that can evaluate both the content of the law and its psychological and symbolic projections. We need a philosophy of an 'active we'. The picture then becomes less edifying. The colours fade, and countless contradictions and inconsistencies appear. Nelson Mandela quite rightly remarked one day that the way it treats its 'minorities' is the standard by which a democracy should be judged. In doing so, he immediately posed the debate in practical, political, concrete and everyday terms. The concept of a minority then becomes both legal and psychological: 'minority' status is usually given to those who, in legal, psychological and even symbolic terms, are regarded, either formally or informally, as not being part of the original society, its culture or its 'collective psyche'. A cultural community whose small numbers make it a minority may also be seen as such in the eyes of the law.

As sociologists from Weber to Bourdieu remind us, we also have to remember that outdated economic and social categories can determine the way individuals are treated in both modern and traditional societies. Discrimination and injustice are primarily, and above all, a matter of 'social class', even though discourse now tends to 'culturalize' the debates and to turn them into religious issues. Social exclusion, unemployment and the marginalization of the poor, and women, are still the main evils of contemporary societies. There is obviously nothing new about this phenomenon, but the way we approach these questions turns socio-economic and political power relations into the so-called 'new' problem of cultural or 'civilizational' differentiation. The most disturbing thing is that the unemployed concur with this new reading of social problems and, rather than emphasizing that they all share the same fate of exploitation and poverty, are tempted to invoke the cultural and religious differences between their own marginalization and that of others. Psychology and social and media representations have an unrivalled ability to split the ranks of any potential resistance movement. Religious and cultural factors may well be grafted on to socioeconomic realities, but they can never totally replace them: they are aggravating factors in the sense that cultural and religious discrimination can compound social exclusion and make it even more complex. The economic, political and sociological theories that try to explain the mechanisms of exclusion still provide our initial and objective analytic framework. We are still talking about classic relations of domination.

Armed with these tools, we can begin to study the new phenomenon of discrimination on the basis of culture and religion. Anyone who is now poor, 'African, Arab or Asian' (or perceived as such) and 'Muslim' (or perceived as such) is disadvantaged in more than one sense. In day-to-day life, this may mean that she or he faces spontaneous and/or institutional racism in the form of bad treatment and may find that access to jobs and upward social mobility is blocked (representatives of cultural diversity who have reached a certain level are assumed to have reached the natural limits of their competence). The letter of the law says otherwise, but practices are, as we have said, bound up with representations, projections and fears. Structural racism and institutional discrimination set in insidiously, but in the long term they result in a very negative twofold phenomenon. On the one hand, they have an effect on their victims – and they really are the victims of discrimination and injustice on a daily basis – who develop a very negative 'victim' attitude. Everything is explained and justified in terms of racism, and not in terms of their lack of competence or their failure to understand institutions and codes. The 'symbolic majority', on the other hand, comes to justify unequal treatment in terms of a difference of origins. The result is the normalization, on a large scale, of the stigmatization of the other and a mass racism that recalls the darkest hours of history.

Women and men may well have internalized the three 'Ls' principles that should grant them recognition as citizens (respect for the *l*aw, knowledge of the *l*anguage and critical *l*oyalty), but they still have to justify themselves and prove that they are not dangerous and are assets to the society in which they live. Citizens 'of immigrant origin' who look like Arabs, Africans or Asians are not faced with these problems so often if they are wealthy, musicians or high-level sportspersons. The application of the law and collective representations give them a very different welcome: 'they belong with us', and represent us if we like their music and if their talents help 'us' to win in sporting contests. Here, we are in the realm of psychology and representations, which is not really surprising given that we live in the era of global communications, of media supremacy and perpetual migrations. We now have to get used to the idea that values and laws do not protect us from anything unless we make the effort to educate ourselves, critically evaluate the information we are given, and learn to understand representations. The means of mass persuasion are so powerful that anything is possible: even the most educated people and the masses are increasingly vulnerable and are potential objects of the most hateful populist campaigns and media manipulations. Sixty years after the ratification of the Declaration of Human Rights, nothing can be taken for granted, and everything is possible. As former Prime Minister Tony Blair once said, 'The rules of the game have changed.' That was an understatement. Surveillance, the loss of the right to privacy, summary extraditions, 'civilized' torture camps all over the world, places where the writ of law does not run. The normalization of violence appears to have desensitized us, and we are more and more indifferent to the inhuman treatment we see all around us. It is true that we have often lost the ability to marvel at the simple things in life, as a result of either pessimism or lassitude, but we can only conclude that we have also – and to a dangerous extent – lost our capacity for outrage and revolt. Our representations are becoming standardized just as our intellect and sensibilities are atrophying. Our fine laws may still delude us, but they will do nothing to protect us or to promote respect for human dignity unless our conscience imbues them with substance, meaning and humanity.

'WE'?

A holistic approach to these realities requires us to rediscover, respectively, together and in practical terms, some basic principles and values. Education, everyday life and interaction with fellow citizens of different origins, cultures and religions are the things that will allow us to apprehend our common humanity in concrete terms, and to understand that it is, by its very essence, made up of diversity and of many different identities and traditions. Our fellow human beings act as mirrors, and they allow us to understand that we too have multiple identities, and that we are not reducible to one origin, one religion, one colour or one nationality. This education and these relations forge knowledge and shape a psychology. It takes time, patience and commitment: changing mentalities and transforming perceptions and representations means that we have to work with our fellow human beings at both the local and the national level. We have to give a 'philosophy of pluralism' substance through our practical commitment, and through the projects of actors who represent a diversity of cultures and religions but who are also inspired by their common willingness to take up the same challenges. We can thus create a collective psyche, a common sensibility and a mutual feeling of belonging.

None of this can be done at the legal level; we have to begin long before the law intervenes. How and why, at a given moment in history or life, does a group acquire the ability to say 'we', and to allow its members to feel at ease with themselves, to feel that they are recognized and that they are at home? A group or a society ... regulated and organized by legislation and cemented and unified by a common sensibility. This is not a matter of recognizing the formal limitations of the law, but of coming into contact with the other's sensibility, values, doubts and quest. We encounter new trajectories, and the efforts others are making to belong, and to find their equilibrium and peace. We learn to empathize, as we have already said, and to identify the sacred spaces of the 'other' who is our neighbour. We learn to understand the importance of our neighbour's values, loves and convictions, and even the geography of his or her psychology and sensibility. As Mircea Eliade points out, even the most modern amongst us have their personal maps of their sacred and profane spaces and elements. We become a society when two, three, thousands or millions of us learn to decipher the main lines of our respective routes and to respect them because we understand their general meaning.

As we have said again and again, we need the law. But building a society means going beyond the legislative level and entering the realm of civility. At this level, it is not a matter of using the law in order to know the extent to which I can exercise my rights to impose my will or to attack the other who stands in my way (or whom I mistrust), but it is important to concern ourselves with conviviality, to adopt the welcome vocabulary and aspirations of the political ecologist Ivan Illich. There are, as we have said, some things that are legal but that we shun because of our sense of dignity and decency. Knowing how to make use of our rights is indeed important, but we also have to have some sense of our common humanity, a concern for the others, a shared sensibility and a shared emotional life. We are talking about an ethics and a humanism that precedes (and succeeds) the law. Illich was hostile to schools, to that 'new church' that promised 'salvation' in the light of an economic order that oriented knowledge and shaped behaviours in such a way as to make them competitive and profitable. Taking his inspiration from the biblical parables, he adopted the adage 'the corruption of the best becomes the worst' and tried to think about the future of our modern societies. And our desire for speed, profit and social success, together with our fear of the other, of difference and insecurity, are indeed turning the best into the worst. Our constitutional states are becoming fortresses within which we defend our interests, and a lot of our selfishness. Our rights, the most important of which is the right to self-expression, are being used to delineate territories and to provoke – for no good reason – the anger and reactions of those we distrust, or simply those whose presence and beliefs offend us. Our democracies used 'legal' mass persuasion and manipulation to justify – with or without the approval of the masses – new wars between civilizations in the name of civilization and democratization. These perversions stir up fears and distrust and block the development, at both the local and the international level, of the conviviality that gives individuals a sense of belonging. We have become the creators of ghettoes at both the international and the national level. Our affiliations are becoming more and more narrowly defined, our humanism is becoming a matter of tribal instincts, and our universalism is not very generous.

We must learn to say 'we' again. Just as I can say 'I' and still belong to myself, we must be able to say 'we' whilst acknowledging our common sense of belonging. Some would like us to sit down at a table and discuss the best way of saying 'we' and of respecting 'one another'. And yet it is quite possible that the method itself is what is preventing us from getting the results we want. The same applies to the concept of integration: the best way to prevent 'integration' from becoming a reality is to go on talking about it so obsessively. A common sense of belonging is not something that can be willed into existence: it is born of day-to-day life in the street, at school and in the face of the challenges we all face. Theories and debates about 'the sense of belonging' actually make it impossible for us to feel that we belong. We are talking about a feeling: we come to feel that we belong because we live that feeling, because we experience it. The common law protects us, but it is common causes that allow us to respect and love one another (by acting together 'for' some cause and not just 'against' a threat). A common commitment *to* respect for human dignity and saving the planet, or to the struggle *against* poverty, discrimination, every type of racism, and *to* promote the arts, the sciences, sports and culture, responsibility and creativity: these are, as we have already said, the best ways of developing a real conviviality that is both lived and effective. When we trust one another, we no longer attack our neighbours in order to test their reactions without reason, and we can keep our critical intellectual distance from their ill temper or provocations. We become subjects who can say 'I' when we have discovered the meaning of our personal projects: we become a 'we', a community or a society when we can decide upon a common collective project. In most circumstances, it is not dialogue between human subjects that changes the way they see others; it is the awareness that they are on the same path, the same road and have the same aspirations (and their interminable dialogue sometimes blinds them to this). When our consciousness acknowledges that we are travelling the same road, it has already half-opened the door to the heart: we always have a little love for those who share our hopes. 'We' exist by the sides of roads that lead to the same goals.

13

Of Civilizations

We are always talking about 'civilizations', and we cannot even agree on the definition of the term or determine what substance the concept might have. Some refer to more or less precise definitions, or refer to a set of ideas which they relate to the notion of 'civilization', whilst others rely upon the 'intuition' that 'somewhere' there is an entity that expresses the natural bonds that exist between men and societies that share the same values. The alternative view is that 'civilization' is part of the paternalist vocabulary of the dominant. Whilst this confusion is disturbing, it is still true to say that the constant reference to the concept of 'civilization' has indeed created categories and perceptions that recognize the existence of entities, large groups and frames of reference in which people say 'we' and use that word to identify 'them'.

The concept's etymology and evolution, and the different ways in which it has been interpreted in the course of history are illuminating. The Latin root relates to *civilis*, which is the adjectival form of *civis* ('citizen'): it refers to a society that is regulated by law, that allows the emergence of a civil or public space and that organizes interpersonal relations between its members. To begin with, we therefore have human beings, a legal framework, the establishment of a differential status for individuals (inside and outside the group in question) and, at a later stage, an organized society with formal or informal behavioural norms (a 'civility', to use the term we used earlier). We have here a preliminary definition that attempts to determine objectively the elements that turn a collection of human beings into a society that is 'civilized' in the sense that it is regulated by laws. And yet it quickly becomes apparent that this way of describing the preconditions for the emergence of a civil space and civility can give rise to value judgements as to the extent to which any given society is 'civilized'. Is there in fact any such thing as a human society, or even what is pejoratively termed a 'primitive' society, that is not regulated by laws and that does not give its members a specific status? In that sense, all societies, and a fortiori 'primitive societies', are 'civilized' and display the characteristics and conditions of 'civilization'.

The point is that the very origins of the concept lie not only in the way we see 'ourselves' but in an implicit comparison with those we see as the 'other', the other society of 'foreigners' and 'barbarians'. The definition of the term 'civilization' is therefore very relative, which is why the use of the concept can change, depending on how we see ourselves and others, and, of course, on historically defined power relations. The relativity of the definition does not, however, detract from the imperative nature of the process. That is what Ibn Khaldûn is trying to explain in his *Al-Muqaddima* or 'Introduction to Universal History'. Societies, dynasties and civilizations all have a primal need for a bond that can unite them, for a sort of common social point of reference based upon blood ties or a common feeling of belonging (*asabiyya*) that is reinforced by shared interests, the organization of a hierarchy and sovereignty (*mulk*) and the integration of religion as an additional factor that supplies meaning and cohesion. The psychoanalytic analysis made by Freud in the twentieth century demonstrates the same historical need for the process of 'civilization', but in *Civilization and Its Discontents*, he explains that need in terms of fear and anxiety. Our bodies, the outside world and other people can be the source of pain and trauma, and we therefore have to protect ourselves from them. We therefore quite naturally seek out a structured society, civilization or religion in the same way that we seek out a father who can protect and reassure us (by supplying order, laws and a morality). To revert to the image we used in the Introduction, human beings need a frame or window (which identifies and protects the self) through which they can see and contemplate the ocean. And Freud does in fact refer to the 'oceanic feeling' that comes from seeing ourselves as part of a whole or of being 'at one with the world', and asserts that it can only be something that is understood and accepted after the event. The 'civilizing' process that gives us protection is, in other words, precisely the opposite of the process that gives us access to the ocean, but paradoxically, we need protection before we can go to the ocean. It is only when we have protection that we dare to expose ourselves to danger.

EVOLUTIONS

We also have to consider the necessary relationship with others. It is not incidental that the concept of 'civilization' re-emerges and takes on new connotations during the Age of Enlightenment. In his research on the modern usage of the concept of 'civilization', Emile Benveniste points out that Adam Ferguson uses it in English as early as 1759 to suggest the idea that, like human beings, civilizations move from childhood to adulthood: 'civilization' is an expression of the view that societies reach maturity.[1] We find the same idea in Mirabeau (1749–91), who appears to have been the first to use the notion in French to describe the process or dynamic that allows a society to become civilized by 'softening its manners'. The shift from the conception of the state of a 'civilized' society to that of a process of 'civilization' (in the sense of progress) is closely bound up with the rationalism of the Enlightenment and linked to self-image and the view of others. There was a historical evolution of societies and, consequently, a hierarchy between more advanced, more 'adult', more developed and more 'civilized' societies and primitive or 'infantile' social organizations that must of necessity mature and develop. The concept is not, then, neutral (and was never really neutral), but in the eighteenth century it takes on more voluntaristic connotations and acquires a self-conscious status. There is a new certainty of being ahead, or being in the forefront of progress and of showing that way for all other civilizations.

Accordingly, the term 'civilization' was henceforth invested with a value judgement about the 'degree' to which societies are organized, about the 'nature' of their beliefs, about their 'type' of relationship with reason and the sciences and even about the 'justification' for

1. Emile Benveniste, 'Civilization: Contribution to the History of the Word', in *Problems in General Linguistics*, trans. Mary Elizabeth Meek, Miami: Miami University Press, 1971.

their hierarchies. The parameter used to make these judgements is of course of the European societies that were rapidly moving through the stages of their scientific and industrial revolutions. Those societies were, by definition and essentially, the very embodiment of the civilizational process and of access to a higher form of civility. These considerations, later completed by some aspects of nineteenth-century theories about the evolution and selection of species and societies, provided the philosophical and scientific justification for 'civilizing' operations in the most literal of senses. The goal was to 'civilize' 'infantile' and backward peoples, and to colonize them in order to free them from their own alienation, or in other words to help them grow up at last. They had to follow the march of history. This was what Kipling described as the heavy 'white man's burden' who 'had to' colonize the Philippines, Asia, Africa and, of course, South America. Whilst the white man sometimes had to use violence (or even resort to slavery, though 'whites' did not have a monopoly on slavery by any means), that was 'justified' in historical terms. From the discoveries of Columbus to the colonization of the nineteenth century, humanist, economic and missionary considerations overlapped and reinforced one another. 'Higher' values were imposed, economic profits were definitely made, and populations were Christianized: the irreversible process of civilization (in the sense of civilizing) was under way, and the possibility of regression, and still less decline, was unimaginable.

It took a long time for these messianic visions, or even the concept of 'civilization', to be critically reconsidered. Even in the nineteenth century, there were critical voices that expressed doubts about the benefits of progress and civilizing missions, and it is mainly in the Marxist critique of imperialism that we find in-depth analyses of the ideological and economic mechanisms behind the processes of colonization. According to Marx and Engels, colonization takes us to the very heart of the capitalist system of exploitation and expansion. The goal was to enslave and to exploit, and not to civilize. Over a century later, Edward Said, who adopts a different approach that is more philosophical and cultural than economic, tries to uncover the ideological mechanisms behind the *Orientalism* that constructs civilizations of the other in order to distinguish itself from them and to subdue them. The outcome is the same: the reference to 'civilization' seems in all cases to conceal the real terms of the relationship, and to distract our attention from a relationship of philosophical, cultural, political and/or economic domination.

It took the two 'world' wars of the twentieth century, the rise of fascism and the economic crises of the 1920s and 1930s to raise certain doubts about Western civilization's 'definite superiority' over all other civilizations. Communist protests and then communist revolution and the increasingly widespread and organized resistance of the peoples of the South undermined certain beliefs and certainties. The process began in the nineteenth century in South America and then intensified in Africa and Asia. It was not just that 'Western civilization' was characterized by frequent failures, wars, crises and regressions; the way it treated and 'civilized' the human beings it had colonized revealed temptations that were scarcely 'humanist', somewhat 'barbarous' and very often inhuman and dehumanized. The 'colonial exhibitions' that were shown in Europe until the Second World War were real 'human zoos' in which 'civilized Europeans' could stare at flesh-and-blood 'exotic', 'colonized' and 'primitive' men and women who had been deliberately displaced and exported from the colonies. History then seemed to change direction as peoples began to resist in the name of their dignity, their beliefs, their independence and their own civilizations. Decolonization was under way, and it was bringing a new form of civilization with it.

In the West, some intellectuals and politicians still think that colonization had 'its positive side' and that it was indeed a way of giving the peoples of the South some elements of civilization. The knowledge and economic and social progress of the countries of the South owe, in their view, a great deal to the contributions of the countries that colonized them. Opinions can be either critical, positive or to a greater or lesser extent nuanced, but we are slowly coming around to a rather different idea of what is meant by the notion of 'civilization'. That idea is not in itself new, but the circumstances of history are slowly normalizing it: the emphasis is no longer on a historical dynamic but on the intrinsic conditions that allow us to define what is meant by civilization. This approach is more normative, and takes the view that the characteristic features of any given society can explain its unity at the level of values, moral principles, intellectual points of reference, behavioural norms and artistic expressions. It is no longer a question of being 'primitive' or 'civilized' or of any other value judgements. There is no such thing as a series of stages that realize the historical process of civilization. There are a multitude of civilizations, each with its own points of reference and its own development. In the mid-twentieth century, the historian Arnold Toynbee's *Study of History* (twelve volumes, 1934–61) lists twenty or twenty-five civilizations that have emerged, evolved and developed, and sometimes declined and disappeared. More recently, Samuel Huntington developed the same plural approach and integrated it into his theory of the 'clash of civilizations'.

These recent developments and what appear to be more normative definitions do not necessarily signal the emergence of a more egalitarian idea of civilizations. And nor does the acceptance of diversity mean that the idea of superiority has vanished. In both North and South critiques of economic and cultural postcolonial imperialism and neocolonialism have been directed against the logic of domination, which still predominates even though it no longer involves political control or an actual physical presence in the nations they control. Some in the alter-globalization movement (and elsewhere) see in the displacement of the debate on to 'civilizations' and 'cultures' at a global level the same strategy of displacement that we saw with socio-economic problems at the national level. The self-justifying rhetoric that emerges concentrates on the sustained and manipulated tensions of the 'clash' and 'dialogue' of civilizations and thus masks power relations whilst mobilizing populations by reviving their sense of belonging, stirring up fears and exacerbating the natural need for security. In the predominantly Muslim societies of the South, violent extremist movements and anti-Western Islamist currents play on the same register in order to galvanize crowds and use emotional reactions and popular frustrations to capitalize on their ability to give them a political representation. The polarization of the debate around questions of 'civilizations' and 'religions' finds objective allies on both sides of the potential clash of civilizations. At the same time, other and more reasonable minds are beginning to argue what is now the imperative case for dialogue.

In this dialectic process of 'clash and dialogue', concepts are vague, 'civilizations' are ill-defined or not defined at all, and feelings of superiority and logics of domination persist. An emergent ideology appears to assert that we are living in a new era characterized by the end, or absence, of ideologies, or even in a era of 'non-ideology' brought about by postmodernist globalization. Noam Chomsky has said ironically that he does not understand this inflation of terms and concepts, but it cleverly masks some very classic, and very old, issues to do with power relations. Fukuyama's theory of the 'end of history' and his claim that history finds its apotheosis in the experience of the West is basically very revealing: we can readily accept that there are different civilizations, but there is one civilization that is ahead of all the rest and it is superior because of its ultimate political achievement – democracy – and its mastery of scientific knowledge and technological know-how. The theory does have its supporters, but it has also been heavily criticized: the West's achievements are indeed remarkable, but it is impossible to understand them without subjecting them to a general assessment of relations between the 'West' and other civilizations. And besides, the development of the world economy is now seeing the rise of contradictory economic forces (such as India and China), of politico-religious resistance, and of elites and/or entire populations (and not just small groups of violent extremists) that are anything but resigned to the status quo. A fair, reasonable and lucid acknowledgement of diversity means that we have to change the way we see the world, 'civilizations' and relations between civilizations.

RELIGION AND PHILOSOPHY

We really must see things in a new light, or at least look at the question of civilizations and cultures through a different window. We would do well to question the values, systems, meanings and hopes that use intrinsically different sets of references (rather than immediately engaging in dialogues that can sometimes confine us with in the limits of what we think we know) in order to reach a better understanding of what we have in common and what divides us. We appear to be obsessed with avoiding conflict or, at the opposite extreme, with stoking up conflict for political purposes. Our points of reference are no longer fields of knowledge, of intellectual culture and of mediations about human diversity: we use them to impose our will, to justify (ourselves), to make accusations, to defend ourselves, to regulate, to bring peace and to kill. They tell about 'oneself' only through the mediating gaze of the other: outlooks are distorted and quite literally alienated from the outset and by the very nature of the exercise.

And yet spiritualities, religion and philosophy are not dead. Some did express the hope that they would either disappear or be transcended (they hoped that religion would be transcended by philosophy, or that religion and philosophy would be transcended by science, as in the case of the positivist Auguste Comte), but the fact remains that they have a life of their own, that they underlie conceptions of the universe, organize systems of thought, determine relations with reality, with politics and with society, and that they formulate hopes. They have to be taken seriously, whatever we may think of religion or metaphysics, and whatever our political responsibilities may be at the international, national or local level. The men and women of our day, like those of the past, need meaning and not just management.

The disturbing thing is that we are now witnessing a twofold phenomenon. It is not just that the fundamentals of our different philosophies, religions and civilizations are becoming unfamiliar and are being studied less and less, but that we are content with 'self-evident truths' that allow us to establish a hierarchy of civilizations or religions that classifies them as 'progressive', 'open' and 'modern', or 'problematic', 'retrograde' or openly 'dangerous'. Given that spiritualities, religions and philosophies are neither 'exact' nor 'experimental' sciences, we supposedly have the right, in this age of scientific and technological revolution, to rely upon a few articles published here and there, on 'impressions' of varying accuracy, on old school memories and on truisms reported and repeated on the internet. The surprising and saddening thing about the new atheists, from Richard Dawkins and Christopher Hitchens in Great Britain to Sami Harris in the United States or Michel Onfray in France, is that these scientists and thinkers seem to have only a very superficial understanding of the religions they criticize. Whilst they may, like Dawkins and Dennett, be rigorous when it comes to their respective scientific domains, they are real amateurs when it comes to religion. Their generalizations are excessive and their comments on religion sometimes betray a smug arrogance. We also find that the way they describe religions and spiritualities is based upon an implicit hierarchy: Islam is often at the top of their list of dangerous references, followed by Christianity, whereas Judaism and Hinduism are rarely discussed, and Buddhism is of course seen as the least dangerous of all spiritualities. There is a curious similarity between their hierarchy and the popular impressions and feelings that are so influenced by crises and media coverage: these scientists and thinkers are very much 'of their times', and far removed from the transhistorical preconditions for rigorous and constructive critical thinking.

And yet we need to engage in an in-depth dialogue about these questions. Idealist and apologetic responses to these criticisms of religion usually display little objectivity, and are badly argued and 'on the defensive'. They place the emphasis on religions' higher or humanistic values, or on their human and social importance or usefulness, but their critical remarks are as superficial as those of their critics. They call for dialogue and mutual respect, as though dialogues 'between' civilizations, religions and philosophies were enough to justify them or told us anything about them. We need knowledge and intellectual rigour, but we are offered 'positions' based upon 'good intentions' and hopes. There are contradictory tendencies at work here, and they do not get us out of the vicious circle: there seems to be a new revival of interest in religious, spiritual and philosophical 'feelings' at the very time when schools are doing less and less to promote any objective understanding of these subjects (and when these disciplines are regarded as being of secondary importance when it comes to planning a future and thinking of how to make a living).

Any serious consideration of 'civilizations' that wishes to avoid ideological manoeuvres and political calculations (and that also keeps its distance from paternalist relations of domination or analyses) requires a commitment to the study of systems of thought, metaphysics and different conceptions of man and life. Even before we know how we can enter into a dialogue and what we can agree or differ about, we must study and identify what our different sets of references have to say about meaning, postulates, realm of values and ends.

This means reading, studying, knowledge and effort. Reconciliation with thought, the intellect and culture: rigorous critical thought should not just be the servant of productive and efficient sciences and technologies; it should also be the servant of systems of thought, religions and spiritualities. We too are of our times when we accept the existence of a hierarchy of sciences and methodologies when it comes to the rigour of their approach, the coherence of their exposition and their critical thinking. We are in fact seeing some disturbing developments. Intellectual arenas, from schools to academic circles, ought to be able to protect themselves from media coverage and fake 'obvious facts', to keep in touch with the population at large and to promote critical and autonomous thinking. All too often, such arenas are themselves greatly influenced by media debates and impassioned controversies, and it is therefore impossible to get away from the clichés and the general mood of hysteria.

Superficiality and idealism are bad advisers at a time when there is a growing lack of self-confidence, when fear of the other is becoming more widespread, and when exclusive and closed identities, distrust and emotional overexposure are everywhere. Wishful thinking, optimistic statements of intent and complacent dialogues will not get us out of this crisis. As we have already said throughout this book, a holistic approach cannot rely upon superficial remarks about different domains of knowledge. We also require both specialists and a dynamic and effective interdisciplinarity. In our era, the 'universal man' can no longer be a single individual or a single mind with a global vision. Groups of intellectuals, scholars and scientists should pool their knowledge, resist the majority trend to divide and fragment knowledge and establish critical but profound links between different domains of human activity. Every universe of references, and every civilization, philosophy and religion, needs to forge these internal links. We have already said that the study of philosophies, religions and the arts must adopt a historical and memory-based approach. Their relationship with the modern sciences and applied ethics is a further dimension that we cannot afford to ignore. This brings us back to the idea of reconciliation, but we are now talking about reconciliation within the various domains of the intellectual realm. We have to begin with the simple but profound things that allow us to distinguish between values and norms, the immutable and the historical, and similarities and differences.

PRINCIPLES AND MODELS

It is difficult to deny the existence of 'civilizations': throughout human history, there have always been communities, 'areas' and 'universes of references' that can be identified with societies that have, on either an essential or a temporary basis, certain things in common, such as values, principles, cultural elements, intellectual attitudes, technologies, and so on. It is just as difficult to list them in either diachronic or synchronic order. Doing so would require us to have pre-established categories, and we still know very little about certain civilizations or societies, either because they have vanished or because they were very localized. We now speak of eighteen, sixteen, eight or four 'great civilizations', but those figures mean very little. We sometimes identify civilizations with the cultures they embody, with organized religions, philosophies or spiritualities, with a language or with a geographical space. The criteria are, to say the least, vague, and the legitimacy of some classifications can be highly debatable. Categorizations can easily be revised in the light of the political or geostrategic needs of the moment. Turkey is an interesting example. In the nineteenth and early twentieth centuries, the country was regarded as 'European', but some now regard it as completely 'Asiatic' and predominantly 'Islamic' (and therefore not very 'European'). There is little objectivity where civilizations are concerned!

We can, however, identify certain distinctive features and dominant trends, and therefore circumscribe civilizational zones. We can, for example, refer to Buddhism, with its various traditions and the internal distinctions between the area of China and the very different civilization of Japan. We can also refer to Islam, to the distinctions that have to be made within a broader Islamic civilization, and to its specifically Persian, African, Arabic (and even Western) specificities. Then there are overriding common features, just as there are distinctions at the cultural and linguistic levels, and particular national features. Western civilization is influenced by the same dynamics. There are, for instance, differences between North America and Europe (not to mention Australia and New Zealand): they have a number of basic common, founding principles, but they also represent sub-sets that are integrated into a greater whole. We find the same plural reality in South America and Asia.

One primary truth emerges, and it completely contradicts those perceptions that tend to confine civilizations within monolithic categories. There is no such thing as a 'pure' or closed civilization, that has received no inputs from outside its sphere of existence and influence. Traders, intellectuals, travellers and scholars have always imported and exported ideas, customs and technologies that promote the cross-fertilization of civilizations. Civilizations have multiple roots and constituent elements, and are subject to countless influences that constantly transform one another, intertwine and interact. Just as there is no such thing as an exclusive or pure identity, there is no such thing as a uniform or homogeneous civilization. Essentialist approaches in fact defend an ideological, and often dogmatic, position on issues of nationhood, culture and civilization. There is nothing scientific about their relationship with memory and other people, and they conceal considerations as to the purity of the self and its references. 'Dangerous civilizations' echo Amin Maalouf's 'murderous identities'[2] . . . and the damage they can do is indeed frightening.

Then there is the historical dimension that intrinsically affects all civilizations. Like identities, civilizations are always in motion. They change and evolve, undergo transformations, make progress and regress, go through crises, face up to tensions and even come under attack and face various challenges. These historical changes go hand in hand with redefinitions and changes affecting their geographical zones, their spheres of influence and their relations with their cultural neighbours. Frontiers shift and become rigid or porous, and these very dynamics renew civilizations. The phenomenon has been observable for centuries in China, India and Japan, around the Mediterranean and in Europe, as well as in North and South America and even Australia. All 'civilizations' have undergone historical and geographical

2. Amin Maalouf, *In the Name of Identity: Violence and the Need to Belong*, trans. Barbara Bray, London: Penguin, 2003.

transformations, and whether we do or do not support Ibn Khaldûn's idea of 'cycles of dynasties and civilizations', we have to agree that we can always detect periods of greatness and periods of decadence that succeed one other. Sometimes the process speeds up and sometimes it comes to a halt, but it is always at work.

Another major phenomenon is observable within civilizational zones, and it can have a major impact on relations between different universes of references. Even when they are considered to be universal, the same values and principles can give rise to very different concrete applications and historical models. The principles on which democracy, for example, is based (the rule of law, equal citizenship, universal suffrage, accountability and the separation of powers) may well be common to most European (and Western) societies, but no one model of democracy is identical to all the others. The same universal principles do not give rise to the same historical models. The latter depend upon the national memories, collective psychologies and cultures that give historical creations particular forms. What is true of individual 'civilizations' becomes even more pronounced when we adopt a comparative approach to civilizations in the plural. If we are to debate and discuss shared and different values, we require a different type of constructive and critical comparison when we come to look at historical formations. One can certainly take the view that one model is more successful at this or that level (social management, political organization, and so on), but ultimately our evaluation of a civilization or society only make sense when we compare its practical achievements with the principles it claims to recognize. In absolute terms or in terms of applied ethics, comparing models is often pointless and can be influenced by nationalistic and chauvinistic feelings, or by power relations that dare not speak their name.

This last point is important. Just as there is no such thing as a couple without power relations, there can be no such thing as a civilization without potential relations of domination. We may well wish to enter into a dialogue, understand one another and build something together, but the fact remains that the whole apparatus that defines civilizations, identities and the universal integrates them, wittingly or not (and never innocently), into a system of categorizations that determines hierarchies, whether we like it or not, and whether or not we pretend that this does not happen. The terminology that is used to express principles and the temporality that is used to evaluate history's stages, the hierarchy of values and the celebration of certain 'models' (which are confused with the principles that underlie them) are all elements that have to do with the quest for power that influences debates, self-representations and representations of others. As we have said, the same intuition determined the stances taken by the Frankfurt School, Herbert Marcuse and then the economist Serge Latouche and his critique of the Western mega-machine and of some of the myths that surround progress.

DIALOGUES

The obsessional reference to 'civilizations' and to the possibility of conflict between them has given way to repeated, and sometimes equally obsessional, calls for 'dialogue'. They became increasingly common, and Spain resolved to take the international lead after the attacks of March 2004. Turkey, the United Nations and UNESCO then became associated with the project. The 'Alliance of Civilizations' has organized numerous seminars, meetings and lectures. The Saudi, Malaysian, Iranian, Turkish, US governments and the European Union have made a positive, and constructive, commitment to multinational debates involving states, NGOs and intellectuals. The 'dialogue between civilizations' has certainly been very lively at the diplomatic level.

We cannot but rejoice at that, but we should be wary of lapsing into a naive complacency. It should also be noted that what is referred to as 'civilizations' in the plural is actually referring to only two civilizations – the West and Islam – that seem, in terms of values, cultures, historical development and economic and geostrategic interests, to be in direct competition with one another. Whilst this perception has become more pronounced since the terrorist attacks, there is nothing new about it. It is as though we were talking about two different worlds and as though we had to make a clear distinction between ourselves and the other world and its values in order to enter into a constructive debate with it. Fine words and good intentions are not enough. And the worst thing that could happen in a dialogue between civilizations is a lack of self-understanding and the fantasy construct of a closed and ghettoized 'civilizational identity' based upon fear and scarred by historical traumas and wounds. A recognition of the diversity of the past, of ourselves and the other, of the other within us, and of our multiple and complex memories is a sine qua non condition for any dialogue or any alliance. In both the West and in Islam, representations are stereotypical and memories are alienated, and both sides have serious doubts. The point is not so much to reach an agreement with the 'other' as to decide where the boundaries of our neighbouring territories lie so as to feel comfortable with ourselves and get to know ourselves better. The other civilization is a mirror that should facilitate a collective form of therapy. Once again, the dangerous thing about the concert of civilizations is not the presence of the other, but the ignorance of self.

A dialogue with oneself is a sort of collective introspection. This kind of psychological and/or spiritual exercise is unavoidable. And so is politics. And so are political calculations. An inter-civilizational dialogue or alliance that was interested only in the 'philosophy of fine feelings' and never openly tackled political philosophy, power relations, popular frustrations or the respective breaches of elementary consistency would be seen as a delaying tactic or a way of forgetting, through dialogue, the sometimes cynical policies that are used to protect geostrategic and economic interests. And yet we face so many challenges. Even the most democratic societies have to recognize that their citizens are increasingly reluctant to accept any responsibilities, as Paul Ginsbourg demonstrates in his critical but optimistic *Democracy, Crisis and Renewal*.[3] The central theme of the dialogue between Marx and Mill described by the author is the need for involvement on the part of citizens with a sense of responsibility. Ginsbourg highlights the crisis facing Western societies, and the 'apathy and cynicism' that dominates them. Whilst powers are delegated democratically, there seems to be a widespread ignorance of the meaning of the power of responsibility. Elsewhere, dictatorship and/or corruption rules, and we would do well not to ignore economic relations and their impact

3. Paul Ginsbourg, *Democracy, Crisis and Renewal*, London: Profile, 2008.

upon societies, democracy and governments. Entering into a dialogue also means discussing in critical terms these themes, these difficulties and our contradictions. What, basically, are our intentions?

Do we mean to hide our respective crises and contradictions? To blame others in order better to hide from ourselves? To avoid the real issue? To have a dialogue despite everything, and leave out the 'important things', which will be decided elsewhere? Perhaps we have to be at once more humble and more ambitious: in our plural societies, the 'dialogue between civilizations' may well begin very close to home and may well be about very concrete issues. Humility here consists in apprehending values and ideas through daily experiences and the actions of everyday life. Ambition implies the belief that nothing is impossible if we begin with real local issues. There are many such issues and they, in historical terms, are inevitably part of the process of renewal at both the national and the international level. We need to have dialogues, debates and dreams. And we need to be lucid. The ideal lucidity we dream of is that of a lucid dream: observing the world as it is, *knowing* that nothing is impossible, and that the other is not the frontier of my impossibility but the stimulating multiplication of our common possibilities.

14

Love, Forgiveness and Love

To live is to suffer, said Schopenhauer and Nietzsche, who were both steeped in the teachings of Buddhism. To live is to love, asserted St Augustine, recalling the teachings of Christianity and the monotheistic religions. Aristotle's syllogism is unanswerable: if to live is to suffer, and if to live is to love, then to love is to suffer. There is also another universal truth that we cannot escape, even on the remotest island on the planet: if love goes there with us, suffering inevitably follows us there. The most beautiful dispositions of the heart inevitably have their dark, sad side, and can sometimes be especially painful. Being lucid and developing our memories is fine, but it is also true to say that the things we forget, our mental blanks and the things we are not aware of are forms of protection: there is no other way to bear our humanity. Unless we are to lose our minds, losing our memory is sometimes good for us. When we look into the eyes of the man or woman we love or glance at our parents, children or friends, how can we bear the truth of life without flinching: one day, we will have to separate, leave or perhaps divorce, or perhaps go into exile or disown one another. And whatever happens, and without a shadow of a doubt, we will die. In any case, we live between heaven and earth and the Meursault of Camus' *The Outsider* is right: 'There is no way out.' Then we should 'divert ourselves' in Pascal's sense of the term: forget, think about something else, or avoid thinking. That is the wisest and most intelligent course. Cassius 'thinks too much', said Shakespeare's Julius Caesar, who wanted to have about him 'fat, sleek-headed men and such as sleep nights'. Helicon, the advisor to Camus' Caligula, adds, 'You know full well that I never think. I am far too intelligent for that.' The alternative is to love in order not to think. To love is to suffer . . . to love is to forget. Hecate has two faces. By night she is the moon, and by day she is the sun. The contradictions of life are inextricable.

We sometimes use the same words, but we do not say the same things. The path or way (*tao*) that leads to enlightenment and regeneration in Taoism allows us to reach a higher level of fulfilment through work on oneself, on the totality of one's being. We are a long way from Greek dualism and the categories of the West. Taoism teaches us to use self-control, breathing and sexuality to rediscover within our own bodies the cosmic energy that is the essence of the Whole, and to blend and become as one with it. There is no boundary between the profane and the sacred, and love therefore does not mean forgetting, but going beyond contingencies, finding eternity and therefore the transcendence of the suffering that is bound up with death. The earlier and later influences of Buddhism give these teachings of Taoism many different nuances of meaning, depending on whether or not we believe in the cycles of reincarnation (*samsara*) and the liberation of Nirvana. Despite their diversity, the one thing these traditions have in common is their rejection of dualism. The stages that lead from body to mind – liberation, compassion and detachment – involve a process of asceticism. The energy we require and the goal we seek is a love that has been freed from all instinctual and emotional dependency and fuses with the vital energy of the macrocosm. Everything can be part of the same impetus, the same inspiration: eating, breathing and caring for our bodies, being and our inner life are mystical, sacred acts that allow us to reach an absolute by transcending the self through Love-Compassion. It is the love that is veiled and imprisoned, or the love we undergo, that causes us to suffer, that makes us forget or that momentarily diverts us. This is a love that is 'corporealized' without a mind, or that is 'sentimentalized' and without a soul. It is a 'natural' love, but it is incomplete and handicapped. We must know the straight but demanding path that leads from the body to the self (inner breath), from the self to the soul, and from the soul to the Whole. Dualism is a trap, and individuation is a prison. Our sufferings inevitably increase when we are trapped and in prison. To go back to the categories we used earlier, we might say that we have to make a distinction between the love-emotion we undergo (and which can take possession of us) and the love-spirituality that we master, that we choose and that allows us to reach out of ourselves and find well-being. Love-spirituality is said to be a more lucid form of asceticism. Some, like Chaung Tzu, who was one of the masters of Taoism, took the view that we must 'empty ourselves' and free ourselves from our intentions and from language, whilst others apparently took the opposite view (as in some of Confucianism's teachings) and argued that we should seek 'fullness' without denying our intentions. On the contrary, the latter group argues, we should direct them by developing through exercise an attitude and actions that can both transcend and liberate.

When St Augustine says 'Love and do as thou wilt', he is not thinking of the teachings of one of the currents within Taoism which, like Chaung Tzu, calls upon us to rediscover the Path, natural lightness, the absence of will, letting go or the 'fullness of the void'. The words are similar but the demands and finalities are quite different. We have to work on ourselves, and self-control and transcendence are certainly essential but, given his belief in the duality of being and morals, St Augustine is referring to Christian ethics: experiencing love in Jesus means being freed from sin, and overcoming our natural corporality so as to find the spirit or soul in its purity and proximity to the divine. Such love is very demanding and acquires its status because it does not deny any of its human attributes: the body, its instincts and its temptations are products of original sin. If we are lucid from the outset, we can be free and 'do as we will' in the Love of Christ and God. The Jewish and Muslim traditions are similar in terms of their teachings about love. They do not have the same relationship with sin and salvation through Christ as Christianity, but their basic teachings are the same: love is an indispensable element in the relationship with the One, as are the teaching, effort and personal discipline required to transform it, spiritualize it and to experience the proximity of the divine.

'Love is the key,' said the young poet Rimbaud, who eventually chose to go alone into exile. The poet Nerval, who wrote in the same century, was afraid that he had chosen the wrong love (the creature Aurélia rather than the Creator) and eventually committed suicide. The literatures of the world are full of these hopes, contradictions and pains. Indeed, they are what sustain them. Shakespeare uses drama to express the truths of what it means to be human. Juliet is the archetype of love, of the happiness that causes us pain. Carried away by love, she realizes that Romeo is both the man she loves and the enemy: her love is impossible. Shakespeare's formula then reveals the secret: 'Love is a smoke raised with the fume of sighs; being purg'd, a fire sparkling in lovers' eyes; being vex'd, a sea nourished with lovers' tears.' The tormented Hamlet laughs and cries as he tries to find an answer to the agonizing question 'to be or not to be' in the eyes and love of Ophelia. Her death by drowning sends him back to his existential questions: the absence of love is, in a strange way, an invitation to commit suicide. Tension, contradiction, pain and death appear to be the food of love. They are also the salt of love.

All spiritualities and religions seek reconciliation and harmony and try to overcome the intrinsic and basic tension within man: the tension between love and suffering. That tension is another way of expressing the hope that we will find the freedom that lies beyond the realities of dependency. All spiritualities and religions teach us the same thing: if we seek the self-confidence and well-being that lies at the end of the initiatory path, we must begin by learning to take heed of ourselves. Whilst the feelings we instantly feel in our hearts make love seem simple and obvious, we must still take time to study that love and those hearts. We must learn to love, and to imbue ourselves with the forms of 'the key' . . . and of the doors it fits.

ME

Love too is a journey. We have to set out, get away from ourselves. We have to take the first step, and keep our balance. And, ultimately, it is all a question of balance. The one thing that the teachings of all spiritualities, religions, philosophies and modern psychologies have in common has to do with the fact that we always have to begin with ourselves. There is no escaping that. We must learn to know ourselves, learn to accept ourselves and learn to love ourselves. Once again, we are talking about processes and stages, and about the evolution that allows individuals to understand themselves better, to gain maturity and, ultimately, to accept themselves for what they are. In the beginning, we are carefree, natural, and put our feelings on display; loving means feeling love, showing it and talking about it. And then we begin to have, express and formulate expectations. We have to go further. Love's first journey is a journey to the inside: again and again, we come back to ourselves, watch ourselves, study ourselves and become completely imbued with ourselves. Not in order to drown in a blind and arrogant egocentrism, but in order to find a balance. It is in fact possible that going back to ourselves is the best way to avoid egocentrism. We have here a relative paradox: on the periphery of the self, the ego is both prominent and hypertrophied.

Learning to love ourselves means learning to accept ourselves. It means entering oneself, in the way that we enter a foreign or 'other' world, and taking stock of the qualities, achievements and potential of our being and personality. A searching gaze can also be a positive gaze, and a positive gaze requires an intellectual predisposition. It will be noted that all religious, philosophical and spiritual teachings are from the outset imbued with the basically positive attitude that invites human beings to become initiates, to change, to reform themselves and to find inner resources that will lift them up. That is their essence. It is when they are perverted that their teachings become rigid and dogmatic, and solidify into moral codes that inspire a feeling of guilt, that stigmatize what is natural, or lead to an obsession with limits, flaws or 'sin'. It is at this point that things become inverted and that we begin to see ourselves in a negative and deprecatory light. When it is not one's own gaze or final judgement that condemns one to condemn oneself, one begins to feel uncomfortable, and feel that one cannot live up to one's ideals. Now, love really is the 'key', and it means, first and foremost, love of oneself, of one's qualities, will power and ability to make progress. With determination, strength and humility; once more, it is a question of balance. We must observe ourselves through our qualities, the efforts and the progress we have made, the resistances we have overcome, the struggles we have won, and the failures we have recovered from. Rather than counting, as Labro suggests, the number of times we have 'fallen', we should count the number of times we have been able to pick ourselves up again. Lao Tsu said that 'failure is the basis of success', and success consists, in the same way, in fully understanding the existence of that inner energy that allowed and allows us to overcome failures . . . that have become successes. What do we see when we look in our own mirror? The gaze is more important than the evaluation because, ultimately, it is the gaze that determines the evaluation. Our relationship with ethics begins with our relationship with our being: if we began by deprecating ourselves or even hating ourselves, the harm has already been done. That is the criticism Nietzsche makes of the moralists in *The Genealogy of Morals*: when we are taught to hate what is human, morals become a prison for some, and an instrument of power for others. To go towards the self, towards our liberation, towards the Cosmos or God, is to go . . . and we cannot go unless we begin to love ourselves. Without any illusions about ourselves, of course, but without fear and without hesitation.

This self-love can be expressed in various ways: lucidity consists in denying nothing of ourselves, and especially not our needs. We can certainly try to overcome certain needs and certain expectations, but there can be no question of denying their existence from the outset. Our needs – for protection, to be listened to, to communicate and for tenderness, affection and love – are, to a greater or lesser extent, both deep-rooted and natural, and both the monist oriental traditions and the dualist Semitic or Western traditions teach us that it is physically and spiritually impossible to find our balance and to achieve inner well-being without taking them into account. A love for someone else that fuses with the other to such an extent as to lead us to deny our own being and our own needs is a love that is fragile, unstable and unbalanced and that will lead, in the long term, to suffering and failure (unless it merges into the experience of absolute self-sacrifice). The ability to give ourselves presupposes and demands, by definition, that there really is a 'self' to give: we give ourselves in love without denying any of our needs or expectations. This obviously does not mean that we have to accept everything from ourselves, or that the 'self' forces itself on us. It means primarily that we must learn to listen to ourselves, to respect ourselves and, when we experience love, to make ourselves heard and respected. We must love ourselves with humility and dignity: we must expect ourselves to change and make constant progress, and expect others to help us on our way without denying us in any circumstances. We must learn to love ourselves, and to make ourselves loved.

'Self'-centred approaches have all too often been described as the antithesis of spiritual experience and the inclination towards altruism. This is a serious misunderstanding. All experience of transcendence, detachment, liberation and proximity to God begin with the 'self': we have to work on ourselves, our gaze, our desires and our intentions. Self-love is no exception to this requirement: far from becoming trapped within the ego and its desires, we start with what exists, and, as we learn to love ourselves better and more deeply, we gradually learn to love others better, and to love their needs, expectations, doubts and hopes. Prophets, sages and philosophers unanimously recommend that we should question our intentions and objectives. Nothing has changed: listening to ourselves teaches us to listen but if we listen only to ourselves, we become deaf to others, and eventually to ourselves. Some begin with the 'self' in order to reach a higher finality; others can see nothing but themselves and smugly come to a standstill at the very point where their apprenticeship begins. The world's religions and philosophies have always warned us against the latter attitude and invite us to follow the difficult, but so much more illuminating, prospect of the former. Love and be what you are, for that is the path that will make you what you would like to be.

YOU

We are short of love. That much is certain. It seems that we do not have enough to give, and that we never receive enough. That should be enough to convince us that emotional outpourings are not always outpourings of love. The key is to be found elsewhere: as we have said, it consists in coming back to ourselves, 'leading out' and educating ourselves in order to learn, mature and give form and substance to our being. It consists in listening to ourselves rather than seeing – and alienating – ourselves through the gaze of the other. The age of the image gives rise to a deep unease: standards of beauty are forced upon us, appearance becomes oppressive and, whether we like it or not, our self-image is distorted and 'mediatized'. This is a cruel age, and our unease is painful. The same is increasingly true of all societies, without exception.

It will be noted that the ancient spiritual traditions of both East and West systematically direct the human consciousness towards Nature. Nature is a school, and an initiation. The elements are there, they have surrounded us since childhood, and we are used to them. The awakening of spirituality consists in seeing them differently, in seeing in them signs, celebrations and songs, hymns and prayers to the cosmic order, universal archetypes, the gods or the One. That conversion in our gaze is a conversion of the heart, and marks the transition from the state of one who observes to that of one who loves. Our capacity for knowledge, recognition and wonder comes from the depths of our subjectivity, from the 'self', our consciousness or our hearts. It means that we must distance ourselves from the 'immediate' gaze, for proximity, and often for meaning.

The old and the familiar then become new. We see other things, things we had overlooked, failed to see or notice . . . or neglected altogether. The elements reveal themselves to us to the precise extent that we are revealed to ourselves, that we see more deeply into things, and that our gaze changes and becomes more intense. Our hearts become more understanding, our spiritual discernment grows, our imaginary horizons expand . . . and we feel more love. Whilst the age of frenetic progress and speed encourages us to escape boredom by constantly offering us something new and an ever-expanding range of 'new products' and blind consumerism, spiritualities, religions and philosophies ask us to look more closely at what is old, and to find something that is perpetually new within it because, to paraphrase Heraclitus, we never look at it twice in the same way. It is a question of finding something extraordinary in the most familiar and ordinary things: Nature, the sky, the elements, our environment and the people with whom we are most familiar. It is a matter of changing the way we see.

The most ancient traditions invite us to bring about this inner conversion, and it is the initial stage of all spiritual teachings. Traditional African spiritualities (which are too quickly and very inaccurately described as 'animist') and Amerindian spiritualities echo the teachings of Hinduism, Buddhism and the revelations of the monotheisms: the metaphysical exists within the physical, the extraordinary lies hidden in the ordinary, the sacred haunts the profane, and meaning lies hidden in the essence of the elements. In her *Weavings* (1988), Esther de Waal notes that, in our technological age, we are capable of seeing 'more' but actually see 'less'. Surface area is inversely proportional to depth: the Celtic spiritual traditions, she points out, integrate God, the sacred and the extraordinary into the most ordinary aspects of daily life. The English poet William Blake had the same intuition and tried to revolutionize the way we see things when he wrote: 'To see a world in a grain of sand / And a heaven in a wild flower / Hold infinity in the palm of your hand / And eternity in an hour.' The French poet Baudelaire experienced the same revelation. *The Flowers of Evil* already displayed his interest in vision, but it was between the publication of that collection and *Petits Poèmes en Prose* (*Little Prose Poems*) that he realized that the poet must seek to extract the extraordinary from the ordinary. The alchemist of the word, who 'extracts the quintessence from all things' and turns 'mud' into 'gold', must change the way he sees things. For anyone with an uncommon vision, Beauty lies in what is common. Rainer Maria Rilke repeats the same truths about the spirituality of art: learning to look is one way of learning to love. Or perhaps it is the other way around. Perhaps learning to love teaches us to see better. Or perhaps both are true at the same time and in contradictory fashion, with both a tension and a harmony between them. The French poet Eluard argued that we have to love in order to understand, but that truth does not exclude the possibility that we may have to understand in order to love. When it comes to love, Aristotle's logic is probably incomplete or relative: two conflicting theses can be true at the same time, for the same person.

It is with this gaze from within that we should observe the women and men around us. We should learn to love and learn to look; learn to look and learn to love. Going beyond appearances, roles and functions, and familiarizing ourselves with the inner horizons of those we love out of habit, or because our drives or a sudden flash of desire make us love them. We must rediscover the paths of wonderment, and try to find something original, extraordinary and new, not 'in the depths of the unknown' (Baudelaire) or in the 'latest model', but in what we know best and what is most naturally in front of our eyes. Transform the presence of beings into landscapes we have yet to discover, and the elements that constitute them into signs. Rather than multiplying things in a quantitative sense, make their qualities denser: this is the exact opposite of consumerism in love, as it is in friendship, and as it is in our relationship with technological progress. A different gaze at oneself a different gaze at you. Observe our mother, father, children and those around us with the particular attentiveness of the love that goes in search of the extraordinary miracle of presence, the gift of the heart and the singularity that is 'you'. 'Thank' God, the cosmos, Nature and 'the other' who created us, in their mirror, with their presence and through their gaze. Look, love, thank . . . love, look, thank . . . thank, love, look . . . etc. Infinite combinations of love.

'You' are like no one else. My heart knows it, and my gaze proves it to you. As all hearts know, love needs proof. Learning to love those we love better is a constant spiritual exercise. Modern psychologies keep going back to the first truths that the world's first spiritualities have already transmitted to us. 'Love must be reinvented,' said Rimbaud in his adolescent keenness and disappointment, but perhaps it just has to be rediscovered. Taking time, standing back, pondering, evaluating and setting out: love is like the spiritual quest because it is a quest for meaning and well-being. It is up to every one of us to discover the extraordinary that lies hidden in the heart of the all too ordinary presences in our daily lives. A character trait, an emotion, a smile, an expression, a look, a feeling, a wound, a silence or an absence: everything speaks to those who know how to listen. Listen without passing judgement, or rather judge that there is nothing on which to pass judgement. To judge is human, and to judge is to love. Suspending one's judgement is a better way of loving . . . and to love, in spite of judgement, is truly to love.

FORGIVING

Some people forgive themselves everything and condemn everyone else. Some condemn everything about themselves and find extenuating circumstances for others. Some do not forgive themselves for anything and forgive nothing. And others forgive everything and (almost) everyone. To love and forgive is to be both demanding and indulgent. Once again, this is a matter of balance. An Islamic prophetic tradition says: 'Find seventy excuses for your brother (sister), and if you cannot find any, imagine that there is one excuse you do not know.' This suggestion echoes the Christian maxim 'Love they neighbour as thyself,' and 'Thou shalt not judge.' It is about loving and suspending one's judgement. This does not mean accepting everything that others do (in which case there would be no love), but it does mean taking the view that their mistakes or sins do not tell us the whole truth about them. In *Measure for Measure,* Shakespeare suggests that we 'Condemn the fault and not the actor of it' if we wish to ensure that we do not punish the wrong person. All the monotheisms recommend that we make that distinction: human beings can judge acts, but only God is in a position to judge human beings. When human beings turn into judges, they invent not the hereafter on earth but hell, for then hell really does become 'other people', to paraphrase Sartre.

What, basically, does the expression 'No one's perfect' mean, if not that we all – and not least you and I – make mistakes, get things wrong, and that we sometimes lack courage, generosity, love and/or understanding. We have to begin by learning to forgive ourselves, and that, as it happens, means two very different things. We must, on the one hand, be aware that we are at fault and, on the other, hope that our faults will be forgiven or transcended. Some people seem to find it easy to forgive themselves and to ignore their own failings, and we know that they are not really aware of the nature of the harm they can do. They offend, insult, ignore, despise and humiliate others without any real awareness of what they are doing. They may be blinded by prejudice, by their emotions, their wounds, their vengeance or their certainties, but they have no perception of the process of their own dehumanization. Their reasons mean that they are, by definition, in the right. Learning to put a critical distance between us and ourselves, our intentions and our behaviour, is the elementary basis of spirituality and psychology: a human mind cannot develop unless it acquires the ability to take a critical moral view of its own actions. What we said earlier about tolerance, respect, freedom and love partakes in the basic teachings that allow us to resist the thoughtlessness, dehumanization and bestiality of human beings. By acquiring that awareness, the human mind acquires a sense of forgiveness.

This awareness must not become another trap. All spiritualities and religions teach us to be both demanding and indulgent towards ourselves. The reason why sages and prophets were human beings is that they had to convey to us the message of their humanity, which was sometimes strong and sometimes fragile, sometimes determined and sometimes vulnerable, sometimes alert and sometimes weary. Their mistakes and failings are signs, reminders and calls against being smug, arrogant or pretentious as we go on our way. At the same time, they are expressions of the need to be watched, forgiven and loved. Our faults make us human, and we must accept them, not as fatalities but as initiations that raise us up. Forgiving others teaches us our need for humility. Begging forgiveness, and being forgiven or unforgiven, is the essence of our humanity. Alone before God and/or our conscience, we must have the humility to ask for forgiveness, and to forgive. To forgive is to love. To love is to forgive. We must love what lies, or might lie, beyond what exists or what has been done.

We must also learn 'to put ourselves in the place of the other' and practise the empathy we discussed earlier. We must try to understand others' motivations and actions, as that will give us a better understanding of the meaning and import of their gestures and actions. That is not always easy. It is never easy. Let me tell you a story. Thierry was fifteen when, in a fit of anger, he violently struck his mother one day. She had to be rushed to hospital: the blow had been so violent that it had smashed her upper lip into her upper teeth. Thierry's sister called his teacher for help, because he and Thierry enjoyed a relationship based upon a deep trust and complicity. When he got to the hospital, the teacher was beside himself with rage. He was ready to scold, or even to hit Thierry himself because he found his behaviour as unacceptable as it was shameful: there was no excuse for hitting his mother. Thierry's sister took him to one side: 'That's how our father behaved. He used to hit our mother, and us: violence has always been the way we communicate in our family. Thierry shouldn't have done it, and I hate him for doing that to Mum, but ... ' She did not finish her sentence, and then added, with a tense, hurt expression on her face: 'You understand?' The teacher said nothing: he understood, and he calmed down. It was not a matter of condoning violence, but of understanding where it came from. Thierry's sister had helped him to revise his initial moral judgement and to take into account the complexities of the boy's life. He was now able to revise his moral judgement, to realize that things were more complex than he had thought and to forgive Thierry without condoning what he had done. All spiritualities, from Hinduism to Confucianism, and from Buddhism to Judaism, Christianity and Islam teach us the same lesson: forgiveness does not mean passive acceptance but an active human commitment to reforming and transforming ourselves. God indeed forgives mistakes, and men can sometimes forget them in a positive sense. For the moral consciousness, forgiving mistakes and forgetting about them is not a way of denying that mistakes have been committed, but a way of asserting that our conscience has the ability to overcome them, or that it is trying to do so.

Thierry was a victim, and he became a bully. Did he become a bully because he had been a victim? Psychological and psychoanalytic studies support that view. Or did he become a bully simply because he was human and because inhumanity lies dormant in all of us? Spiritualities, religions and philosophies support that view, and postulate that it is a truth that is borne out by the history of humanity. We have to distrust both feelings of pity and abuses of authority, and forgiveness can become either a feeling of charitable condescension towards the victim or an instrument of authority in the hands of a former victim and/or future bully. Who forgives whom? Who forgives what? Forgiving, like loving, is not feeling pity. It is very easy to feel pity, and the ability to forgive forces us to question the intentions of those who do so: pity can be the dark side of authoritarianism or psychological manipulation as well as the brightest side of love and of an active, constructive empathy. The difference between the two kinds of forgiveness is, of course, love: we forgive out of love, forgive with love, and go on loving.

LOVE AND DETACHMENT

All spiritualities highlight the ambivalence and ambiguity of love; its different natures and its two faces. Love is an initiatory school in which we learn to make progress, to rise above ourselves and then to free ourselves, but it can also be a prison in which we are bound by more and more chains. We go under, get lost and eventually become totally dependent. The universal teachings of spiritualities, philosophies and all religions are in agreement about this and proffer the same truths: in love, the individual rediscovers what she or he went there to look for, because love is a mirror as well as a revelation. Because she/he is under the sway of her/his emotions and her/his need to possess, her/his love will always turn against her/him and cause her/him the sufferings of dissatisfaction and a chained heart. Imbued with spirituality and mastery, her/his love will take her/him out of the self and enable her/him to attain fulfilment and self-giving.

Love is therefore like education. It involves 'going with' and learning to detach ourselves with an ever-greater awareness of the ambivalence of things and of the need for balance, which is always so difficult to achieve and so fragile. Knowing oneself, loving oneself sufficiently, learning to love better, to give, to give oneself and to forgive are lifelong learning processes that are never complete, never finished, always to be renewed. Loving without becoming attached and loving without becoming an object of attachment are probably both attitudes that require human beings to develop an acute discernment and to arm themselves with deep qualities of being and courage. Loving life and watching it fade away, loving ourselves without any illusions about ourselves, loving one's loves in the knowledge that times will take them away, loving without idolatry, and loving with an awareness of the relativity of all things. That is the profound meaning of the loving compassion that must, in the Buddhist tradition, set us free. In the monotheist religions, the oneness of God has the same deep meaning. We must free ourselves from our illusions, from the false worship of our desires and idols of one's inner self if we wish to accede to a love-lucidity as we seek a proximity that can perceive the extent of distance in the absolute. That is the mystical experience that al-Jilâni (1077–1166) and Rûmi (1207–1273) try to convey, as do all spiritual and mystical experiences. Gibran's *Prophet* sums up how the love of the Whole and/or God leads us to abandon the self when he says: 'When you love, you should not say "God is in my heart", but rather "I am in the heart of God".'

To love without being dependent. Nothing could be more difficult, and doing so requires a long apprenticeship that is both demanding and sometimes painful. The goal is to love without any illusions. That is all the more difficult in that we sometimes have the impression that love means being deluded. How can we graduate from the illusion of love to the lucidity of love? How can we detach ourselves from the very thing to which we are, by definition, attached? Gibran's Prophet also says: 'Love possess not, nor would it be possessed', but what becomes of those who are possessed, of the women and men who are 'blinded by love' and who are in chains? How can we reach out of ourselves to merge into the heart of the Whole or the Light of the One? Love is indeed a promise of good, beauty and well-being, but that promise has always come with so many tears, so much suffering, and so much pain. To live is to suffer; to live is to love ... to love is to suffer. And if we wish to live, must we therefore come to love our suffering until we die?

The love that transcends love is a love that liberates. It brings both fullness and a sense of contingency. We therefore have to teach our consciousness and our hearts to love in the absolute of the moment and in full awareness of time, to be there and to know that we will pass away. To love whilst learning to go away: the finest love never forgets separation, and still less does it forget death. Love and death are the most human of all couples: the deepest human love tries to have no illusions about the inevitability of death. That fragility is its strength. The power of humility lies hidden on the edge of that awareness – in love – of death.

To go back to the beginning. The sacred texts, the ancient traditions and all philosophies of all ages tell us to look at and learn from Nature, its beauty and its cycles, and to the ephemeral and eternity. We know that we love, naturally, but they still teach us to love better, to love consciously and spiritually, and to learn to apprehend meaning in detachment. And we have to choose between the reserve of Kant's and Nietzsche's impetuosity, between the way of Buddha and that of Dionysus, between the love of God and the love of Desire. Between an idea of freedom and the management of needs, between independence and dependence, and between detachment and bondage. One does not choose to love but one can choose how to love. Nature is the mirror before which we must raise our faces, gaze into proximity and distance, in the knowledge that, whilst we are now fully present, the earth will give the same fullness to others as it sanctifies our absence. The mirror of time and the infinite spaces reflect it, the liberated self understands it, and the One repeats it: to love is to be there, in proximity to the extraordinary in the ordinary, and to offer, give and forgive. To love is to reconcile the sedentary presence with nomadic migration, the roots of the tree with the strength of the winds. To love is to receive and to learn to let beings go. To love is to give and to learn to go. And vice versa.

Through the Ocean, Windows

This really is a Copernican revolution. Look out over the ocean we were talking about when we set out. The ocean is the window, and the windows are the ocean. We have reached the end of our journey, but our initiation is not yet over. And besides, these are only the first steps on a never-ending journey that is always new and that we always have to begin again. But there are still a few visions on the other side of the ocean: the windows are so similar, with the transparency of their glass, the edges of their frames and the relativity of their viewpoints. But from here, from the ocean, relativizing the windows' truths is out of the question. That would be as pretentious as claiming to have a monopoly on the one true 'point of view'. From the ocean, we can only conclude that there are a lot of windows and that we share the same experiences. That is all and that is enough ... provided that we set out. We have to go, learn and be initiated. With determination, we said ... and with humility.

In the course of our travels, we have been able to talk about human beings, faith, reason, tolerance, the universal and the quest for meaning. But we have also been able to talk about freedom, equality, women and men, as well as ethics, the sense of belonging and love. In that ocean, there were paths, ways, valleys and mountains, questions, doubts, suggestions and a few theses. We saw broad horizons, and a host of mirrors when we met the spiritualities of Africa and the East, the philosophies of the East and the West, and the monotheistic religions. We have been on distant expeditions, and then returned in cyclical fashion to certain questions or certain issues by taking other paths reflected in other windows that were neither quite the same nor completely different. This initiation is a mirror.

The architecture of the text reflects it. The fourteen chapters represent two cycles of seven. The figure '7' is a universal symbol that is present in almost all traditions. The four cardinal points and the three heavenly spheres make seven: the seven chakras of Hinduism, the seven emblems of Buddha, the seven heavens, the seven days of the week. In the Jewish Kabala, seven is the symbol of completion. Jesus used seven vessels, there are seven sacraments, the seven verses of the Opening (*Al-Fatiha*) to the Quran and the seven circumambulations around the Ka'aba and so on. Twice seven, then, to reflect linearity, evolution and the cyclical return of the same and the different through the universality of the symbol. With mirrors and echoes: the first chapter, which deals with the quest for the universal, echoes the eighth, which deals with the independence and universality of ethics. The seventh, which looks at women and men, echoes the fourteenth, which deals with love and detachment. Two cycles of seven chapters dealing with time and themes that disappear and reappear. There are correspondences between them, as well as bridges, echoes and repetitions that are not repetitions.

The pages of this book are a strange mixture of analytic thought, Cartesianism, strict rationalism and flights of mysticism, some of them quite ethereal. It really has been a strange journey through the lands of Eastern philosophies, religions, the sciences, psychology and the arts, flying from one to another, weaving links, and opening up horizons by starting out from the one and the multiple, as though the presence of the ocean were enough to reconcile the windows rather than separating them. So is this the work of an Eastern mind or a Western intellect? Is logic more important than the imaginary, structure more important than form, or science more important than art? How can we describe this book and how can we define the mind that conceived and produced it? Surely it has its own window, through which it could be identified and categorized. Then there are the correspondences, the 'fourteen chapters' that make 'twice seven', the themes and stages that speak to and complement one another: is that a coincidence, or is it the product of a will that systematically planned the symbolic structure of its quest? Or might it be the coincidence of writing encountering, like a sign, the imperative contingency of meaningful signs? A contingency discovered a posteriori, indeed, but which must have been there, a priori, whether or not the author was aware of it, in his unconscious perhaps or in divine purposes. So who can answer these questions? What textual analysis can have the last word to say about the secrets that guide a consciousness, a mind or a heart, and which are the hidden jewels of spiritualities, philosophies and art?

We said that this initiatory journey is a mirror. In it, the reader will sometimes find doubts, sometimes hopes and sometimes certainties. Some will take the view that its architecture is pure coincidence, and that it is very flawed. Others will see in it the expression of psychic or psychological determinisms that are veiled by a sublimation that is by definition involuntary. Some will find it inconceivable that this order is not deliberate or planned, and they will find other and deeper correspondences that will enrich the text still further as its dialogue with itself is mediated through the reader. And some will see nothing, or almost nothing, in it. One reads a book as one reads the world, after all. There is what it says objectively and what we project into it subjectively. There are things there that exist, things that we see and things that we hope to see.

We plunged into the ocean. Sometimes we lost our way, sometimes deliberately and sometimes by chance. It depends. The goal of the expedition was to get away from windows and points of view and to become as one with the open sea – the common object observed – and to try to approach the shores of a shared universal and of diversity. We hoped to land upon the shores of that philosophy of pluralism in which the differences between men, religions and cultures are as similar as their experiences, sufferings and hopes. We have been on a journey towards the Whole that took us far away from the 'self' and the 'ego'. The ocean embraced us and revealed its secrets as we were tossed from wave to wave, from shore to shore: the ocean is also a mirror. We see our own image reflected in it. The self went to the self, and the 'me' to the 'me', and our mirror-voyage took us to the edge of the ocean-mirror. And we watch ourselves, watch the me in the Whole, tossed by the waves that are so close and so ephemeral in the immensity of the vast surface of the sea. That is what happened to Narcissus: he saw himself, rediscovered himself, found himself beautiful, drowned and was lost. The point here is not to drown in the image of our own certainties, to become trapped within them, to delude ourselves or to become lost because we believe we have found ourselves. The dog-matic spirit confuses its exclusive convictions with the ocean of quests and human truths. Dogmatism is to thought what narcissism is to a self-image: a hypertrophic ego that reduces the sea to its mirror. Even at sea, even on the road, we are not safe from anything.

Time is linear or cyclical. The paths are steep, and sometimes there are mountains, plains and vast expanses of desert or water. We go on, in order to make progress or simply to go and then come back, and we learn to be, to live, to think and to love. Inside our being, there is the ego that sometimes traps us, oppresses us and blinds us, and then there are the attractions of the power that colonizes us, our friends or enemies, and sometimes all of us at once. All the sufferings of life, its separations and death hurt us, break us or simply kill us. Poverty, hunger, unemployment and the paths of exile make us strangers to ourselves, to our roots and to the world. So where should we go, when there seems to be no point in going anywhere? The world is a prison where we amuse ourselves by painting the bars. Life is a prison, life is a game . . . but do we have to be satisfied with playing in gaol? We look around us – at ourselves, our friends, our enemies – and we are overwhelmed with sadness: so little critical thinking, so little curi-osity, and so little love. When reflected in the ocean, our convictions may be reason enough for us to drown ourselves: perhaps it is better to be blind to men rather than to watch the depressing spectacle of endless fratricidal struggles, human ambitions and relationships of domination and power.

And yet, in the distance, in the silence of our subjectivity and in that of the infinitive spaces, we hear the murmur of other voices and other hopes. We have to lift up our faces, look towards the open sea and feel a different aspiration to understand the depths of its being. The deep silence speaks to us and summons us. This is a quest, an initiation, and we have to set off. Really set off. Leave our windows, and take the road of questions, truths, beauties, inspiration and love. Seek, with our eyes on the horizon, and plunge directly into the ocean . . . find ourselves within ourselves, rediscover ourselves, know and recognize ourselves in the infinite forces and inestimable wealth of knowledge, communications, gifts and fraternity. Our gaze changes, and the universe has changed. This new gaze has extraordinary power!

There is such a thing as meaning, and we must give meaning. And give of ourselves for the sake of meaning.

We must also be able to resist ourselves, Men, all shortcomings and all excesses. The most beautiful words can become the most dangerous of weapons when they are in the hands of human beings. Vigilance and commitment are essential if we are to protect our dignity, justice and the critical spirit as we move from ourselves back to ourselves, from ourselves to those who are close to us, and from ourselves to others. The consciousness of all the humanisms born of religions, spiritualities and philosophies is concerned with coherence. And the open sea now adds a new dimension, a new landscape and another gaze to our hearts. Silence and encounters. The winds give birth to a new inspiration and to the strength of intimacy. It gradually gains in confidence. The call comes from the world as well as from the heart, and the two echo one another. The experience of the quest, of the gift of the self, or resistance and coherence will indeed be accompanied by difficulties, doubts, tears and pain, but they open the horizon up to diversity, pluralism, humanity and a shared universal. As we regain confidence, the windows open and love speaks to us of the beauty of the ocean, which is both unique and plural. The ocean-mirror that reflects our image now reflects that of a humanity that is in quest of reason, God, truth, happiness or love . . . always in search of meaning, serenity and peace.